Napoleon's Chicken Marengo

Napoleon as First Consul.

Napoleon's
Chicken Marengo

CREATING THE MYTH
OF THE
EMPEROR'S FAVOURITE DISH

Andrew Uffindell

Frontline Books
London

Napoleon's Chicken Marengo
This edition published in 2011 by Frontline Books,
an imprint of Pen & Sword Books Ltd,
47 Church Street, Barnsley, S. Yorkshire, S70 2AS
www.frontline-books.com

Copyright © Andrew Uffindell, 2011

The right of Andrew Uffindell to be identified as Author of
this Work has been asserted by him in accordance with the
Copyright, Designs and Patents Act 1988.

ISBN: 978-1-84832-578-4

CIP data records for this title are available
from the British Library

For more information on our books, please visit
www.frontline-books.com, email info@frontline-books.com
or write to us at the above address.

Printed and bound CPI Group (UK) Ltd, Croydon, CR0 4YY

Typeset in 11.5/15.5 point Caslon 540

Contents

Maps and Illustrations

Maps

Diagram

Plates

Illustrations in Text

Author's Note

Historical Background

Napoleon seized power in a *coup d'état* at Paris in November 1799. During the Consulate, as the new regime was known, he ruled as the foremost of three consuls, and steadily tightened his grip on power. In May 1804, the Consulate gave way to the Empire with a proclamation that Napoleon was now Emperor of the French. He fell from power a decade later, abdicating in April 1814 after a succession of military disasters and the occupation of Paris by a coalition of hostile powers. Exiled to the small Mediterranean island of Elba, which he ruled as a sovereign, he was replaced in France by a Bourbon monarch, King Louis XVIII. But Napoleon added a final chapter to his career. In March 1815, after boldly landing in Provence with a small escort, he marched on Paris and regained power. Defeat at Waterloo three months later resulted in his second and final abdication. This time, he was exiled to the remote South Atlantic island of Saint Helena, where he spent the last six years of his life as a closely guarded prisoner of the British. He had married twice. His first marriage, to Joséphine de Beauharnais in 1796, ended in divorce in January 1810 following her failure to produce an heir. He then wed Marie-Louise, the eighteen-year-old daughter of the Austrian Emperor, and this second, dynastic, marriage produced a son and heir, known as the King of Rome, in March 1811.

For simplicity, I have referred throughout this book to Napoleon, although he was more commonly known, until he became Emperor, as Bonaparte, or Buonaparte (the Italian spelling). Similarly, I have given all dates in their Gregorian form, including those between 24 October 1793 and the end of 1805 when France used the Republican calendar. Ranks are shown in their original language, as they often lack an exact English equivalent. Similarly, the original French or Austrian unit titles have been retained. In the French infantry, the term *demi-brigade* ('half-brigade') was the Republican equivalent of a regiment. The unit title was often contracted: for instance, the 9e demi-brigade d'infanterie légère might appear as simply the 9e légère.

The data in the diagram showing the exchange rates of the *tiers consolidé* have been extracted from the daily reports published at the time in the *Journal de Paris*.

Napoleon at Waterloo.

Acknowledgements

For their help and encouragement during the writing of this book, I am very grateful to my family and friends, including Michael Leventhal, Deborah Hercun, and the staff of Frontline Books; Peter and Mel Arnold; and Agostino von Hassell, the author of *Military High Life: Elegant Food Histories and Recipes*, for his helpful advice in the early stages of this book. I am much obliged to Peter Harrington and the Anne S. K. Brown Military Collection at the Brown University Library for kindly providing the image of Napoleon for the cover of the book, Shona Andrew for designing the dustjacket, and Donald Sommerville for copy-editing and typesetting. I also wish to thank Alexander Swanston, who drew the superb maps, and Philip Haythornthwaite, who kindly read the manuscript and gave me the benefit of his expertise.

I am indebted to the staff of the Bodleian Library at Oxford, of Hertfordshire Libraries, and of the British Library, including the Newspaper Library at Colindale. In Paris, I am grateful to the Service historique de la défense, the Archives nationales, and the Bibliothèque Sainte-Geneviève. I also wish to thank the staff at the excellent museum on the battlefield of Marengo, and the helpful attendants at the Hospice of the Grand Saint-Bernard in Switzerland.

Chapter 1

The Myth

Poulet à la Marengo! Bellowed over the din, the order provokes a flurry of activity in the restaurant's kitchens. The chef quickly assembles the dish, arranging some fried pieces of chicken on a bed of *croûtons*, and then pouring on top a tomato-and-mushroom sauce richly flavoured with garlic and wine. Pungent slices of truffles provide the garnish, while a fried egg, sunny side up, adds a splash of colour. Perched right on the summit as a final, theatrical flourish, a bright red crayfish arches its tail and brandishes its hefty pair of claws like a miniature lobster. Whisked away by the waiter with a deftness that speaks of years of experience, the plate appears moments later on the table of a hungry diner.

This bizarre concoction has become famous around the world as one of the classic creations of French *haute cuisine*. Within the first two decades of the nineteenth century, chicken Marengo had already pervaded Paris, and its heyday lasted for 150 years. Even today, it is still respected as one of the truly great dishes of history, one that has acquired a legendary status. Its name alone would have been enough to guarantee it a footnote in the history books, for it commemorated a victory – and no ordinary victory, but one of Napoleon's most important in his nineteen years as an army commander. By winning Marengo, he not only wrested north-western Italy back from the Austrians, but tightened his grip on France just seven months after he had seized power in a *coup d'état*. If Waterloo fifteen years later saw the setting of Napoleon's star, then it was Marengo that marked its ascent.

Yet this pivotal battle was desperately contested, and left at least 2,000 corpses strewn over the plain. 'Our demi-brigade lost 850 men,' lamented Chef de bataillon Antoine Gruyer of the French 43e de ligne. 'For my part, in my company alone, I have lost my *lieutenant* killed, the *sous-lieutenant*, who is minus a leg, and forty-seven *grenadiers*.'[1] In fact, of the 56,000 soldiers present in the opposing armies, as many as one in every three became a casualty or a prisoner – proportionately as heavy as at, for example, the notorious Battle of Antietam in 1862, the bloodiest day of the US Civil War.[2]

Besides being so costly, Marengo remains a confused and intensely controversial action. Napoleon himself deliberately falsified the official account to conceal just how close he had come to defeat, and this web of deceit became even more entangled when several of his key subordinates bitterly contested the credit for the outcome. Marengo soon became so enshrouded in myth and political spin-doctoring that even today, after decades of accumulated research, historians cannot be sure exactly what happened.

The battlefield itself was deceptive. At first glance, it seemed to be just a monotonously flat plain, ideal for cavalry charges and devoid of any obvious defensive positions. Yet a closer examination revealed that its apparent openness did not apply to the western edge, which was ideally suited for a delaying action against an enemy onslaught. The ground in this part of the battlefield was wet, cut by brooks and drainage ditches, and made still more intricate by woods and marshes. Even the drier and more open plain further east had hidden strengths for a defender, being studded with massive, stone farmhouses, along with a scattering of small towns or villages, all of which made formidable bastions. The combination of the flatness of the ground and its abundant vegetation deprived generals of the viewpoints they needed to see the action as a whole, and made it difficult to coordinate an offensive.[3]

The battle began in the morning of 14 June 1800, when Napoleon's advanced guard unexpectedly came under attack from the Austrian army of General der Kavallerie Michael, Freiherr von Melas. For the entire day, the two sides grappled in the plain outside

Melas's base, the Piedmontese fortress city of Alessandria. During the morning, the Austrians strove to break out and clear enough ground on which to deploy. At this stage, the French were able to commit only their most advanced two corps, supported by cavalry, for the reserves had spent the night up to 6 miles further east. They found themselves massively outnumbered, and were fortunate that the nature of the terrain prevented the Austrians from moving swiftly enough to exploit their initial superiority.

The importance of the tiny, but centrally located, hamlet of Marengo became obvious as soon as the Austrians began their attack. Standing right on the axis of their principal thrust, it straddled the main road from Alessandria, and blocked the tracks that branched off to either side. Without Marengo, the Austrians would be bottled up, and unable to deploy in the open plain. The hamlet simply had to be taken, yet it lay on the eastern side of a stream called the Fontanone, whose steep and slippery banks were overgrown by dense curtains of trees and bushes. In a series of brutal, head-on assaults, the Austrians took sickeningly high casualties – unacceptably so amongst the officers, who courageously led the way. Losses were also appalling on the French side. A senior officer, Général de brigade Olivier Rivaud, described a vicious firefight that lasted for more than a quarter of an hour. 'Men fell like hail on both sides,' he wrote. 'I lost half my line at this time, and it was just a field of carnage. In my brigade, anyone on horseback was killed or injured. The *chefs de bataillon* and the *capitaines* were dangerously wounded, my orderlies were killed, my ADC had a ball pass through his right leg, and I myself was hit in the leg by a canister shot.'[4]

By early afternoon, the French positions on either side of Marengo were being overwhelmed. Their troops were exhausted, short of ammunition, and on the verge of being outflanked. By 2.30 pm, more than six hours after coming under attack, they were forced to abandon Marengo, leaving their opponents free at last to deploy the full might of their army. An Austrian company commander, Hauptmann Joseph von Rauch, advanced along the main road through Marengo. 'To the right and left', he wrote, 'were strewn guns with smashed wheels, piles of bodies, and heaps of dead horses. Officers and men were bursting with delight and jubilation over the news of the advantages we had won.'[5]

At this stage, Napoleon himself belatedly arrived from his head-quarters in the rear, having finally realized that the Austrian offensive was more than a mere feint. He committed his reserves to try and stem the tide, only to see them overwhelmed by the Austrian firepower and weight of numbers. Even the infantry of the élite Consular Guard was overtaken by disaster when a cavalry regiment burst in on its flank and rear. By now, the French were in full retreat. As the disorder grew, the road eastwards became jammed with a mass of carts, along with crowds of servants, sutlers, and soldiers seizing the chance to escort wounded comrades to the rear as an excuse to leave the firing line. A member of Melas's staff scribbled a hurried letter from the battlefield. 'Everything is going better,' he exulted. 'The enemy's left is completely routed; the centre and right have been driven in . . . Tell your mother to pray hard. Farewell.'[6] Melas himself entrusted the rest of the battle to a subordinate in the belief that it was as good as won, and returned to his headquarters in Alessandria, for at the age of seventy-one he needed to rest and recover from his bruises after having two horses shot beneath him.[7]

Napoleon was lucky to escape disaster. Outnumbered, out-gunned, and on the brink of disintegration, his army stumbled back in an apparently unstoppable, 4-mile retreat. It was saved by the timely reappearance of a division that had previously been detached to the south under Général de division Louis-Charles Desaix to cover that flank. By now it was late in the afternoon, yet the arrival of these 5,000 fresh infantrymen made it possible to rally the army and organise a dramatic counter-attack.

Fortunately for Napoleon, the Austrians were decidedly sluggish in pursuit. Flushed with success, they became complacent, and allowed discipline to slacken. It took time to disentangle their units after the morning's fighting, especially as several senior officers had become casualties. What the Austrians should have done was hurl

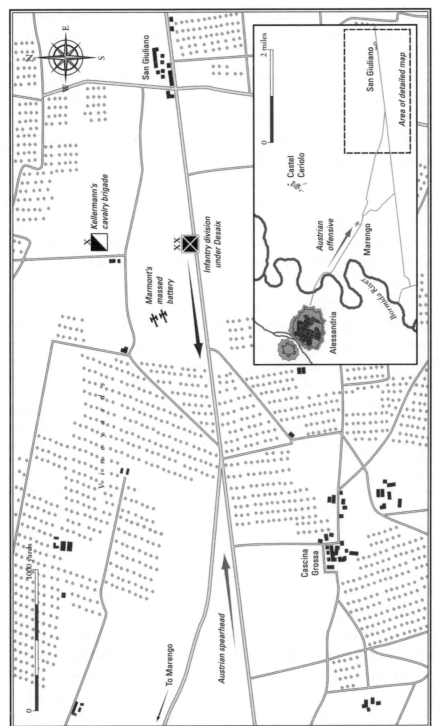

The Climax of Marengo.

their numerous cavalry eastwards in mass to harry the French relentlessly across the plain until the retreat turned into a rout. Yet they had dispersed their horsemen in small detachments to support the infantry during the opening stages of the battle, and several of these detachments had become exhausted, or had been knocked out by the better-handled French squadrons. In the absence of a proper cavalry screen, the Austrian infantry columns were now advancing blind, and risked suddenly blundering into a French rearguard. Even so, they made an impressive sight. 'It was marvellous to see the victoriously advancing troops,' wrote Hauptmann von Rauch. 'They looked as if they were advancing on the drill ground, and the march continued for some hours over the finest plains without a check.'[8]

Spearheading the push along the main road from Marengo was an advanced column of 4,000 infantry, supported by artillery and a regiment of light dragoons, and it was this column that collided with Desaix's division as the day reached an abrupt and decisive climax in the fields west of the village of San Giuliano. Suddenly coming under fire, the column halted and deployed into a formation more suited to combat, and an artillery duel developed, lasting perhaps twenty minutes, with heavy losses on both sides. Then the leading Austrian infantry regiment was sent forward to clear the way, only to be shattered by a murderous hail of musketry fired from behind a screen of trees and vines, and thrown back in disorder. It had run into Desaix's most advanced unit, the 9e légère, which now surged forward in pursuit. But it was the turn of the French light infantry-men to be surprised, for the Austrians brought up some crack grenadier battalions for a renewed push. Desaix himself was shot dead in a sudden blaze of fire, and the fighting became ferocious. 'In some positions, the enemy's resistance was terrible,' reported Desaix's chief subordinate, Général de division Jean Boudet. 'Trying to expel them with musketry would have been an idle waste of time. Bayonet charges alone were able to evict them, and they were carried out with an unparalleled agility and boldness.'[9]

For a while, the battle hung in the balance, and at least part of the 9e légère seems to have been driven back by the Austrian grenadiers. But then came the turning point. A French cavalry commander, Général de brigade François-Etienne Kellermann, seized his chance. Formed in column, and hidden until the last minute by vines, his brigade of heavy horsemen suddenly smashed into the northern flank of the grenadiers. Kellermann could not have timed it better, for he caught them with empty muskets following their firefight with Desaix, with their ranks disordered as they pressed forward, and immediately after they had received a blast of canister from three French guns.

No infantry could resist such a sudden, determined, and unexpected onslaught. Within minutes, Kellermann had crushed the bulk of the Austrian spearhead, and captured over 1,600 men, including the army's chief-of-staff, Generalmajor Anton, Ritter von Zach. Stunned by this abrupt reversal of fortune, the rest of the Austrian army was too shaken to try and retrieve the situation. Melas's absence, Zach's capture, and heavy casualties among the officers since the start of the fighting had decapitated the high command, and paralysed attempts to restore order. Fleeing cavalry units spread panic, precipitating a general rout. Some battalions fled without firing a shot, while others, amid the dust and confusion, fired wildly into the air, or even into their own comrades.

Yet the bulk of the French army was too bloodied and exhausted to be able to exploit the Austrian collapse, and even those units that attempted to do so pursued cautiously. 'The fear of falling into some new disorder caused us to advance everywhere only at a steady rate,' admitted a staff officer.[10] Even so, the Austrians were unable to do more than cover their rout by forming a defensive line with a few reserves. By the end of the battle, they were back in the positions from which they had marched out so optimistically at the start of the day. A few, isolated cannonshots were heard at intervals, like the last, insolent claps of a spent thunderstorm, and then everything lapsed into the darkness and silence of night.

That evening, Napoleon rode back to his headquarters, a massive, old farmhouse complex called the Torre Garofoli, 3 miles behind the battlefield. Still only thirty-one years old, he could not be called strikingly handsome, yet his pale, sallow skin was offset by the regularity of his face, a long, slightly aquiline nose, and a well-shaped mouth that was capable of a bewitching smile. Despite the popular notion, fostered by hostile caricaturists, that he was a short man, he was actually of average height, yet it was his personality more than his physical appearance that made him such a dominant figure, for his character was steeled with a ruthless, calculating egotism. His bluish-grey eyes were piercing in their intensity, while his quick glance and brusque, impatient gestures betrayed the intense, nervous energy that boiled like the lava of a perpetually smoking volcano beneath the crust of the commander's mask.

Inner confidence and an ingrained habit of authority had replaced the gawkiness of his youth, but although he had taken within the last two years to having his fine, auburn hair cut shorter, his trim and angular body had yet to fill out into the more familiar, pot-bellied figure that we recall from his later years as Emperor. His uniform, too, had only some of the elements that later merged into the instantly recognizable outfit witnessed on battlefields the length and breadth of Europe. His dark blue, double-breasted general's coat, with its long tails and scarlet collar and cuffs, was embroidered with gold oak-leaves that symbolised the strength of the French Republic. A long overcoat protected this uniform from the smoke and dust, while on his head was a black, cocked hat, decorated with a large, tricolour cockade, and a broad band of gold on the upper edges.

When Napoleon reached his quarters, he called for his cook, François-Claude Guignet, who was better known by his adopted name of Dunant.[11] Using whatever varied and unpromising ingredients the foragers could lay their hands on, Dunant hurriedly prepared a meal. There was a scrawny chicken or two, along with a handful of tomatoes, some eggs, mushrooms, garlic, onions, and truffles, as well as wine, a piece of bread, and even some crayfish. Dicing the chicken with a sabre, in rough-and-ready soldier's fashion, Dunant fried it in olive oil in the absence of any butter, and then combined the other, disparate ingredients to produce a startling new *fricassée*.

Astonishingly, Napoleon actually liked the improvised dinner. Perhaps, with his appetite sharpened by hunger, he would have appreciated anything, especially in the sudden release of tension after those endless, agonizing hours when the outcome of the battle had wavered precariously on a knife edge. 'It was one further conquest for this victorious day,' exulted a French writer sixty years later. 'The hero applauded, and thereafter *poulet à la Marengo* has always appeared on the best-served tables.'[12] Despite its accidental origins, chicken Marengo proved a remarkable success story. Born out of the chaos of an Italian battlefield, it became a quintessentially French dish that appeared in the finest and most elegant restaurants in Paris, before being exported around the world.

🐦🧍🐦

In eating chicken Marengo, people want to believe the story of its birth, and to enjoy a tangible link with one of the great men of history, yet the tale has grown increasingly convoluted. One version even alleges, ludicrously, that Napoleon did not like chicken, and has a peasant woman including vegetables to mask the taste. Another omits the chicken altogether, and claims that when Napoleon stopped at Turin on his way to the Battle of Marengo, he was served some lampreys – thin, eel-like creatures from the Po river – and found them so delicious that he ate the lot. Alas, the colourful tale is spoiled by the fact that Napoleon did not go through Turin in the weeks leading up to the battle, and the only way he could have eaten lampreys there before Marengo would have been at Melas's table and as his prisoner.[13]

These obvious distortions raise a host of niggling doubts that soon erode the foundations of the popular and yet constantly varying story of chicken Marengo. For a start, Dunant, the supposed creator of the dish, was not even in Napoleon's service at the time of Marengo. Born at Paris in August 1755, he was employed during the *ancien régime* in the household of the prestigious Condé family, where his father was a cook, and he followed it into exile at the time of the Revolution. Only after twelve years as an *émigré* did he return to Paris, where he entered Napoleon's service as *premier chef de cuisine* in August 1802 – a full two years after Marengo. In 1807, he was promoted to *maître d'hôtel ordinaire*, and he continued to serve for the rest of the Empire. He was not, in fact, the only Dunant in Napoleon's household, for two relatives joined him there. In November 1802, just three months after his own admission, his nineteen-year-old son, François-Joseph, arrived as a *garçon de fourneau*, or kitchen assistant. In addition, Dunant's brother, Jean-Marie, entered service in June 1804 as a *maître d'hôtel ordinaire*.[14]

Although the younger of the two brothers, Jean-Marie actually occupied more senior positions while working for Napoleon, and it was only the older Dunant's association with chicken Marengo that has made him the better known. This makes it all the more surprising that Dunant himself apparently laid no claim to being the father of the dish. At any rate, that is what emerges from a conversation he had in March 1830 – fifteen years after the fall of the Empire – with Marie-Antoine Carême, the greatest celebrity chef of the age. Carême published a record of their discussion: it was a long and detailed interview about Dunant's service with Napoleon, and yet contained not a word about him creating chicken Marengo, even though that alone is how he is remembered today.[15]

Nor were some of the dish's classic ingredients commonly found near the battlefield where it was supposedly invented. The area was famed for producing silk and good quality wine, rather than the olive oil used in chicken Marengo. In fact, olive oil was hardly ever used locally, for despite Italy's reputation as a hot and sunny country, it is actually a land of stark regional contrasts. Whereas the Ligurian coast basks in the warmth of the Mediterranean, the Po plain further inland endures winters that are usually colder than those in Paris. Olive trees cannot survive mean winter temperatures below 6 °C, whereas in January the mean temperature near the Po hovers around freezing. 'This is why the olive tree grows here only with great difficulty', explained a statistical databook of 1805, 'but its fruit is replaced by nuts, which provide a fairly good oil that the inhabitants use.' Walnut, not olive, oil is what one would expect to find in a dish created at Marengo.[16]

Could the dish really have been improvised on the evening of the battle? It seems unlikely, and not simply because of the rarity of one of the core ingredients. The most memorable dishes are created not in a sudden, effortless flash of inspiration, but as a result of long, painstaking months of thought. Rarely are they completely new creations. Some small changes, the addition of an extra ingredient or two, or a different style of presentation, are enough to rebaptize and elevate a dish whose antecedents might stretch back into antiquity.

Equally remarkable is the absence of any reference to the dish in eyewitness accounts of the battle. When some of the key French participants wrote their memoirs, they did not mention chicken Marengo at all. Neither Napoleon's stepson, Eugène de Beau-harnais, nor his artillery commander, Général de brigade Auguste Viesse de Marmont, referred to it. Nor did an ADC, Chef de brigade Anne-Jean-Marie-René Savary, even though he followed Napoleon back to his quarters at the end of the day. Nor did Napoleon's valet, Louis-Constant Wairy (known as Constant), whose memoirs contain not a word about the hurriedly concocted dish being eaten that night. In fact, one witness, Louis-Antoine Fauvelet de Bourrienne, stated that Napoleon was not fed by his cook at all. Instead, he and his staff enjoyed the hospitality of one of his generals, Kellermann, the man who had made the decisive cavalry charge at the climax of the battle. 'This was no small service, deprived as we were of everything,' wrote Bourrienne, who was one of those fed in this way:

> We were very lucky to benefit from the precaution Kellermann had taken of having foraging parties sent to one of these religious sanctuaries that are always well-stocked, and that are a welcome find on campaign. It was the Convent del Bosco

that had to provide requisitions, and as a just reward for the plentiful food and good wine with which they supplied the heavy cavalry commander, the good fathers were given a safeguard, and were thereby preserved from the looting and misfortunes of war.[17]

This is a crucial piece of evidence, but can it be trusted? Bourrienne was certainly in a position to know, for he was Napoleon's personal secretary, and a long-standing friend from their schooldays together at the military school of Brienne. Yet Bourrienne had a fatal flaw in his character. He lived beyond his means, and became involved in some scandalous financial transactions involving the supply of equipment for the army. Napoleon liked to retain familiar faces around him, but his tolerance had its limits, and he dismissed Bourrienne in 1802. Entering his office one day, he abruptly told Bourrienne to hand over his papers and keys. 'I never want to see you here again,' he snapped, and then walked out, slamming the door behind him.

Bourrienne received another post as plenipoteniary minister at Hamburg in 1805, but the friendship was over. When Napoleon fell from power in 1814, Bourrienne switched his loyalties to the restored Bourbon monarchy, but was then forced into exile in Belgium by his debts. It was this need for money that made his memoirs so unreliable. Instead of producing them personally, he simply accepted a large sum for his co-operation. 'He agreed to lend the authority of his name to cover memoirs for whose composition he contributed only some confused and incomplete notes – papers that professional writers were then entrusted with working up,' noted Claude-François Méneval, who had succeeded him as Napoleon's secretary. These ghost-writers had to fill in the gaps with other material they had uncovered in the course of their research.[18]

Bourrienne's memoirs were hardly unique in being artificially patched together. The desire to exploit Napoleon's fame spawned a host of dubious reminiscences in the decades after his fall. Many popular anecdotes about him stem from these early accounts, and are highly questionable, despite being endlessly repeated by historians. Bourrienne's account is just one example of the almost industrial way in which the supposedly trustworthy recollections of well-placed eyewitnesses were mass produced by so-called 'editors'. The chief of these ghost-writers was Charles-Maxime Catherinet de Villemarest, who managed a whole team of them.[19] It was a lucrative business. Villemarest created no fewer than ten volumes of Bourrienne's memoirs, and they have to be used with particular caution in that they were published while the Bourbons were still in power, which meant that the inclusion of scandalous or derisory tales about Napoleon and his family were an obvious way of ensuring sales. The core problem with Bourrienne's memoirs is the impossibility of knowing which parts were genuinely provided by him, and which were fabricated by others, yet they cannot be ignored altogether, for Bourrienne was a key, and sometimes credible, witness, and few other men worked so closely with Napoleon during the early stages of his career.

✿

What is not in doubt is Napoleon's partiality for chicken. According to one of his chamberlains, Charles-Philibert Barthelot de Rambuteau, he often had fried chicken for his morning meal or *déjeuner*: 'in general, he was brought some braised or grilled mutton, a fried chicken, sometimes some fish, a dish of vegetables, some fruit and cheese, and always some Chambertin wine'.[20]

Rambuteau's testimony was confirmed by other members of the imperial household. 'The dish that the Emperor liked the most', recorded Constant, 'was this type of chicken *fricassée* that was dubbed *poulet à la Marengo* because it was the favourite of the conqueror of Italy.'[21] Constant – or at least his ghost-writers – implied that the dish acquired its name not because it was invented on the battlefield, but simply because it came to be associated with

Napoleon. This interpretation is supported by a passage in Bourrienne's memoirs dating from the first months of the Consulate:

> We went to eat *déjeuner*, and the meal was extremely frugal. At that time, [Napoleon] would eat almost every morning some chicken dressed with oil and onions. This simple *ragoût* was, I believe, called *poulet à la provençale*, but since then it has perpetuated on the menus of our *restaurateurs* the memory of a famous battle, under the more ambitious title of *poulet à la Marengo*.[22]

In Bourrienne's view, therefore, chicken Marengo was simply a variation of a dish from Provence in southern France, and its combination of tomatoes, garlic, and olive oil is indeed a distinctive characteristic of *provençale* cooking. This reinforces the suspicion that the dish was neither a new invention, nor born in Piedmont, but at the same time it raises the puzzling question of how it became so popular with Parisian diners, for it was not an obvious dish to win them over, being cooked with olive oil rather than with the butter more generally used in French *haute cuisine*. Whereas olives were widely grown in Provence, it was butter that was favoured in the cooler north of the country, where dairy farming was more prevalent. Was this why some recipes for chicken Marengo did not insist on using oil, and suggested butter, fat, or dripping as alternatives?[23] Claiming that it was cooked the way it was because no butter was available on the evening of Marengo might have been an ingenious attempt to persuade Parisians to try a dish fried with oil. If so, Napoleon's association with chicken Marengo would have been doubly appropriate, since he, too, came to Paris as a provincial import from the Mediterranean, and yet managed to conquer the sophisticated city despite his unpromising origins.

Yet the notion that the people of Provence cooked everything in oil, and Parisians used only butter, is an exaggerated stereotype. Oil was, in fact, used in the capital, even if its inhabitants were less fussy about the quality, while books of recipes from the south of France included such dishes as *riz au beurre*, or used lard rather than oil for cooking chicken *fricassées*. *Provençale* cuisine actually enjoyed a certain popularity. 'Those who are familiar with the history of cooking know just how far several *ragoûts* from Provence have won favour at Paris in the last fifteen years,' noted an early gastronomic periodical, the *Almanach des gourmands*, in 1805.[24] Of course, it would be easy to overstate the prevalence of *provençale* food, and we have to remember that even the Trois frères provençaux, one of the most famous Parisian restaurants of Napoleon's time, had a surprisingly wide-ranging menu, including such distinctly un-*provençale* options as Bayonne ham, pig's trotters *à la Sainte-Menéhould*, Italian *macaroni*, and Cheshire cheese.[25] All the same, it is clear that instead of having to overcome unpromising origins, chicken Marengo is more likely to have been created to exploit an appetite for *provençale* food.

Even if chicken Marengo had its origins in Provence, it soon acquired a separate identity of its own, and by 1815 some restaurants were offering both *poulet à la Marengo* and *poulet à la provençale* simultaneously. Cookery books provide different recipes for the two dishes, with chicken Marengo tending to omit the olives or anchovies often found in chicken Provençale, while adding fried eggs or crayfish. The story contains yet another twist, since chicken Provençale's own links with Provence are surprisingly superficial. Regional cuisines have evolved with time, and supposedly traditional characteristics emerged only relatively recently. Today, the classic trio of tomatoes, garlic, and olive oil is immediately recognised as a peculiarity of Provence, and yet none of these three individual ingredients truly belongs to the region. Tomatoes had originated in the New World, and became fully absorbed into *provençale* cooking only in the fifteenth or sixteenth century. Garlic was common throughout the south of France, rather than being limited to one particular province, while olive oil was used only to a limited extent in Provence in the Middle Ages, even if it had become widespread there by Napoleon's reign. Even the apparently *provençale* elements of chicken Marengo are therefore deceptive, leaving the origins of Napoleon's favourite dish shrouded by multiple layers of illusion. It cannot be pinned down to a particular region, let alone to a specific point in time. In fact, the basic concept of frying chicken in oil stretches back to antiquity.[26]

Such niceties were of little concern to the restaurants of Paris intent on exploiting any opportunity to make their fortune. The choices they offered to diners were immense. In 1801, the menu at one restaurant listed, for poultry alone, no fewer than thirty-two different *entrées*, besides numerous roast options.[27] Amidst such a profusion of restaurants and different dishes, it took a degree of deceit to attract customers. Reputation was all-important, and surrounding a new dish with the mystique of Marengo artificially increased its profile. A prominent *restaurateur* of Napoleon's time, Antoine Beauvilliers, confessed how frequently old dishes were reinvented and made fashionable again:

> Curiosity can undoubtedly result in the creation of new experiences. The need for variety can lead to changes which, without altering the basis of a dish, modify it with a simple decoration, and thereby allow you to call it whatever you wish. An ingenious chef . . . adds or removes something from a familiar dish, in the way it is made or decorated. He gives it a fanciful name, for example that of the patron to whom he is attached. The existence of this variety of expressions for the same concept can mislead pupils who are striving for perfection, and can cause some confusion in the way the dish is prepared. But the new label bestows the charm of novelty on the familiar dish, which loses its former name and is adopted in every kitchen under its modern title. This, for example, was how the name *côtelettes à la Soubise* was given to cutlets *à la purée d'oignons*.[28]

The name chicken Marengo was therefore applied as a marketing device some time after the battle. The claim that the dish was invented for Napoleon on the spur of a moment, on the evening of a great victory, endowed it with an invaluable prestige, but was just a colourful, beguiling fiction, one of those romanticized stories that draw their strength from people's preference for a simple and memorable tale.

Far from ending there, the story of chicken Marengo is only just beginning, for the dish has become inextricably intertwined with a host of other popular misconceptions. Instead of being considered in isolation, it should be seen as a key for unlocking some of the mysteries surrounding the battle, and for uncovering the startling contradictions in Napoleon's own, extraordinary personality. We will start by exploring the myths that he spun so assiduously around Marengo, and by seeing how these contributed to the confusion over the dish's origins. More so than after any other of his victories, Napoleon used propaganda to transform awkward or lacklustre realities into a glittering, faultless display of his generalship, for he knew that in war and politics alike, perception was as important as reality, and that a mighty reputation, constantly inflated and burnished, could intimidate his enemies even before a shot had been fired. So pervasive was his spin-doctoring that it had an effect on anything connected with the Marengo campaign, and involved men of every variety of talent in a compulsive drive to capture, commemorate, and interpret events in a way that left his image indelibly stamped on the era and gave birth to one of the most powerful legends of history.

Napoleon's hat and sword.

Chapter 2

The Campaign

For Napoleon, the most dramatic phase of the Marengo campaign was not the concluding battle, but the opening act, when he marched an army over the Alps to fall on the Austrians in northern Italy. His crossing of the snow-bound Grand Saint-Bernard pass became so vaunted an achievement because of its sheer boldness and ambition. It seized the popular imagination, for the wild and dramatic mountains evoked a sense of sublime beauty, mingled with feelings of awe and fear. Napoleon portrayed his exploit as an epic venture that achieved the near-impossible by triumphing over nature. It also had grand echoes of antiquity, of Hannibal's passage 2,000 years earlier. Above all, it occurred right at the outset of the campaign. It was an immediate proof of the capabilities of the army's leaders, and provided an invaluable boost to morale.

In the first half of May, Napoleon's strike-force, the deceptively named Armée de réserve, had concentrated on the shores of Lake Geneva, before moving southwards along the Rhône valley to the small Swiss town of Martigny, where it began the long and difficult ascent. Napoleon himself stayed three days in Martigny before setting out for the pass in the early hours of 20 May. Entering a gap in the mountain chain, he followed a road that became progressively narrower the higher he climbed. Few troops were present, for most of the army had already completed the crossing during the previous days. The most difficult stretch began at the village of Saint-Pierre, where the track degenerated into a mere snow-covered path that no vehicle could negotiate. All supplies now had to be carried by hand or on the backs of mules, while guns were dismantled, and their heavy, bronze barrels laid in hollowed-out tree trunks that were laboriously dragged by teams of men.

Trees and shrubs could not grow at this altitude, and their absence exposed an immense, unbroken perspective of the mountain chain, made dazzlingly beautiful by the blanket of snow reflecting the rays of the rising sun.[1] An eerie silence reigned, disturbed only by the wind and the noise of a nearby stream. The climb became steeper, and wound its way round a sequence of twists and turns. During their passage, the soldiers had been obliged to walk in single file, carefully following the footprints of the men in front so as not to stray to either side and slip over a precipice. To minimize the risk of avalanches, they crossed early in the morning, before the sun had time to weaken the cohesion of the snow.

A large, stone building appeared at last around the corner of a rock. It was the Hospice of the Grand Saint-Bernard, perched on the highest point of the pass, at an altitude of 8,100 feet. Monks had been living here for eight centuries in order to help travellers, and over the past few days they had handed out thousands of bottles of wine, along with bread, cheese, and meat to supplement the passing soldiers' rations. Men who became lost in the snow were rescued by the Saint-Bernard dogs, which carried not the barrel of brandy of popular myth, but a small basket of food. This was more suitable for reviving a victim of hypothermia, although the dogs inspired such affection that they seem to have been fed by Napoleon's soldiers more than the other way round.[2]

Napoleon had covered 25 miles since leaving Martigny, but stopped for little more than an hour at the Hospice, where he ate *déjeuner*, his morning meal, before beginning the descent into Italy.[3] After another 8 miles, he halted at the village of Etroubles to spend the night. From there, the road continued down to the old Roman town of Aosta, before heading south-eastwards along the valley of the Dora Baltea, until the mighty mountains on either side gradually diminished into mere foothills, and then gave way at last to the immense, fertile plains of the River Po.

The war had to be won in northern Italy. Neither side could afford to abandon this key strategic region. In Austrian hands, it would keep a perpetual invasion threat hanging over southern France, whereas if it fell to Napoleon, he could dominate the Mediterranean, and be within striking distance of Vienna itself. These were the stakes that drove him into so difficult a venture, that of bringing an army over the Alps before the snows had relaxed their icy grip on the passes.

A year earlier, in 1799, fortune had turned against the young French Republic. Confronted with a powerful new coalition – which included not only three of the great powers (Britain, Austria and Russia) but also Portugal, Naples, the Papal States, and the Ottoman Empire – the French found themselves assailed on a whole array of fronts. In both Holland and Switzerland, they managed to hold their own, but in Italy they suffered a string of defeats. By the end of the year, their Armée d'Italie was a shrunken and demoralized shadow of its former self, and had been driven right back into the Alps and the Italian Riviera at the very fringes of the campaign theatre.

Against the background of these reverses, and with the Republic's government, the Directory, becoming increasingly de-stabilized, Napoleon returned from Egypt, where he had been commanding an expedition. On 9–10 November, he toppled the Directory in a *coup d'état*, and immediately began tightening his grip on power. By the end of the year, he had established himself as First Consul, and the new constitution was then approved by a plebiscite, with the results being falsified to conceal the low turn-out. The need to resort to such fraud made it all the more important for Napoleon to resolve quickly the problems that beset the exhausted and strife-torn country, in order to enthuse its largely apathetic population and strengthen his regime's tenuous claim to legitimacy.

Within months, Napoleon could point to solid progress. By May 1800, he had stabilized public confidence, staved off the threat of bankruptcy, strengthened law and order, and suppressed, at least for the moment, the civil war in the west of France. At the same time, he had continued to concentrate power in his own hands by emasculating the legislature and improving the efficiency of the state's administrative machine. The military situation had also improved, not least as Tsar Paul I had effectively withdrawn Russia from the war after becoming disenchanted with his allies. That left Britain and Austria as Napoleon's two main enemies. He wrote personally to both their monarchs, expressing a general desire for peace, but without offering any concrete proposals. It was little more than a cynical bid to gain domestic support by posing as a peace-maker, and to rally the country behind the war effort when his vague approach inevitably came to nothing. The truth was that he needed a peace won on the battlefield, for nothing could consolidate his regime more effectively than peace with military glory. By winning a decisive victory, he could deliver France from its peril, and produce a wave of relief and gratitude.

Whereas Britain was shielded by the sea, Austria could be forced to make peace by direct military pressure. The Austrians fielded two armies, each of roughly 100,000 men. One was in southern Germany, where it faced the largest and best-equipped French force, the Armée du Rhin under Général de division Jean-Victor Moreau. The other, under Melas, was on the far side of the Alps, in northern Italy, where Général de division André Massena's heavily depleted Armée d'Italie of little more than 30,000 troops stood between it and the south of France.

Napoleon hurriedly assembled a new formation, the Armée de réserve, with which to intervene in person and tip the balance. The key to his strategy was Switzerland, a French satellite republic from which the Austrians and Russians had been driven the previous year. Protected by its mountains, it offered a central location from which to attack the inner flank of either of the Austrian armies. Napoleon's plan was for the Armée du Rhin to take the offensive and drive back the Austrian army in southern Germany. That would enable the Armée de réserve to pour through the Alps and descend on Melas's rear in northern Italy, cutting his line of retreat and forcing him to fight a decisive battle while trapped against the Armée d'Italie.

The danger was that Melas might move his forces northwards to block the exits from the Alpine valleys, thus bottling up the Armée de réserve before it could emerge into the plains. It was therefore vital for the Armée d'Italie to keep Melas occupied. Deception could also help, and Napoleon later boasted in his memoirs that he misled the Austrians with a fiendishly cunning double-bluff. Rather than try and hide the existence of the Armée de réserve, he disclosed it so openly that the Austrians dismissed it as a ruse intended to distract them from the vulnerable Armée d'Italie.[4] Napoleon encouraged them to reach precisely that conclusion by announcing that the Armée de réserve was being assembled at the city of Dijon in Burgundy, while actually organising its divisions at several isolated locations over a wide area. As a result, he claimed, Austrian spies at Dijon found an army of just a few thousand conscripts and former soldiers, many of them crippled by old wounds. He sowed further doubt with forged pamphlets, purportedly written by opponents of his regime, which ridiculed the combat-readiness of the Armée de réserve.[5]

It all reads like a masterstroke, but was it? In fact, Napoleon misled posterity more than the Austrians, for his deception plan was an elaborate fiction dreamed up retrospectively to enhance his reputation. At the time, he seems to have been focused more on maintaining order and stability within France than on misleading Melas, and the reason he publicized the existence of the Armée de réserve was to reassure the population, especially in volatile Paris. From the beginning of March, a flurry of annoucements appeared in the press, building up the impression that a powerful army was taking shape. 'The Armée de réserve grows in strength every day,' read a report from Dijon published in the official newspaper, *Le Moniteur*, on 17 April:

> Our city is full of soldiers. Corps of all arms pass through it in quick succession ... The conscripts are arriving from every part of the Republic, and now number more than 40,000. Muskets are sent from the factories of the Forez region. The stores are filling up with food, and everything affirms the foresight of a government that must have calculated the effects of the enthusiasm it inspires. The imposing appearance of the Armée de réserve already justifies the hopes of every Frenchman who desires peace and cherishes glory.[6]

A remarkable amount of militarily useful information was made public, precisely because of the need to reassure the French people. In any case, Napoleon would have found it impossible to hide an entire army, or to conceal his own departure from Paris, and he made no attempt to do so. It is true, as he claimed in his memoirs, that French newspapers focused attention specifically on Dijon, but they did so to conceal the army's ultimate destination, since the city was much the same distance from both the Italian and the German theatres of war. Napoleon's focus on Dijon was unlikely to mislead spies about the true strength of the army, and he was certainly dishonest in claiming that only inexperienced or decrepit soldiers were present there, for some of the very first units to arrive, as early as March, contained a high proportion of veterans.[7] The reason he kept the army dispersed until the last moment was not deception, but simply because he would have found it physically impossible to feed so many troops for weeks on end had he concentrated them all at Dijon.

The pamphlets mocking the state of the Armée de réserve seem to have been genuine anti-government propaganda, rather than documents forged by the regime itself as Napoleon later claimed. Indeed, confidential police reports at the time blamed rumours about the army's deprivations on foreigners and royalist conspirators intent on encouraging desertion.[8] Nor were the British and Austrians wholly misled, despite Napoleon's claims to the contrary.[9] In Britain, the *Morning Chronicle* reviewed the military situation on 19 April, and, far from dismissing the existence of the Armée de réserve, predicted that it 'will in a few days be assembled in great strength (at least 60,000 men), as troops are on their march at once from every quarter', adding that 'it will very soon be a formidable [and] effective force'.[10] As for Melas, his correspondence shows that as early as 8 May, almost a week before the crossing of the Alps had even begun, he had reliable information that part of the Armée de réserve would be entering Italy, even if he remained unaware of the scale of the threat or which pass would be used.[11] Rather than react immediately, Melas decided to remain focused on finishing off the Armée d'Italie, so he could subsequently turn with all his strength on the Armée de réserve. In the absence of precise, definite intelligence, this was surely more sensible than abandoning his operations against the Armée d'Italie prematurely, which would leave him facing two intact enemy armies at the same time. The belated Austrian response to Napoleon's passage of the Alps was therefore due not so much to French deception as to Melas's desire to avoid half-measures.

Melas had intended to take the offensive against the Armée d'Italie as early as 25 February, which would have given him time to crush it before the Alps were practicable enough for Napoleon to intervene. But bad weather caused the operation to be postponed, and the five-and-a-half week delay ultimately proved fatal. Even so, when Melas finally attacked on 6 April, he split the Armée d'Italie in two, trapping its commander, Massena, and 10,000 of his men inside Genoa, while driving the rest, under Général de division Louis-Gabriel Suchet, back westwards along the Mediterranean coast beyond the city of Nice. With Genoa under siege, the Armée d'Italie in imminent danger of destruction, and the border of southern France breached, Napoleon had to race against time. He recognized that the Austrian offensive could actually work to his advantage, since it shifted Melas's centre of gravity away from the Alps, and tied him down near the coast, but he knew that this benefit would not last for ever. He had to strike with the Armée de réserve before Genoa was forced to surrender, and before Melas could move back northwards against Switzerland.

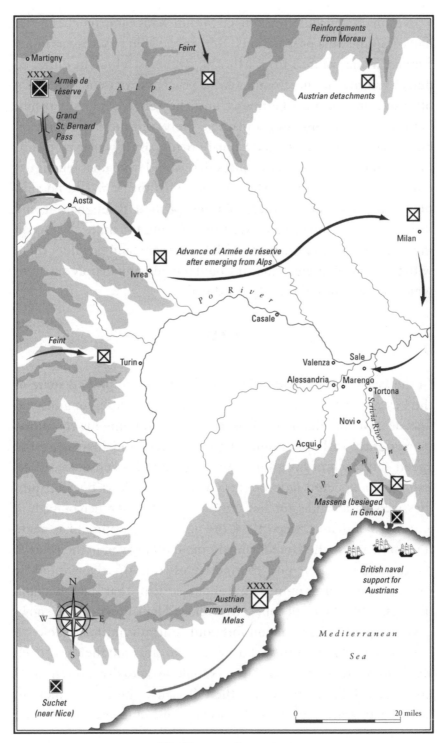

The Marengo Campaign.

Napoleon was therefore obliged to launch his campaign before he had completed his preparations. Nor was he able to secure as much support as he wanted from Moreau, who was reluctant either to detach reinforcements from his Armée du Rhin, or to open his own offensive in southern Germany until he felt ready. As a result, Napoleon had to amend his plan: he preserved the basic concept, but decided to use the Grand Saint-Bernard pass for his main thrust, instead of the more easterly routes that would have enabled him to emerge more directly in Melas's rear. This thrust would be supplemented by four smaller columns pushed through as many different passes, along a concave front of some 115 miles. Napoleon intended to stun the Austrians with his descent, and bewilder them with the array of prongs, since it would not be immediately apparent which of them posed the biggest threat.

♥♦♥

In the years that followed Marengo, Napoleon improved some of the key routes over the Alps, making them praticable for guns and vehicles. Good, reliable roads were a way of binding his conquests more tightly to Paris, promoting commerce, and increasing the speed and reach of his armies. Yet upgrading his communications had an unexpected side-effect. Crossing the Alps became progressively easier and safer, but at the same time lost much of its thrill and sense of drama. Since 1964, the opening of a tunnel has made it possible to use the Grand Saint-Bernard route even in the heart of winter, and travellers now routinely cross the Alps, captivated by the scenery, but complacent about a trip that has become unremarkable. Many of course fly over, and look down on the snow-covered peaks from a comfort and warmth unimaginable to Napoleon's soldiers as they slid, swore, and shivered their way over. By helping to tame the Alps, Napoleon actually undermined posterity's ability to appreciate the full scale of his achievement in bringing an army over them. It was an ironic outcome for one who put such effort into commemorating the venture, and shaping public perceptions of it.

Of the various artists who painted the passage of the Alps, only Jacques-Louis David produced a truly great work. Napoleon stares directly out of his canvas with supreme self-confidence, mastering the mountains with the same consummate ease as he controls his rearing horse. His cloak billows in the wind, highlighting the tempestuous nature of the undertaking, and reflecting Napoleon's own tendency to visualize the Alps as a living opponent. 'At last the Armée de réserve is entering the campaign theatre,' he wrote at the time. 'The Saint-Bernard has put some difficulties in our way. Not since Charlemagne has it seen so large an army. It wanted in particular to obstruct the passage of our heavy field guns, but half of our artillery is finally at Aosta.'[12] In reality, Napoleon was remarkably lucky with the weather, for he enjoyed a fine spell during his passage, sandwiched between bad conditions immediately before and afterwards, yet it suited him to exaggerate the challenges he had overcome.[13]

David made little pretence of historical accuracy. Instead, he painted an overt piece of propaganda, showing Napoleon not simply as a commander, but as a great ruler. He even inscribed on the rocks at the foot of the painting the names of Bonaparte, of Charlemagne, the King of the Franks, and of the great Carthaginian general, Hannibal, all of whom had brought an army over the Alps at the age of thirty. The inclusion of their names was not entirely a figment of David's imagination. Some medieval historians claimed to have seen inscriptions about Hannibal's passage carved into a crag at the side of the road in the Aosta valley.[14] Yet it is not the trio of names etched into the rocks that forms the most arresting feature of the painting, but Napoleon's right hand. David drew inspiration from several sources, but appears to have based Napoleon's pointing gesture, and the way he is enveloped in his cloak, partly on Michelangelo's painting of God creating Adam on the ceiling of the Sistine Chapel in the Vatican. This can hardly have been mere coincidence, for David had spent five formative years in Rome before the French

Revolution, producing several volumes of sketches of the city's artworks from which he ceaselessly drew ideas for the rest of his life.[15] His message was unmistakeable: Napoleon, with a grand and godlike gesture, was stretching out across the mountainous void of the Alps to bring new life and freedom to Italy.

David depicted Napoleon as a leader, yet this was misleading. Napoleon did not lead his army over the Alps. He did not even formally command it. Out of all the campaigns he ever fought, that of 1800 was unique because of this remote and informal style of control. The usual explanation is that, as First Consul, he was con-stitutionally barred from personally commanding the army, yet this is not strictly true. The Constitution of Year VIII, which took effect in December 1799, contained no such clause. It was only the previous constitution, that of Year III, that had banned any member of the executive Directory from commanding the military.[16] Napoleon appears to have yielded simply to a sense of caution over too blatant a break with the principle of the separation of the powers, and this reflected the political fragility of his position so soon after his *coup d'état*. But there could be no objection to him accompanying, rather then commanding, the Armée de réserve, and so he simply made his Minister of War, Louis-Alexandre Berthier, its nominal commander, while taking the key, strategic decisions himself.

Napoleon found it a convenient arrangement, and one that reflected his new position as a soldier-statesman; for the first time, he was going on campaign not purely as a general, but as a head of state. Taking personal command of the Armée de réserve would have placed him on the same level as the commanders of France's other armies, whereas exercising an indirect control preserved a sense of his elevation. He was cautious about exercising authority too overtly. 'You see that I am concerning myself very much with your details,' he wrote almost apologetically to Berthier at the beginning of May, 'but the success of the campaign truly lies in your operation, and I have no doubt that you will have the glory of regaining [northern Italy].'[17] Not until half-way through the actual battle of Marengo did Napoleon take tactical control of the Armée de réserve. Up until then, he usually remained in the army's rear, and often behind Berthier's headquarters, exercising a broad, operational supervision. Berthier's position as the army's commander was not wholly fictional – it is true that Napoleon sometimes ignored Berthier's official status, but this was more particularly the case after the campaign was over. Thus, when special sabres were ordered to reward deserving generals, the inscription read: 'Battle of Marengo, commanded in person by the First Consul'.[18]

Napoleon's role, therefore, was largely that of a manager and figurehead. Far from setting the Armée de réserve an example as it toiled its way over the pass, he actually followed it. The passage of the Alps was a triumph not of heroic leadership, but of paperwork; not of dynamic gestures, but of planning, organization, and logistics. As head of the government, Napoleon had to remain in touch with Paris, and take an overview of all France's armies rather than focus solely on the Armée de réserve. By remaining in the rear, he could regulate the flow of units through the Alps, and try to prevent congestion from building up further forward. He could also use his personal authority to overcome logistical problems as they arose, and hasten the requisitioning of mules. Not until the 20th, the seventh of the ten days the army took to go through the Grand Saint-Bernard pass, did he cross it himself, by which time the advanced guard had already penetrated 40 miles into Piedmont.

David's iconic image was rightly acclaimed as a masterpiece, but so blatant were its exaggerations that in 1848 another artist, Hippolyte Delaroche, decided to paint a more realistic version. He seems to have based his picture on the description published three years earlier in the first volume of Adolphe Thiers's epic *Histoire du consulat et de l'empire*. '[Napoleon] has been depicted in art crossing the snowy Alps on a fiery horse', Thiers explained,

> but the simple truth is as follows. He went up the Saint-Bernard while mounted on a mule and wrapped in the grey overcoat that he always wore, led by a local guide, showing in the difficult stretches the absent-mindedness of one whose

brain was absorbed in other things, speaking to the officers along the route, and then, from time to time, questioning the guide . . . like an idle traveller with nothing better to do.[19]

The Napoleon that Delaroche painted was not David's superhero, but a deflated figure who was clearly feeling the cold.

Dwelling on this contrast would be unfair to David, however straightforward it might at first seem, for in fact Delaroche rarely let historical truth stand in the way of an atmospheric scene, as he demonstrated most notoriously with his earlier painting of the execution of the would-be Queen of England, Lady Jane Grey. His depiction of the passage of the Alps is littered with inaccuracies: the costume of the guide is not that of a local inhabitant, the mule is improbably equipped with a decorative harness, and Napoleon's pose, with his right hand tucked into his coat, is an unlikely one for this particular time and place, being more suited for formal portraits. Furthermore, both artists show Napoleon wearing a military uniform, and yet he apparently did not do so during the crossing.[20]

Delaroche relied too heavily on tales spun by Napoleon, or equally unreliable legends told by local inhabitants. The story of Napoleon's guide is a good example. According to Napoleon himself, the guide was a man of twenty-two, who confided his hopes of some day being able to afford a house of his own. Other versions of the story added a romantic angle, by stating that owning a house would enable the guide to marry the woman he loved. When they finally reached the top of the pass, Napoleon reputedly handed his guide a note, and told him to take it to the address shown – it turned out to be an order to the authorities that made all his ambitions come true.[21] Yet in reality, the guide was twenty-seven at the time of Napoleon's passage, nor twenty-two, and records show that he had already married in 1798. Rather than handing the man a note at the time, Napoleon ordered inquiries to be made about him later. He learned that his name was Pierre-Nicolas Dorsaz, and in July 1801 instructed the French plenipotentiary minister in Helvetia to buy a house for him. When it turned out that Dorsaz had already bought a home for 1,200 francs, Napoleon instead had him paid that amount as a reward for his dedication. Some accounts claim that there was a particular reason for such gratitude, since Dorsaz had supposedly saved Napoleon's life when his mule stumbled, but it is doubtful if this incident actually occurred.[22]

Historians have preferred to ignore Delaroche's subtle flaws, and simply decry David's shameless propaganda, yet in doing so they oversimplify Napoleon's own attitude. However much he appreciated the powerful symbolism of David's image, he would not necessarily have disapproved of Delaroche's had he still been alive to see it, for he was actually proud of having shared the discomforts of his men. In the official bulletin, he even boasted of the unheroic way he had gone down the far side of the pass: 'The First Consul descended from the top of the Saint-Bernard by riding a luge on the snow, crossing abysses, and sliding over frozen torrents.'[23] It was a claim he repeated while dictating his memoirs on Saint Helena, this time with the ludicrous statement that he had used a luge to go down an almost perpendicular glacier. Napoleon even stated openly that he rode a mule for the most difficult stretches of the crossing, and described scenes altogether closer to Delaroche's interpretation than David's.[24]

Some of the most strident criticisms of David are actually mistaken, including the protests about him depicting Napoleon on a horse rather than a mule. If Napoleon rode a mule, it would have been only for the worst stretch, above the village of Saint-Pierre, and David shows him on the lower slopes, with some of the artillery in the background yet to be dismantled.[25] The contrast between David's and Delaroche's paintings is therefore less stark than it at first seems, and David's iconic version may actually be the less flawed of the two. For all Delaroche's apparent desire to capture an authentic image, the reality was even more prosaic than he realized. The simple truth is that hardly anyone would have seen Napoleon during his passage, particularly since he covered the first stage of the ascent in the darkness before dawn. The bulk of his soldiers had already gone through the Grand Saint-Bernard ahead of him, while many of the local inhabitants had abandoned their homes.[26] Simply by portraying Napoleon as the central figure of the crossing of the Alps, therefore, David and Delaroche are equally misleading. But their paintings highlight the schism in attitudes that set the tone for the rest of the campaign, as perceptions of even the most basic points connected with Marengo rapidly became polarised and distorted by myth.

$$\text{🐓 🐓 🐓}$$

'We have fallen here like a thunderbolt', Napoleon boasted four days after his passage of the Grand Saint-Bernard, 'and the enemy, who did not expect it at all, can scarcely believe it. Very great events are going to occur, and will, I hope, have great results for the happiness and glory of the Republic.'[27]

Emerging from the Alps, he entered a vast plain, but instead of heading directly south-eastwards to relieve the besieged garrison of Genoa, he swerved to the east, advancing 60 miles through Lombardy to enter the city of Milan on 2 June. By taking this indirect approach, he avoided running into a major battle on flat, exposed terrain where the Austrians could make the most of their superior numbers of cavalry and artillery, and before his hurriedly improvised army had been properly tested in minor clashes.[28] Marching on Milan also promised greater rewards, for by circling clockwise round Melas's northern flank, Napoleon could cut his line of retreat, and trap his entire army rather than simply defeating it.

Only gradually did Melas realize the full extent of his peril, as he received a progressively worsening series of reports. He therefore found it difficult to devise an effective response, all the more so given his reluctance to abandon the siege of Genoa and the gains he had made against the Armée d'Italie. On 19 May, he left the city of Nice on the Mediterranean coast, intending to concentrate part of his army at the central location of Turin, so as to cover the siege of Genoa until it surrendered; he would then be free to reunite his army and launch a full-scale onslaught against the Armée de réserve.

But Melas was taken aback by the speed with which the French poured through the Alps, and by reports of reinforcements joining them from Moreau's army in Germany. By the end of May, he knew that he could no longer hope to contain the Armée de réserve unless he ordered a general concentration, with his main base at the fortress city of Alessandria, 45 miles east of Turin.[29]

Napoleon was intent on severing Melas's most direct escape route – the main road eastwards along the south bank of the Po – and obliging him to fight a decisive battle on disadvantageous terms to reopen it. The most obvious point at which to check a breakout attempt was the Stradella pass, a strip of flat ground barely 3 miles wide, where the French could rest their flanks securely on the marshes of the Po to the north and a spur of the Apennines to the south. But Napoleon was obliged to revise his plans, for by 8 June he knew that Genoa had been starved into surrender four days earlier, thus removing a key element in the trap he had created around the Austrian army. The next day, the French advanced guard encountered a detachment of 14,000 men in a battle at Montebello, 11 miles south-west of Stradella. The Austrians were defeated, and thus foiled in an initial attempt to reopen a line of retreat. It remained possible that Melas would try again with a larger force, but the next two days passed without an attack, which increased suspicions that he might now be trying to slip past Napoleon by an altogether different, roundabout route.

Passively awaiting events was not in Napoleon's temperament. The only remedy was to advance and seek out a battle, even though this meant leaving behind the security of his position at Stradella. He had the army reorganized for a final, decisive showdown, and then began a westward advance on 12 June. It encountered no opposition, and so on the morning of the 13th two corps, supported by cavalry, were pushed across the Scrivia river to ascertain Melas's whereabouts. As the day progressed, the French moved forward over the wide plain that extended 11 miles westwards to Alessandria, and that evening their foremost division drove an Austrian rearguard from the little hamlet of Marengo.

Where was Melas? What were his plans? Napoleon believed the Austrians to be still concentrating their army, and intent only on escape, which helps explain his boldness in pushing forward into the exposed plain despite his marked inferiority in cavalry and artillery. In reality, the available Austrian forces had already completed their concentration on the 11th. Melas had four options. From Alessandria, he could head 16 miles northwards to cross the Po at Casale, before going round Napoleon's flank, through Milan, to the safety of Venetia. The second option was to retreat 38 miles southwards to Genoa, where he could be supported by Britain's Royal Navy, and find his way back to Austrian territory by a circuitous route. The third alternative was to improve the odds by falling on a surviving part of the Armée d'Italie under Suchet, which was approaching from the south-west to help close the trap around the Austrians. The fourth and final option was to thrust directly eastwards along the south bank of the Po, smashing a way through the Armée de réserve. The one thing Melas could not do was remain inactive, for abandoning the initiative to the French would enable them to tighten their array of forces around him and cut the last of his supply lines. Once that happened, he would have less than a week before his stores ran out, since that summer's crops had yet to be harvested.[30]

Napoleon had become increasingly uncertain which of these options the Austrians would pick. It is often alleged that he was over-confident, and yet it was also concern not to let his quarry escape that exposed him to near-disaster. At noon on the 13th, with anxiety growing that Melas was intent on passing round one or other of his flanks, he broke up the strong corps he had in reserve, and detached Desaix southwards with an infantry division of 5,000 men to cut the main road from Alessandria to Genoa. On the morning of the 14th, Napoleon sent another division, of 3,500 men, to cross to the north bank of the Po in case Melas tried to escape on that side. He was now left with a reserve of just one infantry division and the weak Consular Guard – or fewer than 5,000 men in all.

Napoleon has been roundly condemned for weakening his reserve so dangerously in order to cover his flanks. Yet the stakes were high, and if he let the Austrian army slip past him, he would lose all the advantages he had secured by crossing the Alps. Time was not on his side. Politically, he could not afford to be absent from Paris much longer, and as a result of this constant concern about his power base he was forced to take risks to secure a quick and decisive victory. He did so all the more readily in that everything seemed to indicate the Austrians wanted to avoid battle.

❧❦❧

At seventy-one, Melas was old enough to be Napoleon's grandfather. The serious expression in his portrait, along with his heavy-lidded eyes and double-chin, and the lines etched across his forehead, convey an impression of old-fashioned solidity, with no obvious sign of intelligence, still less of the restless, dynamic energy that drove Napoleon. Yet first impressions can be misleading. It is true that Melas lacked the inner fire and unshakeable self-confidence that make a truly inspirational leader, yet he was actually one of the more capable and conscientious Austrian commanders, and the fact that he has gone down in history as the general who lost Marengo has obscured a distinguished – and largely successful – career spanning more than half a century.

He owed his ascent to his own merit rather than to birth, for he was the son not of a great noble family, but of a Lutheran pastor. Summoned back to active service in 1799, he took command of the Austrian army in Italy, despite having misgivings on account of his age and health. He then won a string of victories, but they came to an abrupt end as the French irruption through the Grand Saint-Bernard left him confronted with one of the most dangerous predicaments of his career. It was unfortunate that he had to face this daunting situation when he was old, tired, and beset by aches and pains.

At first, Melas was inclined to evade Napoleon, and on 11 June actually issued orders to cross to the north bank of the Po. But he then changed his mind and cancelled the move, fearing that his slow-moving army was liable to be checked on one of the river's many tributaries. Equally, a retreat southwards on Genoa was likely to be costly and demoralizing, and might be blocked in the difficult terrain of the Apennines by elements of the Armée d'Italie. Rather than tamely abandon the campaign in this way, Melas concluded that it was better to smash his way out by advancing directly down the main road from Alessandria, along the south bank of the Po.

The Austrian General Staff later claimed that a double-agent misled Napoleon into thinking that its army would escape over the Po at Casale and Valenza. The agent was told to encourage Napoleon to pursue along the Po and through the town of Sale in order to fall on Melas's rear, and the Austrians built a pontoon bridge over the river to make the bluff more credible. In fact, Napoleon does not seem to have given undue credit to this specific information. At any rate, while he detached forces to both flanks, he kept the bulk of his army in a central position, with its components arranged in depth along the main road so they could move in any direction and progressively reinforce any attacked point. 'The fact is that Bonaparte kept his army concentrated as he awaited events, and did not make the detachments that we wanted to induce him to make,' an Austrian staff officer, Major von Neipperg, later admitted. 'Nevertheless, as Général Berthier himself later admitted to me, the French had not the slightest expectation that we would give battle.'[31]

It was actually Melas – not Napoleon – who unbalanced his army, and he did so because he had fallen for his own deception. He firmly believed that he had convinced the French to advance through Sale against his far northern flank, and he planned his own offensive accordingly. His largest column, constituting two-thirds of his strength, would move eastwards along the main road, and then turn to the north to fall on the French flank. Another, northerly, column would distract and delay the French, while the third would act as a covering force in the south. Melas hence based his entire plan of attack on the illusion that the French centre of gravity lay not on the main road, but 5 miles north of it. 'An unexpected appearance on the enemy's flank must have a great effect,' he prophesied in his attack order. 'We can hope to fall on the enemy column, to cut it in two or take it wholly in the rear, to drive back and throw it into the Tanaro and Po. Speed and determination are bound to gain us a splendid victory.'[32]

But speed was not forthcoming. On marching out from Alessandria, Melas would have to cross the Bormida river, and had available only two bridges, followed by just the one exit from a fortified bridgehead on the eastern side. The irony was that by building a pontoon bridge over the Po to try and deceive Napoleon, he had deprived himself of a third crossing over the Bormida. Congestion was inevitable, especially since a French spearhead seized the hamlet of Marengo on the evening of 13 June.[33] Instead of being able to cross the Bormida, pass through Marengo, and form up in the plain under cover of darkness, ready for a general advance at the crack of dawn, the Austrians would now have to wait until full daylight to begin even their preliminary moves, for they had no desire to make a night attack to recapture Marengo, with all the confusion that would entail.

Neither commander had even two-fifths of his troops available, since the rest were dispersed in garrisons, or deployed to protect rearward communications. As a result, each side would concentrate only around 28,000 men on the battlefield. The apparent balance in numbers hid the fact that Napoleon's forces were initially more scattered, and would take most of the day to assemble. In fact, for the first six hours of the fighting, no more than 17,000 French troops would be gradually committed, starting with an infantry division of just 3,000 men. Melas therefore had an opportunity to defeat the French piecemeal. He enjoyed an overwhelming advantage in guns, and had superior numbers of cavalry even after detaching a brigade to Acqui, 18 miles to the south-west, in response to exaggerated reports of Suchet's advance with part of the Armée d'Italie from the Mediterranean coast.

At 8.00 am on 14 June, the first Austrian units moved out across the Bormida bridges, with their bands playing and the sun glittering on a sea of sabres and bayonets.[34] The army had been drained and depleted by its offensive against the Armée d'Italie, its siege of Genoa, and then its marches and deprivations as it hurried to concentrate against Napoleon, but it had benefited from a couple of days in which to recover. Reasonably rested, re-equipped from the stores of Alessandria, and revived with distributions of meat, rice, and wine, the troops had grounds for confidence, for despite partial setbacks such as Montebello, their army as a whole remained undefeated. The day before, Melas had ridden round his camp, from regiment to regiment, gathering the men around him each time to hear what he had to say. One company commander, Hauptmann von Rauch, noted how the commander-in-chief spent a considerable time with his unit, Infanterie-Regiment Nr. 23, praising its courage, boosting morale, and urging the troops to do their duty faithfully. 'As a result of [his] statement that he placed particular confidence on this regiment's bravery', wrote Rauch, 'the officers and men were raised to the highest enthusiasm, and all swore to do wonders on the day of battle'.[35]

So it was in a spirit of hope that the regiments marched off down the road towards Marengo, amid all the freshness and promise of a summer morning. The Austrians had their faults – above all, they tended to be too slow and methodical, and disdained the large-scale use of skirmishers – but they were also tough, resilient, and well-disciplined.[36] Of all the armies pitted against the French Republic during the first decade of its existence, Austria's was unquestionably the most formidable, and within hours of the first shots being fired at Marengo, Napoleon's destiny was hanging by a thread.

Chapter 3

Marengo-Mania

Paris did not have long to wait in suspense. Never in his entire career did Napoleon win a campaign so swiftly: on the morning of 21 June, less than seven weeks after Paris had learned of his departure, a succession of three couriers brought news of his victory at Marengo, putting an end to the tension and uncertainty. Twenty-one cannonshots thundered across the city in salute, while staff officers proclaimed the news by going through the streets and squares, and announcements were posted up on walls.

Paris broke into a frenzy of rejoicing. Everywhere could be heard the excited buzz of people talking. 'Italy is conquered, Italy is conquered!' they told each other. Amid the elation, shops were closed, and work abandoned for the rest of the day, while at the Stock Exchange the news provoked cheers of '*Vive la République! Vive Bonaparte!*', and an immediate surge on the markets. The impact of Marengo is clearly visible in the graph on page 41 showing the value of *tiers consolidé* bonds. *The tiers consolidé* was what remained of the national debt after the notorious default of 1797, and the fluctuating market price served as a barometer of influential public opinion in Paris. Even before Marengo, it had pointed to mounting confidence in the Consulate, and this upward trend was boosted by news of the victory. 'The whole appearance of things has totally changed today,' reported the Prefecture of Police. 'Joy is in everyone's heart, and the name of the General First Consul in everyone's mouth. It is repeated with emotion, and the pleasure is almost incredible. The news from Italy spread instantly from one end of the city to the other . . . It is impossible to describe the mood of Paris today: it is an intoxication, a general rapture.'[1]

Celebrations continued well into the night. Fireworks criss-crossed over the Seine. Verses composed in honour of the army were vigorously applauded in the theatres. A concert was held at the Tuileries, and crowds choked the squares, talking enthusiastically about the battle. 'It was the first popular rejoicing in nine years,' claimed the Second Consul, Jean-Jacques Régis de Cambacérès. 'All the others had given the impression of either coercion or indifference.'[2] He was not being completely honest, for despite the government's assertion that the inhabitants illuminated their houses spontaneously, it actually provided the impulse by ordering the public buildings to be lit up, and by asking civil servants to do the same for their homes.[3] Yet Cambacérès barely exaggerated in adding that there had never been a greater demonstration of national enthusiasm.

Parisians were in no doubt about what the news meant. Marengo meant peace. On the day after the battle, Melas and Berthier had signed a convention at Alessandria, establishing an armistice in the Italian theatre pending the agreement of a definitive peace treaty, and in the meantime the Austrian army was to evacuate the campaign area. The convention suited both sides, for neither was fit for another battle. While the French instantly regained north-western Italy without having to besiege its numerous fortresses, Melas was able to extricate his army and garrisons, and safeguard the remaining Austrian territory in the north-east of the peninsula. In the eyes of the French people, Marengo was a clear-cut victory that not only saved the Republic at a stroke, but also promised a prompt end to the war, and a chance to rebuild France after a decade of conflict.

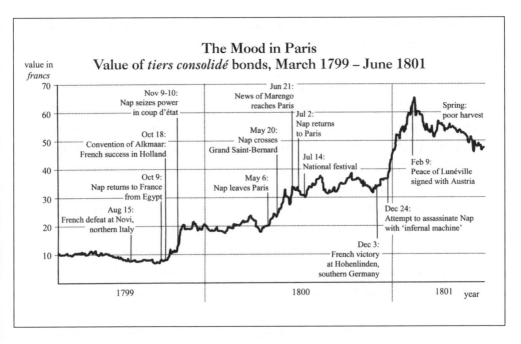

The Mood in Paris
Value of *tiers consolidé* bonds, March 1799 – June 1801

value in francs

Nov 9-10:
Nap seizes power
in coup d'état

Jun 21:
News of Marengo
reaches Paris

Jul 2:
Nap returns
to Paris

Spring:
poor harvest

Oct 18:
Convention of Alkmaar:
French success in Holland

May 20:
Nap crosses
Grand Saint-Bernard

Oct 9:
Nap returns to France
from Egypt

May 6:
Nap leaves Paris

Jul 14:
National festival

Feb 9:
Peace of Lunéville
signed with Austria

Aug 15:
French defeat at Novi,
northern Italy

Dec 24:
Attempt to assassinate Nap
with 'infernal machine'

Dec 3:
French victory
at Hohenlinden,
southern Germany

1799   1800   1801   year

Throughout the campaign, Napoleon had remained nervous about being away from Paris too long. Just seven months had elapsed since his seizure of power, and he had yet to consolidate his position. In letters to his fellow consuls, he repeatedly stated that he would soon return, in the hope that this would stave off alarm and keep potential plotters off balance. 'Events are going to follow each other rapidly,' he predicted on 24 May. 'I hope to be back in Paris in fifteen days. In the meantime, accept my congratulations on the quietness of Paris.'[4]

In order to counter any destabilizing rumours, it was vital for Napoleon to control the flow of information, and shape the public's view of the unfolding operations. At the start of the year, he had tightened his grip on the press by reducing the number of political newspapers by three-quarters, leaving just thirteen, and by April, he was banning the sale of prints harmful to the government, and requiring permits for the sticking of posters on walls, the hawking of pamphlets, or the announcement of theatre plays.[5] These restrictions enabled him to impose a news black-out at the start of the campaign about the Armée de réserve's destination; only after it had completed the crossing of the Grand Saint-Bernard was the news of its presence in Italy released in the newspapers. From then on, Napoleon had frequent accounts sent to Paris for publication, and the benefits of this policy became particularly clear after Marengo, when a plethora of official accounts of the battle appeared in the papers, starting on 22 June, with Napoleon's own bulletins being supplemented by more detailed reports. The result was to keep Marengo in the public eye for a protracted period.

The aftermath of the victory was punctuated by two further bursts of rejoicing, the first of which was triggered by Napoleon's return to Paris. As soon as the Austrians had fulfilled the conditions of the armistice, he left the army in Italy, and set out for Paris on 25 June. 'We travelled with the greatest speed,' remembered Constant, his valet. 'Everywhere, the First Consul was greeted with an almost indescribable enthusiasm.'[6] Napoleon reached Paris soon after 2.00 am on 2 July. As word spread through the city during the day, cheering crowds gathered around the Tuileries, and that evening inhabitants illuminated their homes, just as they had done on hearing the news of Marengo eleven days earlier. The whole of the eastern quarters of the city seemed to be ablaze with all the lights, bonfires, and fireworks, and many people were still out on the streets as dawn began to break the next day.

The climax to the celebrations came on 14 July. For a decade, the day had been an annual festival, marking as it did the anniversary of the storming of the Bastille prison in 1789, but Napoleon was intent on bringing the Revolution to a close, and reuniting the traumatized nation behind him. In subsequent years, the festival would be progressively reduced in importance, and in 1805 would disappear from the official calendar altogether (being reinstated only in 1880 during the Third Republic). The process began in 1800, when the government subtly transformed the festival's character by injecting it with a different meaning, so it no longer commemorated a deeply divisive moment from the recent past, but the start of a new era. 'It is necessary to concentrate on making this a brilliant festival', Napoleon told his two fellow consuls, 'and to ensure it does not ape those that have been held up to now.'[7] The tone was set by its new title, the Festival of Concord and Reconciliation. For this particular year, the festival was also a celebration of Marengo, a tribute to France's armies, and a demonstration of popular support for the newly embedded Consulate, in order to reinforce its dubious claim to legitimacy. It became, in fact, an updated version of the 'bread and games' with which the political leaders of Ancient Rome had sought to win popular approval – on the day before the festival, theatres in Paris even held free performances to enable the lower classes to attend.

Napoleon carefully stage-managed the events. As one of the highlights, he had two of the finest Italian singers specially brought to Paris to perform songs celebrating the liberation of their people from Austrian occupation. Yet, for the Italians, it was liberation with a distinctly French flavour. Just eight days after the festival, Napoleon wrote to encourage Massena, the commander of the Armée d'Italie, to be ruthless in extracting taxes. 'It is necessary to make some examples,' he added. 'The first Piedmontese village that rises in insurrection, have it given over to be pillaged and burned.'[8]

The highpoint of the festival was a military review, held in the afternoon on the open space of the Champ-de-Mars in front of an immense crowd. Twenty-three captured flags were presented to the Consuls: fourteen from Moreau's Armée du Rhin, and the rest from Italy. All were carried by *grenadiers* of the Consular Guard, the élite bodyguard created by Napoleon immediately after his *coup d'état*. They had reached Paris that very morning, after marching all the way from Italy in three weeks, and appeared still covered in dust. They were there to represent the army that had won Marengo, but also to disprove hostile rumours that the Guard had been wiped out by Austrian cavalry during the battle. The claims were exaggerated, yet the Guard's losses were heavy enough to create a potential political danger for Napoleon, for he needed an intact and reliable military force at his personal disposal in case of plots against him. The inclusion of the guardsmen in the review was intended to dispel the more alarmist reports about their fate, although it actually sparked another rumour, this time that the casualties had been replaced by a hurried spate of recruiting.[9]

Despite such controversies, the overwhelming mood in Paris during the festival seems to have been one of genuine rejoicing, with the police reporting only a few, isolated protests. This did not prevent royalists from later playing down the fervour of that day, or even denying it altogether. A former *émigrée*, Henriette-Lucie de La Tour du Pin-Gouvernet, claimed two decades later that she was struck by the indifference with which the crowd supposedly greeted the guardsmen as they arrived in the Champ-de-Mars in their torn and dirty campaign uniforms. 'Some had an arm in a sling, while others had bandages wrapped around their head,' she wrote. 'I expected frenzied and well-deserved applause, yet contrary to my assumptions I detected not one cheer, and very few indications of joy. We were equally surprised and indignant at this, and even later, when we were able to reflect about it at our leisure, we could not grasp the reason for the coldness.'[10]

Yet Napoleon's stepson, Eugène de Beauharnais, remembered a completely different mood. He was just eighteen at the time, and was serving as a cavalry officer in the Consular Guard. 'We went round the Champ-de-Mars', he recalled, 'in front of an immense crowd which covered the banks and greeted us all the way with thunderous applause and cheering. It was one of the finest moments of my life.'[11]

ᴗ🕊ᴗ

The extraordinary wave of enthusiasm that greeted these events found immediate expression in a whole range of outlets in Paris. As early as 24 June, just three days after the arrival of the official news of the victory, one of the theatres was announcing a show entitled *La Conquête de l'Italie, ou la bataille de Maringo*, which opened on the 27th. The first performances followed of *La Nouvelle inattendue, ou la reprise de l'Italie* on 1 July; of *Paris illuminé, ou le retour de Marengo* on the 9th; and of *Desaix au Mont Saint-Bernard* on the 20th. Many of these hurriedly staged plays were unmemorable. *Bientôt la paix, ou la voiture cassée*, first shown in Paris on 3 July, was actually written in a single night, something that was obvious from its poor quality.[12]

Entrepreneurs exploited the excitement by charging for admission to celebratory *fêtes* featuring fireworks, concerts, balls, and even a goddess of victory hovering in the air in a balloon. Songs, poems, and medallions were produced equally quickly, and writers were also busy. Barely a month after Marengo, the *Journal de Paris* was advertising a description of the campaign by Alexandre Foudras, followed that November by an eyewitness account from Joseph Petit of the Guard cavalry.[13]

Within a month of his death, Desaix was even being used to promote a phantasmagoria – a ghost show using magic lanterns to project a series of terrifying, moving images. On 9 July, he was included for the first time in the regular advertisement in the *Journal de Paris* for the Fantasmagorie de Robertson. 'Today, APPARITIONS of GHOSTS, the SHADE of the Prophet DANIEL, of BUFFON, of Général DESAIX, etc.', it promised, before adding some equally intriguing enticements. 'ILLUSIONS, OPTICS, HARMONICA. Experiments with GAS, AIR, GALVANISM or ELECTRICITY. VENTRILOQUIST on even-numbered days. Performance every day at 7.30 pm. You will enjoy the experience and explanation of the INVISIBLE WOMAN.'[14]

It had been three years since the phantasmagoria had first opened in Paris. The man who ran it was a Belgian known by the stage name of Etienne Robertson, and he had found an ideal, spooky location in the crypt of an abandoned convent. Desaix's ghost was just one of the new attractions he was continually adding to attract spectators.[15] So realistic were the performances that some people were left convinced they were witnessing the genuinely supernatural, and the show had even been closed down temporarily following allegations that Robertson might conjure up the ghost of King Louis XVI – a highly alarming prospect for regicidal republicans.

To commemorate Marengo in a more substantial fashion, its name was bestowed on streets, squares, and bridges. Within days of

Napoleon's return from Italy, the toll-gate through which he entered Paris was dubbed the barrière de Marengo. Even babies were named after the battle during the initial wave of rejoicing. A local woman had just given birth to twins at the town of Nogent-sur-Seine when the Consular Guard passed through on its way to Paris to attend the 14 July festivities. She invited two of the Guard's senior officers to name the babies, and they happily accepted, calling the boy Alexandre-Maringo, and the girl Victoire-Alexandrie. (Alexandre was a doubly felicitous choice, since it was not only Berthier's first name, but also a reminder of the city where the convention had been agreed after the battle.)[16]

The mania surrounding the battle embraced a remarkable range of items – some of them as well known in their day as chicken Marengo, but now largely forgotten. The victory lent its name to a dark cloth speckled with tiny white dots, a black grape grown on the banks of the Rhine, and even a type of jumping spider. There is a rose called 'Etendard de Marengo', and another known as 'Souvenir de la bataille de Marengo'. A *marengo* is also a gold coin worth 20 francs. First minted at Turin in 1801, it bore the inscription 'Italy liberated at Marenco'. (The spelling of the name varied during the early years, Maringo being a common alternative.) Coins were an important propaganda tool, and the gold *marenghi* (the plural of *marengo*) became symbols of prosperity, since they were immune from the runaway inflation that had made worthless the paper *assignats* issued during the Revolution. Gold 20-franc coins were also known as *napoléons*, since those issued in France bore his effigy. They served as a model for similar coins produced in other European countries of the Latin Monetary Union, the scheme established in 1865 as an early attempt to standardize national currencies. As a result, the names *marengo* and *napoléon* were applied by extension to all gold coins of the same weight and diameter.[17]

Several ships have been called *Marengo*, including no fewer than six of the French Navy that came into service between 1780 and 1872.[18] (The oldest two were launched under different names, but became *Marengo* in August 1800 and December 1802.) The name

Marengo was also bestowed on a French patrol boat built towards the end of the First World War. Sadly, most of these ships failed to live up to their illustrious title. One, captured by the Royal Navy in 1806, became HMS *Marengo*. A second managed to collide in 1813 with another vessel in Brest harbour, but survived to see action during the Crimean War. Three, including HMS *Marengo*, ended up as prison ships, but the most curious of them all took an astonishing forty-three years to build, and underwent a whole series of name changes to reflect the political upheavals that beset France during that period. Begun in 1807 as the *Marengo*, it later became the *Ville de Vienne*, then the *Comte d'Artois* in 1814, went back to the *Ville de Vienne* during Napoleon's brief resumption of power in 1815, before reverting to *Comte d'Artois* immediately afterwards. Following the 1830 Revolution which toppled the actual comte d'Artois (who by then was King Charles X), it became the *Ville de Paris*, and was finally launched in 1850.[19]

Even places on the far side of the world were named in honour of the battle. Cape Marengo on the coast of Australia was apparently given that title by a French naval captain, Nicolas Baudin, who sailed past it in March 1802.[20] Argentina, Belgium, Canada, Chile, Colombia, and Cuba all have at least one locality called Marengo. Another Marengo was founded in 1848 in the French colony of Algeria, but was renamed Hadjout following independence in 1962. Interestingly, not one commune in France itself is called Marengo, but there are two localities within communes that bear the name.[21] During Napoleon's rule, Marengo was also the name of a *département*, or administrative district, for the battlefield, along with the rest of Piedmont, was absorbed into France. The overwhelming majority of *départements* took their name from a local topographical feature, usually a river, but Marengo was exceptional in being one of just three *départements* in the Empire to be named after a battle, the other two being Jemmapes in Belgium and Montenotte in Italy.

Twelve US states have at least one place called Marengo. The prevalence of the name there is less surprising than it may seem, since the battle had been won by a republic against an imperial monarchy, and supposedly in the cause of Italian freedom. Adopting a famous title such as Marengo was also an effective way of putting a new settlement in the middle of nowhere firmly on the map. In the case of Iowa, the name was reputedly chosen because the town's flat surroundings were similar to the plain on which the battle was fought.[22] In Alabama, the county of Marengo was created in 1818, using land acquired from the North American Indians, and its name was a tribute to the first white settlers in the area, French Bonapartists who had gone into exile after Waterloo. The county's main town was also called Marengo until 1823, when it was renamed Linden, as a shortened version of Hohenlinden, the other great victory won by the French in 1800.[23] In Michigan, a town was called Marengo as a tribute to one of Napoleon's horses, said to have been his favourite, which had become a tourist attraction after being captured at Waterloo and put on show in London. The town in Michigan came into existence around the time of the horse's death in 1832, which explains why it received the name, but the story has a curious postscript in that the official registers in the French archives record no mention of any of Napoleon's horses being called Marengo. The most likely answer is that one of them was given an informal nickname, or else renamed in Britain in order to add to its celebrity status.[24]

One of the public gardens in the city of Algiers in north Africa used to be known as the Jardin de Marengo, but was named after a French *colonel*, rather than after the battle itself.[25] The *colonel*'s real name was Joseph Cappone, but he had received a *nom de guerre* from no less a person than Napoleon himself. During a review in 1807, Napoleon had stopped and asked him what he was called. 'Cappone, Sire,' came the reply. But Napoleon reckoned that was hardly an approriate name for a hero, for *cappone* was Italian for a capon, or castrated rooster. Acceptable it might be to name a chicken after a victory, but for one of his soldiers to be called a castrated rooster certainly was not. Napoleon then learned that Cappone had been born at the town of Casale, which had been incorporated into the French Empire as part of the *département* of Marengo. 'Come,'

Napoleon exclaimed, 'a brave soldier like you cannot be called Cappone; from now on you will be called Marengo.'[26]

Years later, in the 1830s, Cappone was serving in Algiers when he created the garden named in his honour. He was placed in charge of the workshops for the army's convicts, and, being a humane and enlightened man, he decided to supplement the prisoners' meagre diet by establishing a garden in which to grow vegetables. His story is a reminder that not everything called Marengo was named directly after the battle. Indeed, a type of ivy known as 'Gloire de Marengo' has a doubly indirect connection to the battle. It was actually named after Cappone's garden in Algiers, where it appears to have been either discovered or introduced.[27] Similarly, the USS *Marengo*, a cargo ship built in the United States in 1944, was named after the county in Alabama rather than the battle.

The impact of Marengo was therefore felt right around the world, and continued to reverberate long after the event, like the ever-expanding, yet ever-weakening, ripples made by dropping a pebble in a pond. It was at Paris that the effects of Marengo were the most potent. In Italy, those French soldiers who had not fought in the action often seemed indifferent, or even jealous of the glory won by the Armée de réserve. One Marengo veteran, Adjudant-général Achille Dampierre, complained from Milan about the mood there a month after the victory:

> The Armée de réserve is totally forgotten – if people speak of the speed of its march, it is not so much in admiration as to contrast the brevity of its hardships with the long duration of the deprivations and disasters endured by the Armée d'Italie, and partly by the defenders of Genoa. Every conversation is full of praise for the latter, and the name of Marengo is barely uttered. Whilst France and Europe are amazed by this battle, its memory would fade away at the locations where it actually occurred, if the numerous dead – the indelible witnesses of the combatants' courage and determination – did not still threaten this immortal region with disease.[28]

But in France, and among the men who had been present at Marengo, there was no doubt about its significance. 'We have just won the most famous battle we have had since the Revolution,' exulted Chef de bataillon Antoine Gruyer of the 43e demi-brigade. 'On it depended not only the fate of France, but that of Europe.'[29] To such men, the victory's lustre seemed destined never to grow tarnished – that, at least, was how it looked to an officer in the 101e demi-brigade. 'I have no doubt that my presence at the Battle of Marengo will please you,' he informed his father. 'This will be one of the finest times of my life, and the day will forever remain in my memory.'[30]

Austrian infantry in action.

Chapter 4

Creating a Legend

Marengo was a surprisingly small action. In terms of the numbers of troops engaged, it was not even one-third the size of Waterloo, and faded into insignificance beside the massive battles Napoleon fought when his empire was at its height, especially Leipzig in 1813, which involved more than half a million men. Yet its consequences were so momentous that it remained one of the key clashes of his career, on a par with his great battles at Austerlitz, Borodino, or Waterloo. Constantly he evoked its memory, above all on the morning of Friedland in 1807, when, according to his own account, he cheerfully reminded his army that it was exactly seven years since his great triumph. 'This is a lucky day,' he promised. 'It's the anniversary of Marengo.'

Yet the fervour of the celebrations in 1800 hid an awkward truth. Success had resulted more from Napoleon's bold descent from the Alps into Melas's rear than from the Battle of Marengo itself, in which he had failed to profit from his strategic advantage by annihilating the Austrian army. Faced with this gulf between his original ambition and the more disappointing reality, Napoleon sought to obscure it with propaganda, and spun his own version of the battle, progressively distorting events more and more to suit his own ends. Hiding the sheer narrowness with which he had avoided defeat, he instead sought to give the impression that the battle had proceeded in accordance with a masterplan, in which, far from being driven back, he had actually enticed the Austrians forwards into a trap. He tried to impose order on the chaos of Marengo, and make it seem a classic Napoleonic battle, a perfectly planned and executed victory won by skill and foresight, rather than by mere luck and bravery. In this sense, the contradictions that surround chicken Marengo simply reflect the ambiguity at the very heart of Napoleon's victory, and so the story of how the dish originated is actually a double myth, since it rests on this wider legend of the action being a tactical masterpiece.

Napoleon began rewriting the battle as soon as it was over. His official bulletin, dated 15 June and apparently dictated the previous evening, already contained a hint that he had deliberately lured the Austrians forwards. They were allowed, he claimed, to advance as far as musket-range of San Giuliano before being counter-attacked, and during their advance they made the fatal mistake of letting their army become over-extended. The bulletin over-simplified the decisive clash, presenting a neat and flowing sequence of events, and mentioning no check to Desaix's counter-attack. It is true that the bulletin did not entirely veil the closeness of defeat. 'The roads were covered with fugitives, wounded, and debris,' it admitted. 'The battle seemed lost.' But this merely emphasized Napoleon's achievement in turning the situation around. In the bulletin, it was he who dominated the battle, above all by reinvigorating the demoralized troops immediately before the climax. 'Remember lads,' he supposedly told them, 'it is my custom to go to bed on the battle-field.'[1] The message was clear: they were not to abandon the field, nor retreat any further. Instead, they counter-attacked, cheering 'Long live the Republic! Long live the First Consul!', and instantly overthrew the Austrians.[2]

Berthier, who nominally commanded the army, produced his own account of Marengo in a report addressed to Napoleon on the evening of the battle. Before being released for publication, it was amended in the handwriting of Napoleon's secretary, Bourrienne.[3] Significantly, Berthier barely mentioned the fallen Desaix, and attributed the outcome unequivocally to Napoleon, who 'brought about the victory after it had remained indecisive during thirteen hours of the bitterest fighting'. He emphasized Napoleon's role in the counter-attack by Desaix's men. 'Your presence gave the army the impetus that has secured victory on so many occasions,' the report stated. 'The charge was beaten, and the whole of the fresh line moved off, followed by the divisions that had been fighting all day.' Those who read the report might even gain the impression that Napoleon personally led Desaix's onslaught: *'cette division, que vous avez dirigée au combat, a attaqué le centre de l'ennemi au pas de charge'*. The wording was ambiguous, perhaps deliberately so. The word *dirigée* could mean that Napoleon simply sent orders explaining where and when the division was to go into action, or else that he physically placed himself at the head of the attack. Berthier added an unadorned statement that 'Général Desaix has been killed,' leaving it to Napoleon to dictate a further paragraph, which, though brief, at least had the merit of containing some human warmth. 'The Republic has suffered a great loss today,' it read. 'Desaix has been killed; he had arrived two days earlier. His death has deeply moved the whole army.'[4]

The extent to which these initial reports reinterpreted the battle was limited.[5] They imposed a gloss on events, rather than rewriting them altogether, but as Napoleon steadily tightened his grip on power in the years that followed, he grew more ambitious in manipulating the record. In 1803, the Dépôt de la guerre (the French army's topographical department) produced an official account of Marengo. The original aim was to publish an authoritative narrative that could used for training officers by demonstrating the sort of real-life situations they were likely to encounter during their future careers. The staff of the Dépôt therefore researched the battle meticulously, not only reading the published reports, but also interviewing senior officers who had fought there. To accompany the text of this official account, the Depôt had seven or eight maps drawn, showing the movements of the various units. But when these maps were submitted for Napoleon's approval, they came back so covered in corrections that they had to be redrawn from scratch, apart from the first and last of them, which showed the positions before and after the battle.

Some of Napoleon's changes simply deleted insignificant details for the sake of clarity, but others deliberately distorted what had actually happened. He insisted on portraying the retreat of the army in the afternoon as an orderly withdrawal. The reality, of fugitives flooding to the rear, and units being flung back by weight of numbers, was to be replaced by the fiction of Général de division Jean Lannes's corps carrying out a model retirement, with battalions taking it in turns to cover the withdrawal with all the precision of the parade ground.

Napoleon also insisted that, on his far right wing, his troops were forced to retreat from the village of Castel Ceriolo only late in the afternoon, and for just a brief period. During interviews conducted by the Dépôt during its researches, the relevant officers had stated unequivocally that at least an hour and a quarter had elapsed after their abandonment of the village before they learned that the French army had launched a counter-offensive.[6] Yet Napoleon was intent on minimizing the extent and nature of the withdrawal, and on presenting the battle as he wanted it to have happened, not as it actually unfolded.

Napoleon even took the opportunity to eliminate one of his divisional generals from the record, by replacing the name of Jean-Charles Monnier with that of his senior brigade commander, Claude Carra Saint-Cyr. It has been alleged that the switch was the result of Napoleon's displeasure with Monnier's performance at Marengo, but this is misleading. Monnier's eclipse was due to his political views, rather than to any failings on the battlefield, for he was a capable and distinguished soldier who had held out for more than 100 days when besieged in Ancona by the Austrians in 1799. It was his opposition to Napoleon's authoritarianism that caused him to fall out of favour from 1802. The luckless general remained unemployed for over a decade, until the fall of the Empire. He was

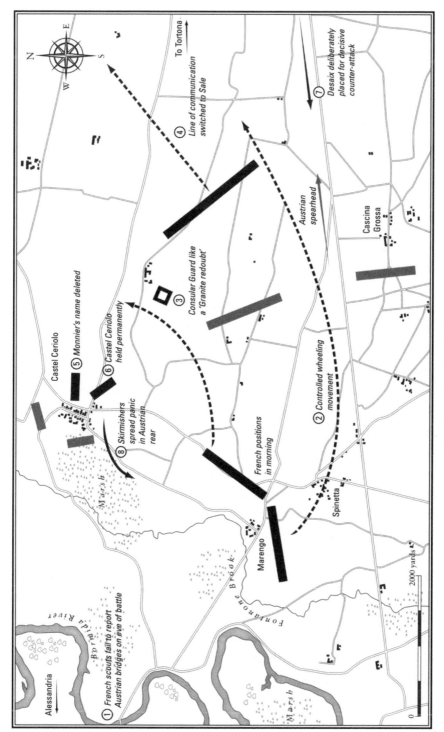

① French scouts fail to report
   Austrian bridges on eve of battle

② Controlled wheeling
   movement

③ Consular Guard like
   a 'Granite redoubt'

④ Line of communication
   switched to Sale

⑤ Monnier's name deleted

⑥ Castel Ceriolo
   held permanently

⑦ Desaix deliberately
   placed for decisive
   counter-attack

⑧ Skirmishers
   spread panic
   in Austrian
   rear

Alessandria

Castel Ceriolo

Marsh

Bormida River

Fontanone Brook

Marsh

Marsh

French positions
in morning

Marengo

Spinetta

Austrian
spearhead

Cascina
Grossa

To Tortona

0   2000 yards

Napoleon Rewrites the Battle.

then restored to activity by the Bourbon monarchy, and made a *comte* and a peer, but died in January 1816. Carra Saint-Cyr, in contrast, enjoyed a distinguished career, but then incurred Napoleon's anger in March 1813 for abandoning the city of Hamburg in the face of insurrections and a major Cossack raid. In fact, Carra Saint-Cyr had little option, because of the weakness of his garrison, and in the event his disgrace proved shortlived, but it was ironic that the man whom Napoleon had falsely credited with a resolute defence of the little village of Castel Ceriolo should have incurred his wrath for failing to hold a city thirteen years later.[7]

The maps for the Dépôt's official account of Marengo were amended in line with these changes, before being engraved. Then, in April 1805, Napoleon set out for Milan in order to be crowned King of Italy, as an additional honour following his recent coronation as Emperor of the French. He took the opportunity to revisit Marengo, and on 5 May – just weeks before the fifth anniversary of the battle – he staged a reenactment on the field itself, involving as many as 25,000 men. The manoeuvres they carried out were clearly based on his revised concept of how the battle had been fought. The troops began drawn up in two lines. One line, representing the Austrians, then advanced against the other, which fell back in a well-ordered movement, with alternate battalions taking it in turns to withdraw, covered by the fire of their neighbours. The retreating line then halted, reformed, and switched to the offensive, while the artillery and cavalry on its left moved round to the right, in order to threaten the flank and rear of the opposing line.[8]

The day ended with the troops marching past Napoleon. He had actually donned the old uniform that he had worn during the battle. The coat had become threadbare, the gold braid tarnished, and the hat damaged. Holes were visible where the cloth had apparently been pierced by Austrian musketballs – at least, that was the story circulated at the time, although it was later suggested that they had been made by moths.[9]

Berthier presented Napoleon with the finished account of Marengo at this review, having brought five printed copies with him to Italy. Yet Napoleon then decided that he wanted further changes made, despite having earlier approved the corrected maps. Seeing the battlefield again seems to have refined his ideas about how he should have fought the action, and it was probably during this visit to the scene of his triumph that he finally cracked the problem of Marengo. The puzzle now had added urgency, for the peace he had secured with Austria eight months after Marengo was on the verge of breaking down. Within four months, Napoleon would be at war with a powerful new coalition led by Britain, Russia, and Austria, and pondering how he could have won Marengo more efficiently generated valuable insights into how best to annihilate the opposing armies in the forthcoming campaign.

The five copies of the official account were hence returned, with the pages of one of them covered in ink corrections. Castel Ceriolo was still a sore point. Napoleon now refused to accept that Carra Saint-Cyr had retreated so far from the village, even though the distance had already been minimized. Even more significantly, he switched the entire axis of his retreat. Rather than falling back eastwards, along the main road from Alessandria, his army was to pivot on its right wing and retire to the north-east. This was the crucial change. It implied a deliberate and controlled retreat, in a direction determined not by Austrian pressure but by Napoleon's own decision. No longer was he to owe the victory to a sudden and undeserved stroke of luck, or a bold flash of inspiration on the part of a subordinate. Instead, it was to be the logical, inevitable result of his own brilliant strategy in drawing the Austrians forward into a carefully laid trap.

Once again, therefore, the maps had to be laboriously redrawn. This time, they were submitted one by one, as they were completed, in case Napoleon required further changes. Sure enough, he was still dissatisfied. In fact, he could no longer stomach the idea of Castel Ceriolo being abandoned at all. Drawing a cross on the relevant map, he scrawled in the margin, as if ordering a move on the battlefield rather than making a correction: 'Carra Saint-Cyr's division into Castel Ceriolo; it barricades itself in there.'[10]

This was the final element, and it resolved the conundrum that had perplexed Napoleon for so long. Castel Ceriolo had been a niggling reminder of how narrowly he had escaped disaster, but now became a strongpoint on which his entire army pivoted as it fell back. In fact, he had not retreated at all, but simply made a wheeling movement as his left wing swung back, and the right remained stationary. 'During the four hours that our army took to make this wheeling move, it presented the most majestic and tremendous sight,' read the final, published account of 1805–6:

> Our echelons retreated in the deepest silence, with their battalions arranged [for mutual support] in a chequerboard pattern. They could be seen under fire from eighty cannon, manoeuvring as if on the drill ground, often halting, and always presenting unbroken ranks, for whenever one of their brave men was hit, the others closed up.[11]

This was far more impressive than the bulletin's bald description five years earlier of roads covered with fugitives, and its admission that the battle appeared to have been lost. The wheeling move brought the left wing to the vicinity of San Giuliano, where Desaix was in position to counter-attack. This meant that the French army was now deployed along a diagonal front, running north-westwards from San Giuliano to Castel Ceriolo, and ready to assail the entire northern flank of the Austrian army. In this final version of the battle, Carra Saint-Cyr was even able to push skirmishers from Castel Ceriolo along the Fontanone stream to the vicinity of Marengo, thus turning the Austrians altogether and sparking panic by threatening their rear.[12]

At last, Napoleon had an official account of Marengo that no longer troubled his mind. He had accomplished the difficult feat of transforming a blunt, attritional battle into a masterpiece of manoeuvre. It remained to dispose of any incriminating evidence, so he ordered the earlier papers to be destroyed, leaving posterity with just the final account of 1805–6. The order was obeyed, but with one, crucial, exception: a copy of the original version of 1803 was secretly squirrelled away in the Dépôt's archives by a *colonel*. In 1828, a decade after the fall of the Empire, it was published, alongside the final text of 1805–6, thus exposing Napoleon's deceptions, and the gradual evolution of his thinking about his victory.[13]

In its essentials, the 1805–6 account remained Napoleon's definitive version of events. Ten years later, when he dictated his memoirs on Saint Helena, he described the battle along the same general lines. He emphasized the wheeling movement; the switch to a new, less exposed, axis of retreat; and the use of Carra Saint-Cyr to threaten the bridges over the Bormida. 'The great art of battles is to change your line of operation during the action,' he boasted. 'This idea of mine is completely new. This is what made me win at Marengo. The enemy advanced on my line of operation in order to cut it, but I had changed it, and then he himself found himself cut off.'[14]

Napoleon did introduce one last change while on Saint Helena. On the day before Marengo, he had sent two corps to reconnoitre in strength towards Alessandria, as a probe to ascertain Melas's location and likely moves. In the evening, the advanced guard of this force took Marengo with such ease that it was entirely logical for Napoleon to conclude that the Austrians had no plans for a counter-offensive, since they would have needed possession of the hamlet if they had intended to advance into the plain. He could not have known at the time that the Austrians had abandoned Marengo simply because they had been taken by surprise, yet he was clearly vexed at his failure to realize this. In the official accounts of both 1803 and 1805–6, he claimed that his advanced guard had been ordered not simply to take Marengo, but to drive the opposing outposts all the way back beyond the Bormida river, and, if possible, to burn the Austrian bridges. This in itself was a dubious claim, since the Austrian bridgehead on the Bormida was so well protected that it looked like a permanent fortress. Yet the crucial question – whether Napoleon was informed that very night of the failure to destroy the bridges – was not even mentioned in the official accounts.[15] Only later, as Napoleon felt increasingly compelled to attribute a faultless performance to himself, did the bridges really become an issue. By the time he dictated his memoirs on Saint Helena, he had decided that the French scouts had, in fact, reported that no bridges spanned the Bormida, and that there was no sign of Melas's army at Alessandria. In reality, it would have been difficult to ascertain either of these two points since dusk was already falling. It was a final, fraudulent twist to the increasingly complex story that Napoleon had spun around his victory.[16]

Napoleon was not the only one to refight Marengo in his mind. One of his subordinates, Général de brigade Jean-Andoche Junot, had returned from Egypt too late to take part in the battle, but listened eagerly to the accounts of more fortunate comrades. 'How many times, during this same year of the Battle of Marengo', recalled Junot's wife, with more than a hint of exasperation, 'did I not see *dîner* carry on until 9.00 pm, because every aspect of this memorable action was being explained. The table became the plain of Marengo, one of its ornate, decorative pieces symbolised the hamlet, the candelabra at the ends were Tortona and Alessandria, and the pears, nuts, and bunches of grapes represented as best they could the Austrian and Hungarian formations, and our own brave French units.'[17]

Despite the ludicrous aspect of such scenes, there was a serious, underlying point to Napoleon's rewriting of history. He was not a born military genius. He had natural gifts, and benefited from a good education, but had to develop his talents through study and first-hand experience. In 1800, just four years had passed since he had first taken up an active army command, and he was still experimenting and refining his ideas. Marengo was a crucial step in his transformation from the young Republican general to the imperial master of war. The battle played a central role in his ongoing process of intellectual development as a commander, and his rewriting of history, rather than being decried as a pointless travesty of the truth, is better regarded as a way of ascertaining and absorbing the lessons of a near-defeat.

In the official accounts, Napoleon described the battle not how it was actually fought, but how he would have fought it with the benefit of hindsight, and this had the added benefit of discouraging potential opponents by portraying himself as an invincible and far-sighted general. The danger, of course, was that he might eventually deceive himself by rewriting history in this way, and lose his edge as a commander by becoming complacent. Yet even as he rewrote Marengo, he recognized his mistakes, learned from them, and formed precepts that became core elements in his art of war, and they can be identified repeatedly throughout his subsequent campaigns, right up until his final battles in 1815.

The need for a powerful, fresh reserve was one of those central conclusions he drew from Marengo. The alarming experience of having to commit the élite Consular Guard early in the battle, leaving him without a reserve, was seared into his memory. Marengo triggered an immediate expansion of the Guard, and reinforced his reluctance in subsequent actions to commit his Old Guard infantry without the clearest necessity. But he also exploited the lesson offensively, for he had seen for himself, with the arrival of Desaix, how the sudden and unexpected intervention of even limited numbers of fresh troops could be enough to tip the balance against an enemy who had already been drained by a prolonged, attritional struggle. The Guard became Napoleon's ultimate reserve, used suddenly – along with a powerful artillery bombardment and an array of heavy cavalry – to shock and awe a beleaguered opponent, and punch a hole through his battleline.

When Napoleon once again took the field at the start of the 1805 campaign, for the first time since Marengo, he showed that he had fully digested the lessons of his near-defeat. The campaign opened with a classic encircling manoeuvre, reminiscent of the sweep through the Alps five years earlier, and this time his forces trapped an Austrian army at Ulm in the Danube valley, forcing it to surrender without even the need for a major battle. This was how the Marengo campaign should have ended: not in the evacuation of Melas's army under an armistice, but in its surrender and captivity.

The 1805 campaign culminated six weeks later in Napoleon's greatest victory, the Battle of Austerlitz. His plan was masterly. By deliberately pulling back from the high ground amid a show of timidity, he enticed the Austro-Russian army forward into striking range, and caused it to become over-stretched as it tried to turn his southern flank. At the same time, he ordered up a detached corps from Vienna to strengthen that supposedly vulnerable flank, and took the added precaution of switching his line of communication to a less exposed route. The result was a crushing triumph, and one deeply influenced by Marengo. The corps of reinforcements from Vienna arrived with the timeliness of Desaix, but by design instead of luck. Despite hard fighting, the Austro-Russian army fell apart as its centre was pierced by a sudden counter-attack, and its southern wing narrowly escaped complete destruction. The lessons of Marengo had been refined and employed to devastating effect.

Yet, if anything, Napoleon learned the lessons of Marengo too well. Austerlitz was so decisive a victory that it encouraged him to over-reach himself, with ultimately disastrous results. As his escalating ambitions embroiled him in yet more wars, Austerlitz became just the first of many battles in which he applied Marengo's lessons. The same basic concepts, simple yet effective, were used to particularly crushing effect against the Russians at Friedland in 1807. In short, Napoleon managed to pick several, semi-accidental events from Marengo, and arrange them into a formidable, battle-winning system, in which he replaced luck by foresight, deception, and the ruthless concentration of force at the right time and place. His greatest victories were the daughters of his narrowest triumph.

Chapter 5

Disputing a Legend

Nothing about Napoleon can be accepted at face value. The Duke of Wellington was particularly scathing. 'Buonaparte's whole life, civil, political and military, was a fraud,' he wrote. 'There was not a transaction, great or small, in which lying or fraud were not introduced.'[1] Yet it was Napoleon's enemies, not just himself, who weaved deceit so closely into the record of Marengo. People alarmed at his tightening grip on power tried to damage him politically by attributing the outcome entirely to his generals, particularly Desaix.[2] Napoleon would surely have been blamed if Marengo had been lost, so it was hardly surprising that he laid full claim to the victory.

After his downfall, Napoleon's lies triggered an inevitable reaction from former subordinates. They now had a chance to seize the credit, and felt all the more compulsion to do so in that they needed to distance themselves from him in order to further their careers under the restored Bourbon monarchy. How better to win official favour than by chipping away at his reputation? Kellermann, for example, became openly critical of Napoleon's generalship, and claimed that the outcome of Marengo was due entirely to his own cavalry charge, which 'won a victory to which Bonaparte personally contributed nothing'.[3] Maréchal Marmont also grew disillusioned, and notoriously abandoned Napoleon in April 1814 – an action that coloured the way he described Marengo in his vain and self-serving memoirs, for he needed to undermine Napoleon's reputation in order to justify his desertion of him. Even if participants had tried to be truthful, their recollections were bound to have been vague and misleading, simply because the battle was so confused, and visibility so limited. Nor should remarks attributed to Napoleon and other key figures be taken too literally; theatrical words enliven a book, and help it to sell, but what soldiers say in the thick of the action is generally more down-to-earth.

The central figure in the battle's controversies was Desaix, despite the fact he had been silenced by the shot that killed him. The reason is quite simply that Marengo would have been lost had he not arrived in time. That inescapable fact has intensified one of the great debates about the battle: whether Desaix marched to the battlefield on his own initiative, or simply obeyed orders to do so. The answer would spell the difference between Napoleon being saved by a combination of luck and the boldness of his subordinate, or saving the situation himself by making the right decisions and issuing timely orders.

At first glance, Desaix was an odd-looking hero. Despite being tall, and blessed with a magnificent mane of long, black hair, he could seem taciturn and absorbed by a touch of melancholy, while his face was pale and distorted by a harelip. Yet his eyes burned with an intensity similar to Napoleon's, and he was adored by his troops. He was brave and talented, but free from any boastfulness, and when he did speak it was clearly and without the foul language with which many generals peppered their commands. His manners, and his aversion to pomp and finery, charmed those who met him. Rarely seen in his general's uniform, he tended to wear a simple blue coat without any embroidery; in fact, a French officer who saw him during the campaign initially thought he was a military storekeeper.[4] Even his harelip was a badge of honour, the result of being shot through both cheeks in August 1793. Despite the pain, he had fought on until nightfall, and only then had his wound bandaged.

The dedication he showed that day had caused him to be raised to general officer rank on the spot.

Such a man was a natural hero for the Republic. He has often been credited with marching on the sound of the guns of Marengo on his own initiative, and some colourful accounts even claim he put his ear to the ground to determine the direction of the firing. Yet in reality, he did little more than obey orders. It was not Desaix's own judgement that enabled him to arrive in time, but a combination of luck, the weather, and the decisions made by Napoleon.

In high summer, the rivers in the Po plain can seem puny, for the drop in water level leaves just a channel of water looking as derisory in comparison with the expanse of stony river bed as a small child wearing his father's boots. Yet in a matter of hours, these deceptively feeble streams can be swollen by heavy rain into torrents, and this was what ensured Desaix was still within reach of the battlefield when he was needed. There had been a downpour on the afternoon of 13 June, the day before the battle, and so Desaix, marching off to the south-west on his detached misson to block the Genoa road, found the Scrivia too high to be forded. During the morning of Marengo, his troops had to be slowly ferried acoss, until 10.00 am, when the water had dropped sufficiently to allow his artillery to drive through it.

Around this time, Desaix may have heard the sound of gunfire to the north-west. He apparently sent an ADC to obtain confirmation of Napoleon's plans, since his reconnaissances had failed to detect any Austrian forces to the south-west. Then, at noon, he actually received an order from Napoleon to continue his march away from the army's main body. But the order was not a response to Desaix's request for confirmation of his mission. It had been sent too soon for that – in fact, it had been sent as early as 9.00 am, when it was still not clear to Napoleon that the Austrian attack on Marengo was a full-scale offensive.[5]

Desaix duly headed off to the south-west, but towards 1.00 pm, after covering less than 2 miles, he received another order, this time informing him that a battle was under way, and bidding him to return. It is unlikely that the message was the desperate, and distinctly unmilitary, appeal that is often quoted by historians. 'I thought I was attacking the enemy, but he has pre-empted me,' Napoleon supposedly wrote. 'Return in God's name, if you are still able to do so.' This colourful version appeared in 1854 in a history of the campaign written by the son of one of the heroes of the battle, Général de brigade Kellermann. The problem was that the son had an interest in portraying Napoleon in an adverse light in order to enhance his father's contribution to the victory. He was also relying on a distinctly dubious source: one of Desaix's orderlies had allegedly seen the contents of Napoleon's note on its arrival, and in a conversation after the battle had mentioned it to an Austrian ADC. It was from the unpublished reminiscences of this ADC that Kellermann junior took the story, and he was therefore using a second-hand anecdote that was liable to have become exaggerated and over-simplified with the telling.[6] All too often, this highly improbable tale has been blindly accepted as historical fact.

What is clear is that Desaix marched to the battlefield only after receiving an order to do so. Heading directly to the north-west, towards the gunfire, he covered the approximately 6 miles to San Giuliano in around three hours, and arrived between 4.00 and 5.00 pm – just in time to save the battle and lose his life.[7] The circumstances of his fall became the next of the great mysteries about Marengo. The official bulletin of 15 June attributed a fine speech to the dying Desaix, which managed at the same time to praise the slain hero, while actually cutting him down to size by making Napoleon the focus of attention. According to the bulletin, Desaix turned to an ADC and told him to inform Napoleon that he regretted he had not done enough to live in posterity.

In fact, if he had been conscious at all, Desaix was more likely to have issued some vigorous commands to close up the ranks, rather than waste time uttering a flowery speech. Four years earlier, he had reacted to the death of one of his divisional commanders in just such a down-to-earth and practical manner. 'We must save the division,' he had exclaimed, 'we can weep for him afterwards.'[8] According to his chief subordinate, Général de division Boudet, Desaix's last words were actually an instruction to conceal his death, in case it undermined morale. This at least had the merit of being in character, yet Boudet did not personally witness the scene, and was writing an official report for public consumption.[9] Another version was provided by a staff officer, who reported that he was riding in front of Desaix as they advanced with the 9e légère. Suddenly, they took an Austrian volley from amid the vines, at a range of just 10 paces. This was when Desaix was shot, just as he launched the charge. 'I turned round in time to see him fall,' wrote the staff officer. 'I went to him, but he was dead.' Desaix had apparently been able to say just one word to a nearby *capitaine* – 'Dead!' – yet the staff officer could not personally vouch for this particular detail.[10]

Other, similar, versions were simply farcical. One second-hand account had an ADC suddenly exclaim 'General, you are wounded!', as he saw Desaix's head sink over his horse's neck. 'Dead!' Desaix replied, and fell lifeless from the saddle.[11] In fact, Desaix was shot through the heart, and probably said nothing at all. The two surgeons who embalmed his body confirmed that he would have been unable to say a single word as he fell. He may simply have given an involuntary grunt, which sounded like a monosyllabic word, and amidst the confusion, his death probably went unnoticed by most of his men at the time, not least because he dressed so unostentatiously. The claim in Berthier's report that his death inflamed his men with a desire for revenge seems to have been no more than empty rhetoric, and his body may actually have been abandoned for a while as the Austrians pressed home their attack.[12]

Desaix may even have been shot by his own men, or so some accounts have alleged. According to Bourrienne's memoirs, a *sergent* of the 9e légère found that Desaix's overcoat had been pierced through the back, which would indicate that he had been hit by friendly fire, or else shot by the Austrians as he turned round to exhort his troops. But the claim is impossible to verify. Another eye-witness – the staff officer who was riding ahead of Desaix at the time of his fall – indicated that he was actually struck in the chest, and that the hole in his back was simply the exit wound. The fatal shot could not have come directly from in front without hitting the staff officer first, but, he explained, it might have been fired in a slanting direction, since it emerged from Desaix's right shoulder.[13]

Yet rumours that Desaix had been shot in the back persisted, and were seized on by conspiracy theorists. In 1815, a scathing piece of anti-Bonapartist propaganda appeared in London, entitled *The Life of Napoleon: a Hudibrastic poem in fifteen cantos*. Embellished by a series of brilliant, and sometimes hilarious, engravings by George Cruikshank, it spun a hostile interpretation of key moments in Napoleon's career. At Marengo, it claimed, he had to be stopped from running away by a stern rebuke from Desaix: 'Citizen Consul, look before you – that is the road to fame and glory.' Napoleon supposedly took offence, and swore to gain revenge for this humiliation after Desaix had won the battle:

> But, while victorious, now we find
> Dessaix received a shot behind,
> His Aid-du-camp was bribed to do it,
> And well too the First Consul knew it;
> Besides the shot, a base attack!
> He got a stab too in the back;
> He fell, and instantly expir'd –
> His death by Boney was desired.[14]

In fact, Napoleon seemed genuinely grieved at Desaix's loss. In the evening of the battle, his valet, Constant, apparently heard him say that France had lost one of its best defenders, and he himself his best friend. 'My good Desaix always wanted to die like this', Napoleon remarked, before adding 'but did death have to be so prompt in granting his wish?'[15] Napoleon's actions on behalf of Desaix's family and friends reinforced the impression that he never forgot his debt to the fallen hero. He immediately added the general's ADCs, Chef de brigade Anne-Jean-Marie-René Savary and Commandant Jean Rapp, to his own staff, and publicized the fact in a bulletin. Desaix's brothers were both rehabilitated by being removed from the list of those who had emigrated during the Revolution. His mother was paid an annual pension, no fewer than five of his relatives were made *barons* of the Empire, and one of his nephews enjoyed such a fast-track career as a result of Napoleon's patronage that he was promoted *colonel* in 1815 at the remarkably young age of twenty-five.[16]

Yet Napoleon's attitude was not as straightforward as it might appear. Grief did not prevent him from cynically exploiting the fallen hero for political gain. Desaix's popular image was that of an untarnished Republican hero, and that in itself made him a politically significant figurehead, precisely because he was believed to be innocent of any political ambitions. Napoleon was able to elevate himself by portraying this apparently pure, Republican martyr as being personally devoted to him. He exaggerated, for despite their mutual respect they had hardly been real friends, but he knew that dead heroes were also silent ones, and that their public image could be readily shaped by the politically unscrupulous.

Even as he rode the wave of emotion unleashed by news of Desaix's death, Napoleon sought to limit it. In death as in life, Desaix was useful to him, but that usefulness would diminish with time, and in distant, pehaps more difficult, years, a fallen Republican idol had the potential to become a politically inconvenient symbol of the alternative, less authoritarian path that France might have followed under different leaders. For this reason, the official bulletin of 15 June subtly sidelined Desaix, while appearing to cover him with praise. As we have seen, it stated that Desaix had fallen with the exclamation: 'Go and tell the First Consul that I die with regret at not having done enough to live in posterity.'[17] These last words were a brazen invention, and were clearly designed to forestall the emergence of a personality cult that might have challenged Napoleon's own preeminence.

The bulletin attributed another dubious remark to Desaix, claiming that two or three days earlier he had foreseen his death. 'It's been a long time since I last fought in Europe,' he supposedly told his ADCs. 'The cannonballs no longer know me, and something is going to happen to us.' The remark conferred a sense of inevitability, of Desaix not suffering a cruel twist of fate, but fulfilling his destiny, and its inclusion in the bulletin was intended to evoke sad resignation rather than a tidal wave of sympathy. Whatever sympathy the bulletin did try to summon was directed at the First Consul himself. When Napoleon was informed of Desaix's death, it reported, only one remark escaped him: 'Why am I not allowed to weep?' It was a stoic and dignified response that emphasized his closeness to the dead man, and at the same time excused him from writing effusive praise.

In fact, Napoleon's ploy rebounded against him. In attributing to Desaix the statement that he had not done enough to live in posterity, the bulletin actually increased his attractiveness by adding modesty to the other qualities of this apparently flawless hero. 'The dying Desaix was mistaken in his modesty,' declared a member of the Tribunate, one of the Republic's assemblies, after the bulletin had been read out. 'He has done enough to live in the gratitude of France, and in the recollection of posterity.' The sentiment was widely echoed. 'Desaix is no more!' lamented another tribune. 'He has dashed from the field of honour into the bosom of immortality!'[18]

If Napoleon was unable to prevent this rising sea of sympathy for Desaix, then he would at least ensure it was channelled and directed by the government until it receded. Within thirteen days of the battle, he announced that Desaix would be buried at the Hospice of the Grand Saint-Bernard pass, although in the event it took six years to construct a suitably grandiose tomb of white marble. The delay was not, in fact, deliberate, for Napoleon actually urged on progress, but it was impossible to create such a massive piece of sculpture in a matter of months, and transporting it up into the Alps was a formidable undertaking in itself, especially over the final stretch inaccessible to vehicles. Its decorative bas-relief alone weighed 2 tons.[19]

Desaix's funeral was finally held at the Hospice on 19 June 1805, shortly after the fifth anniversary of his death, and while his tomb was still being made in Paris. Until then, his embalmed body had remained at a convent near Milan. Napoleon was visiting northern Italy at the time, and had planned to attend the service himself, but in the end found that he was too busy. 'Desaix's funeral ceremony was noble, moving, and had the austere character that you wanted,' his Director-General of Museums reported to him afterwards.[20]

The austerity had its advantages. The Grand Saint-Bernard was an appropriately spartan and noble resting place, in keeping with Desaix's character, but also politically convenient in its remoteness. Far from Paris, Desaix was less likely to eclipse the First Consul, or provide embarrassing points of comparison as a glowing exemplar of Republican virtues. The location of the tomb actually exalted Napoleon more than his fallen subordinate, for Desaix had not personally gone through the Grand Saint-Bernard pass: he had come directly from the French port of Toulon after returning from Egypt, and had caught up with the army only three-and-a-half weeks after its passage.[21] Napoleon undoubtedly had another motive for the choice of location. Laying a French national hero to rest at the Hospice staked a claim to perpetual control of the strategic pass, even more effectively than planting a tricolour flag on it.

If Napoleon's intention in consigning Desaix to the remoteness of the Alps was to minimize rather than honour his memory, then he succeeded. Once the initial outburst of grief became dulled with the passage of time, Desaix was largely forgotten, something that was starkly shown by the fate of the two monuments to him in Paris. The first was erected in the former place Dauphine at the very heart of the city – not by the government, but by a public subscription that had been decided on as soon as the news of Marengo reached Paris. Unveiled on the third anniversary of the battle, it took the form of a fountain with a bust of the fallen hero, and was inscribed with the last words attributed to him by Napoleon, about his regret at not having done enough to live in posterity. Although the fountain survived Napoleon's fall, it soon became dilapidated – the inscriptions were barely legible by the late 1820s – and it was placed in storage when the adjacent Palais de Justice was rebuilt in the 1870s. Finally, in 1905–6, it was transferred 200 miles south of Paris to the town of Riom in the Puy-de-Dôme, the *département* where Desaix had been born.[22]

The second monument, a statue in the place des Victoires, fared no better. Napoleon had felt obliged to provide some sort of official memorial to Desaix in the capital, beyond simply naming in his honour a new quay alongside the Seine river. For a century, the place des Victoires had been occupied by a statue of King Louis XIV, but this had been toppled during the Revolution and melted down in order to be converted into cannon. Its place was taken by a wooden pyramid monument, but that, in turn, became politically outdated following Napoleon's seizure of power, and in September 1800 was destroyed to make way for a joint memorial in honour of both Desaix and another Republican general, Jean-Baptiste Kléber, who had been assassinated in Egypt. The decision for a joint monument was made in the immediate, emotional aftermath of the news of Kléber's death reaching France, and was doubly appropriate in that by chance both men had been killed on the very same day, even though more than 1,500 miles apart.

Yet the passage of time allowed cooler reflection, and in October 1802 the plans were changed, supposedly because of the artistic difficulty in honouring two heroes with a single monument. Instead, Napoleon ordered the erection of a statue of Desaix alone, clearly regarding him as the politically safer choice, since Kléber came from humble origins, and was too blunt and outspoken. Kléber's disillusionment with Napoleon was obvious in the reports he had written from Egypt – reports that were read by Napoleon himself since they reached Paris only after his seizure of power. Small wonder, then, that Napoleon later rated Desaix as the more capable of the two generals, or that he seemingly wanted to consign Kléber to oblivion. When Kléber's body was repatriated in 1801, it was deposited in the island fortress of the Château d'If, off the city of Marseille. This was initially done as a quarantine measure, for bubonic plague had infected the army in Egypt, yet Kléber remained in confinement for the next seventeen years, in as isolated a location as Desaix's lofty resting place in the snow-bound

Alps. There was all the more significance in the fact that the Château d'If was used to imprison men who were deemed a threat to the regime; indeed, it was where Alexandre Dumas incarcerated his fictional hero Edmond Dantès, better known as the Count of Monte-Cristo. The irony of detaining a dead prisoner was not lost on the local prefect, Antoine-Claire, comte Thibaudeau. 'The army brought [Kléber's] body back to France, and it was left in the chapel of the Château d'If,' he explained. 'I had mentioned it to ministers, but apparently they could not be bothered to raise it with the Emperor.' Not until 1818, after Napoleon's fall, was Kléber finally released from detention and laid to rest in his native city of Strasbourg.[23]

As for the monument in the place des Victoires, now assigned to Desaix alone, it ran into further delays, partly because the sheer size of the statue made casting it a challenge. When finally inaugurated on Napoleon's birthday in 1810, it provoked a storm of public protest. Respectable passers-by were offended by the nudity in which Desaix was portrayed, but that was only part of the problem. The statue was quite simply old-fashioned and poorly designed, too heavy and unsophisticated for the elegant square in which it was placed. The only aspect for which one newspaper could find unqualified praise was the marble pedestal. The government resigned itself to starting again from scratch, but was reluctant to risk another failure. A completely different design was now proposed, for an equestrian statue, intended for a new location altogether – not a prestigious public square, but one of the Seine bridges. Meanwhile, the existing, much-disparaged, statue was boarded up, becoming a mute, if unintended, symbol of Napoleon's rewriting of history. After the Bourbons returned to power, Desaix was recast into a statue of King Henri IV to adorn the Pont-Neuf. The empty space in the place des Victoires was then filled with a new statue of Louis XIV, thus bringing the whole process of politically inspired changes full circle.[24]

There were times after Marengo when Napoleon could have done with Desaix's talents. Claude-François Méneval, one of his secretaries, recorded that three or four years after the battle, Napoleon considered sending an expedition to seize British possessions in India, only to shelve the idea, partly because of the problem of finding a suitable commander for such a distant venture. 'On this occasion', recalled Méneval, 'I heard him regret the loss of Général Desaix, for he appreciated his great ability in both military and political spheres . . . He often remembered Desaix when he was pondering some great, independent military expedition, and being deprived of this distinguished general's help may have contributed more than once to making him give up the idea.'[25]

Had Desaix survived, he would almost certainly have been appointed one of Napoleon's marshals – as was every other corps commander at Marengo – and would have been as famous as any of that illustrious band. Napoleon remarked a month after Marengo that 'Desaix would have been the foremost general of the French armies,' and had apparently intended to marry him to his step-daughter Hortense.[26] It has even been suggested that Desaix might have become Napoleon's deputy, and that his beneficial influence could have had an untold effect on the course of history. Maréchal Marmont, another hero of Marengo, had no doubt about the prominence of the role Desaix would have played. 'Since he was truly modest and devoid of ambition,' Marmont reckoned, 'he would have been a useful tool in Bonaparte's hands, and would never have challenged him'.[27] Napoleon himself recorded in his memoirs that Desaix was the most worthy person to have become his lieutenant, or right-hand man, and supposedly commented, during the long sea voyage to Saint Helena, that he and Desaix would always have understood each other, as a result of their similar background and principles. (They were almost the same age, had both come from the minor nobility of limited means, and had been educated at military schools during the *ancien régime*.) Desaix, Napoleon added, would have been content as a subordinate, and would always have remained loyal. At least, that was the view recorded by a companion-in-exile, Emmanuel, comte de Las Cases, although he is known to have heavily dramatized and even invented Napoleon's conversations in writing his best-selling *Mémorial de Sainte-Hélène*.[28]

Would Napoleon really have tolerated anyone, even Desaix, becoming so powerful? He preferred to keep his leading subordinates in check by preserving a balance of power among them, and subtle clues of a more ambivalent attitude to Desaix can be found in his conversation on Saint Helena, if the accounts of his companions can be relied upon. Yes, he still spoke of Desaix as an outstanding general – the best he ever had – and still praised him as a pure and unspoiled hero. 'Desaix was wholly wrapped up in war and glory,' he remarked. 'To him riches and pleasure were valueless, nor did he give them a moment's thought.'[29] Yet even as he praised his character, Napoleon reportedly downplayed his contribution to winning Marengo. He attributed the victory not to Desaix himself, but to one of his units, the 9e légère. 'When I saw it pass by,' he said, 'its determined appearance, with the calmness and decisiveness of its brave men, made me conclude that they were certain of victory, and I took it for granted that the enemy would be checked and overthrown. Then Kellermann charged with his 800 horsemen, in the presence of 10,000 enemy cavalry, who remained passive spectators . . . That was the victory of Marengo: it was due to this outstanding decisiveness. Desaix contributed nothing to it.'[30] Napoleon then added that it had been another corps commander, Général de division Lannes, who had contributed more than anyone to the successes of the campaign. It seems that, even in death, Desaix was not immune from Napoleon's jealousy of potential rivals, or his desire to counter claims from critics that Desaix had saved him from disaster.

Nor can we ignore the related question, left unanswered by Desaix's premature death, of how far he would have supported Napoleon as the Consulate gave way to the more authoritarian Empire. The very nature of Napoleon's rule would have confronted Desaix with a dilemma. He could have continued serving him, thereby abandoning his Republican principles; he could have opted for the path of overt opposition, and be cast into the wilderness with his career in ruins, as happened to Général Monnier; he could have served France's enemies in a bid to bring about regime change, as did Général Moreau; or, if he had sufficient skill, he could have worked from within the regime to limit or undermine Napoleon, as did one of the leading political figures, Charles-Maurice de Talleyrand. Whatever Desaix's decision, his reputation is unlikely to have preserved its lustre.

Indeed, it is difficult to escape the conclusion that Desaix's stature was inflated by the circumstances of his death. A popular hero who falls in battle tends to acquire an almost saintly aura. Desaix's Republican virtues were emphasized, including his devotion to duty, his bravery and self-sacrifice, and his proven ability as a general. Yet he was just one of several men who contributed to winning Marengo, and he was not even the most important of them. Besides, there was always a contradiction lying beneath his popular image. For all his status as a great Republican hero, Desaix was actually of noble birth, and had enjoyed a privileged education at a royal military school before the Revolution. It was a background he had wisely buried during the Terror of 1793 by replacing his original, and unmistakeably noble, surname – des Aix de Veygoux – with the shorter and more politically correct version by which he is remembered. The suppression of these facts, combined with his memorable death during the early, promising months of the Consulate, helped make him a convenient hero, and one of the few men of the Revolutionary era who could be used as a unifying figure. His memory was therefore revived, especially after the July 1830 revolution, which replaced the Bourbons with the more liberal, Orléanist king, Louis-Philippe. For statesmen who pursued a policy of national reconciliation, Desaix was a useful figure because of his ability to transcend the deep schism that continued to divide French society even a century after the Revolution. As late as the Third Republic (1870–1940), he was still being commemorated by those on the Left as a dedicated Republican, and by those on the Right as an heroic patriot. Napoleon was by no means alone in reinterpreting Desaix's life and death in a way that suited his own interests.[31]

❧ ♠ ❧

The other great argument about Marengo rages over Kellermann's role, and at its heart lies a similar question. Did he receive an order to charge with his cavalry brigade, or do so on his own authority? Kellermann himself never wavered in contending that the decision was his alone. 'I thought that there was not a moment to lose', he wrote in his report the next day, 'and that a swift stroke could restore the victory to our flags.' Dashing impetuously at the flank of the Austrian grenadiers, he struck them just after they had fired at Desaix's infantry and before they had time to reload. 'The stroke was decisive', Kellermann stated, 'and the column was destroyed in an instant.'[32]

His version of events was supported by Napoleon's artillery commander, Marmont, who believed that Kellermann had timed the charge perfectly. A delay of three minutes would have allowed the Austrian column to recover from the shock caused by Marmont's final salvo of canister. Charging too soon, on the other hand, before the artillery had fired, might also have led to failure. Thus, Marmont wrote, 'it required this precise coordination to ensure so complete, and, it has to be said, so unexpected, a success. Never did luck intervene more decisively. Never did a general show greater energy, quick thinking, and timely judgement than did Kellermann in this situation.'[33]

Interestingly, Napoleon's first account – his official bulletin of 15 June – made no mention of any orders being sent to Kellermann, and, by praising his vigour and timeliness, actually seemed to confirm that he had charged on his own initiative. Yet by the time the official history was published in 1805–6, Napoleon was appropriating the credit. The official history stated that he had ordered Kellermann's cavalry to advance from reserve, gallop through the intervals between

Desaix's infantry units, and fall on the shaken Austrian column of grenadiers. This was despite the fact that when officers who had taken part in the battle were interviewed during the research for the official history, not one of them contradicted Kellermann's assertion that he had charged on his own initiative.[34]

Kellermann publicly challenged this rewriting of history only after Napoleon's fall from power. In 1818, he spotted an article in a periodical called the *Bibliothèque historique*, about a monument to Desaix being removed from a hill overlooking the city of Marseille. He responded forcefully in a letter that was published later that same year, and claimed that he, not Desaix, had decided the battle. 'The fact is', he argued, 'Général Desaix had no share in the decisive event that restored victory to our flags on the day of Marengo.' By the time he himself charged, Desaix was already dead, and his infantry had been repulsed.[35]

A decade later, in 1828, Kellermann returned to the fray. This time, he clashed bitterly with one of Desaix's former ADCs, Général de division Anne-Jean-Marie-René Savary, who was in the process of publishing his memoirs. The volume about Marengo had just appeared, and disputed the allegations Kellermann had made in the *Bibliothèque historique*. Savary claimed to have been sent by Desaix to ask Napoleon for some cavalry to support his imminent counter-attack. Napoleon then instructed Savary to go and tell Kellermann to charge as soon as Desaix's assault began.[36] Savary had just finished explaining the situation to Kellermann, and giving him Napoleon's order, when Desaix's attack began. According to Savary, Kellermann actually protested against the order for a while, on the grounds that his cavalry was too exhausted after fighting all day, but there was no other brigade available. Savary rejected any idea that Kellermann improvised his charge. He pointed out that the vegetation prevented either Kellermann or Desaix from seeing the other before the counter-attack began, and that meant Napoleon must have played a vital, co-ordinating role in arranging the counter-offensive. In Savary's view, Kellermann's charge succeeded only because it was made as part of Desaix's attack. Desaix gave Kellermann his opportunity.[37]

Kellermann immediately responded to these claims with a pamphlet, which he published anonymously under the pseudonym of Un Ami de la vérité ('A friend of the truth'). When Savary answered back in the final volume of his memoirs, Kellermann published a second refutation of his comments. Extracting the truth from this dispute is complicated by suspicions that Savary's memoirs were produced by a ghost-writer using his notes as a basis.[38] But one thing is clear. For all their vigour, Savary's arguments left Kellermann's core point intact, namely that he received only a broad directive to advance in support of Desaix, and that he personally decided the timing and tactics of his intervention. Only Kellermann, the man on the spot, could have ordered the actual charge, for there had been no time for him to think, let alone consult a superior. He had to react instantly, with all the boldness of his character, lashing out as an instinctive reflex action ingrained in him through his years of training and combat experience. He explained that he dashed to help his comrades, 'like someone instinctively throwing himself into the water to save a drowning fellow man. Fortune gave him the chance, and he seized it by the hair – five minutes sooner or later, and the moment would have been missed!'[39] Napoleon himself seems to have conceded as much in the end, for his final account of Marengo, contained in the memoirs he dictated on Saint Helena, no longer included the claim that he had specifically ordered Kellermann to charge.

Who really decided the battle: Kellermann or Desaix? The question acquires an added sharpness since Kellermann wrote in his report the next day that he had noticed Desaix's infantry south of the main road – the 9e légère – beginning to give way, and the Austrian grenadiers charging it at a run.[40] Desaix was dead, but his subordinate, Boudet, who commanded the infantry division that he had brought to the battlefield, vigorously championed his men in his own after-action report. For Boudet, Kellermann's charge was no more than a supplementary action. He described the bitter resistance his division encountered on assailing the Austrian grenadiers, but explained that this 'was negated by the valour of the 9e légère, and our attack was crowned by a lucky charge of our cavalry'. Boudet firmly attributed the success gained in this sector to the valour and composure of the 9e légère, before conceding that 'the cavalry likewise contributed, with much timeliness and bravery'.[41]

Boudet's report suggests a longer and more complex struggle than might be concluded from the accounts by Kellermann, who probably did not see the whole of the infantry action. Boudet did not mention any disorder or flight among his men, but was not present with the 9e légère, since Desaix had sent him to lead the second brigade of his division. It therefore remains possible that Kellermann did indeed see some men flee, or temporarily stagger back, and mistakenly assumed that the whole of the 9e légère had been defeated. He was not alone in thinking that at least part of Desaix's division had been thrown back. Marmont was with his massed battery north of the main road, urging the men to move their guns forward in support of Desaix's advance. He had just reached the three guns at the southern end of his battery when he suddenly saw one of Desaix's *demi-brigades*, apparently the 30e de ligne, in disorder and flight to his left front. 'I promptly had the three guns readied again and loaded with canister', he wrote, 'but I waited before opening fire.' Amidst the thick dust and smoke, he caught sight of an ordered mass of troops, 50 paces away from the 30e. At first, he mistook them for French, but then realized that they were the head of a large column of Austrian grenadiers. 'We had enough time to fire four canister rounds at them from our three guns', he recalled, 'and immediately afterwards Kellermann passed in front of my muzzles with 400 cavalrymen, the remains of his brigade, and vigorously charged the left flank of the enemy column.'[42]

❧ 🐓 ❧

Most accounts of Marengo state that Napoleon ignored Kellermann and heaped praise instead on Desaix, since it was politically safer to have a dead national hero than a live one. This long-accepted myth can be traced back to Bourrienne's dubious memoirs. 'Little Keller-mann made a providential charge,' Napoleon supposedly told Bourrienne on the evening of the battle. 'He timed it perfectly, and we owe much to him. You see on what threads hang the outcomes of battles!' Bourrienne contrasted this private comment with Napoleon's coldness later that night, when Kellermann appeared. 'You made quite a good charge,' was all Napoleon said. He then turned to the commander of the Guard cavalry, and warmly exclaimed: 'Bessières, the Guard covered itself in glory!'[43]

Bourrienne claimed that Napoleon was deliberately minimizing Kellermann's contribution, and that he provoked bitter resentment in doing so. 'I have just put the crown on your head!' an aggrieved Kellermann supposedly told Napoleon the next day, although even Bourrienne had to admit that he did not personally hear the remark. Bourrienne also alleged that Napoleon saw a furious letter from Kellermann that had been intercepted. 'Can you believe it, my friend,' Kellermann wrote, 'that Bonaparte has not made me *général de division*, when it is I who has just put the crown on his head!'[44]

The problem with this tale is that Bourrienne is so untrustworthy. His ghost-written memoirs were peppered with scandalous anec-dotes and fictionalized speeches, for they were intended to make money rather than provide a true and balanced account for posterity. Kellermann was actually promoted to *général de division* at the beginning of July, little more than three weeks after the battle. Marmont, in contrast, had to wait until September to be appointed to the same rank. Claims that Kellermann's career stagnated after Marengo are simply untrue: he saw active service throughout the duration of the Empire, except for brief periods when he was recovering from illness or wounds. He was his own worst enemy, being an ugly, arrogant, and abrasive little man, who gained an un-enviable reputation as a looter. If anything, he may have been excused too much on account of Marengo, since his conduct there apparently caused Napoleon to overlook much that was unsavoury in his character. Savary claimed to have been present when Kellermann had an audience with Napoleon at Paris a decade after the battle. Kellermann supposedly launched into a justification of some recent actions of his that had attracted controversy, only to be interrupted. 'Général Kellermann,' Napoleon reassured him, 'whenever anyone speaks to me about you, I recall Marengo'.[45]

Modesty was not one of Kellermann's qualities. Yet he waited until 1818 to publish his views about Marengo, after Napoleon's fall, by which time denigrating his former master had become politically correct. Thus far, he wrote, he had 'stuck to a modest silence, and contented himself with the opinion of his comrades', but he now regarded it as a duty to establish the truth about Marengo. He claimed that by winning the battle he had unintentionally placed the crown on Napoleon's head, but that Napoleon had denied him the credit, preferring instead to divert the glory to Desaix, who was safely dead. He added a further swipe by branding Napoleon 'a madman' who had dissipated the benefits won for France at the battle. These were the sentiments that found their way into Bourrienne's memoirs, yet they were expressed in 1818, and did not necessarily reflect Kellermann's true feelings in 1800, nor even as recently as the Hundred Days in 1815, when he accepted a command following Napoleon's return from exile, and made one final charge for him at Waterloo.[46]

Kellermann naturally focused on his own corner of the battlefield, yet in doing so he overlooked the wider picture. Massena, the commander of the Armée d'Italie, actually deserves a greater share of the credit for the victory than either Desaix or Kellermann, but has been forgotten because he played a purely indirect role, and was not personally present on the battlefield. Massena was the man who made Marengo possible. It was his preservation of Switzerland for the French Republic the year before that enabled Napoleon to launch the Armée de réserve over the Alps and into Melas's rear. It was also his defence of Genoa that provided the diversion that Napoleon needed for his campaign plan to work. Despite the numerical odds, and a host of deprivations, Massena's army covered southern France, preoccupied Melas for six vital weeks, and significantly depleted and wore down the Austrian army. Kellermann might lay claim to the key, tactical decision that snatched victory from the jaws of defeat, yet without Massena the battle could not even have been fought.

♥ ♟ ♥

That Napoleon rewrote the official account of Marengo in his favour is unsurprising. What is remarkable, given the scale of his efforts to reshape history, is the fleeting nature of their effect. The lies he constructed around the battle barely survived his fall. As early as 1822, an Austrian officer, Hauptmann Karl Mras, began putting the record straight in a methodical series of articles published in the *Oestreichische militärische Zeitschrift*. Kellermann, as we have seen, was already appropriating the victory for himself. Only in a limited way did Napoleon's spin-doctoring influence popular understanding of the battle in the decades that followed. If anything, historians have actually underestimated his role, and focused on those of Desaix and Kellermann, the generals who took the immediate, tactical decisions. Even Adolphe Thiers, whose account of Marengo in his massive *Histoire du consulat et de l'empire* (1845–62) was generally sympathetic to Napoleon, wrongly attributed Desaix's timely arrival to him marching towards the sound of the guns on his own initiative.

It is particularly ironic that Napoleon's actions should have been so downplayed, since Marengo in a very personal sense was one of his most heroic battles; rarely, if ever, was he more exposed to danger than on the afternoon of Marengo as he strove to rally and exhort the men. After issuing his initial orders in response to the Austrian offensive, he was largely limited to coordinating the battle and inspiring the troops, and he inevitably had a less spectacular profile than some of his chief lieutenants. Yet he did what few other commanders-in-chief would have managed to achieve, in turning such a critical situation around. Above all, he refused to panic. 'I was there when Bonaparte came up to Général Victor,' recalled the latter's ADC, Chef de bataillon Joachim-Jérôme Quiot. 'He did not seem agitated, but I believe he was very annoyed by the retreat. I do not recall any of his words. When he went along the line, he was welcomed by cheers and shouts of Forwards!'[47] Napoleon's apparent calmness formed a stark contrast to his behaviour during his *coup d'état* seven months earlier, when he lost his nerve and antagonized the legislative deputies by haranguing them instead of subtly winning them over. The *coup* had eventually succeeded, but only after Napoleon had resorted to armed force.

Yet Napoleon's calmness and authority at Marengo have usually gone unrecognized, or even been contradicted altogether. Too many of the commonly accepted stories that diminish or falsify his role at Marengo can be traced back to dubious sources. Bourrienne was responsible for one especially ludicrous fabrication, namely that Napoleon predicted three months beforehand that he would fight a battle near Marengo. On 17 March, while they were still in Paris, Napoleon supposedly told Bourrienne to unroll a map of Italy. He then pored over it, and inserted pins to indicate the locations of units. 'Where do you think I will defeat Melas?' he asked. 'The devil take me if I have a clue about that,' answered Bourrienne. 'You're a simpleton,' Napoleon said, and then explained how he planned to cut Melas's communications, and fall on him in the plains of the Scrivia river. As he spoke, he stuck a pin in the village of San Giuliano. Bourrienne claimed that he thought nothing more of the conversation, until he found himself three months later at that very village.[48]

Historians have been surprisingly blind to such distortions, as they have focused instead on exposing Napoleon's own lies. Bourrienne was the origin of another, much-quoted, fable. He claimed to have been told by Napoleon himself what Desaix had said on reaching the battlefield. 'This battle is completely lost,' Desaix had exclaimed dramatically, 'but it is only 2 o'clock, and we still have enough time to win another one today.'[49] The words are dubious, not least as Desaix did not arrive at so early an hour. Nor was Napoleon likely to have repeated a statement that implied he personally had suffered a defeat. Indeed, in 1816, a companion-in-exile, the comte de Las Cases, recorded him telling exactly the opposite story, in which it was Desaix who thought the battle lost. 'Well, things are going very badly for us,' Desaix supposedly exclaimed, 'the battle is lost, I can do no more than secure the retreat. Is it not so?' Napoleon apparently rejected the idea. 'Quite the contrary,' he said. 'I have never had any doubt about the outcome of the battle. Everything that you see in disorder, on the right and left, is on its way to form up in your rear. The battle is won. Push your column forward: all you have to do is gather the fruit of the victory.'[50]

Yet Las Cases's version of the conversation is hardly any more reliable than Bourrienne's. At this stage in the battle it is doubtful if any of the key French participants expected to win an outright victory that day. They had a reasonable hope of sharply checking the Austrian spearheads, and negating the impression of a French defeat. That would enable them to rally their battered army and perhaps renew the fight on more favourable terms the next day. The more sweeping and decisive outcome they actually won was something they might hope for, but could hardly have anticipated. Success on such a scale depended on good fortune and a sudden collapse of Austrian morale, neither of which lay in their direct power to bring about.

What Napoleon and Desaix actually said was probably the completely different exchange reported soon afterwards by a staff officer. Napoleon, according to the officer, greeted Desaix with a smile: 'Well, Général Desaix, what a scuffle!'

'Well, *général*,' Desaix replied, 'I'm here, we're all fresh, and if necessary we'll go and get ourselves killed.' This calm and determined conversation, with its relaxed and almost jocular tone, was more characteristic of both men. The officer who recorded it added that an informal council of war was then held under fire, and the army was readied for a new clash, with guns being deployed to prepare the way for the counter-attack. '*Général*,' Desaix told Napoleon, 'we have only to keep up an intense artillery fire for quarter of an hour, and then we'll get under way.'[51]

Marmont, who also attended this council of war, recalled a similarly businesslike discussion. Desaix told Napoleon that a heavy artillery preparation was vital if his attack was to succeed, whereupon Marmont said that he would go and collect various guns to form a massed battery. 'That's right,' Desaix replied. 'Go, my dear Marmont, find guns, and more guns, and make the best possible use of them.'[52]

Yet another account stated that Napoleon explained the situation clearly and precisely, along with their options – to counter-attack, or simply to try and contain the Austrian advance – and then asked Desaix for his opinion. Desaix calmly replied that there was still time to win a battle, which was the answer Napoleon had been hoping for.[53]

It is untrue that Desaix then simply displaced Napoleon and took over the battle. Instead, he issued tactical orders for the intervention of his division, within the context of Napoleon's overall supervision. The secret of success lay in the effective co-ordination of all three of the army's vital ingredients – Desaix's infantry, Marmont's artillery, and Kellermann's cavalry – and that was Napoleon's role. He actually deserves praise for not trying to control the battle too closely. This is what helped motivate subordinates such as Desaix, and made possible brilliant flashes of initiative by men like Kellermann. Throughout the campaign, he established the political and strategic framework within which the tactical combat leaders could operate to best effect. He was comfortable with the concept of what is now known as mission command, under which he issued broad directives rather than constraining his generals with over-precise orders. His conduct of the battle, after his initial miscalculation of Melas's intentions, was cool, calculated, and courageous. Necessary though it was for him to create the myth of a masterplan, and to counter the claims of potential rivals, the record of what really happened is, on balance, a credit to his ability and nerve as a commander.

The tendency today is to decry the importance of Marengo altogether. Historians point out that it was another eight months before Austria finally made peace. The Convention of Alessandria on the day after the battle had been followed by an armistice on the Rhine front, but the Austrians then stalled on negotiations for a peace treaty. By November, Napoleon had lost patience, and ordered a resumption of hostilities. He himself remained in Paris – partly because Marengo had already stabilized the previously critical situation – but in his absence, four French armies took the offensive in Italy, Switzerland, and Germany. On 3 December, one of them – Moreau's Armée du Rhin – won a crushing triumph at Hohenlinden, 20 miles east of Munich, in a battle two-and-a-half times the size of Marengo. Pursuing swiftly, Moreau was within 50 miles of Vienna when an armistice on 25 December halted hostilities. Peace soon followed, with a treaty signed at Lunéville on 9 February 1801.

Yet placing the emphasis on Hohenlinden rather than Marengo misses the point. Marengo did, in fact, prove decisive, although there was a time lag before the Austrian leaders, who were split over the desirability of continuing the war, accepted its full implications. Before Marengo, Napoleon had been racing against time; after it, time was on the French side. What remained in doubt after Marengo was not the outcome of the war, but just the timing and terms of the peace. It had been a political and psychological victory, one that reinforced him in power, and shocked the Austrians. In less than six weeks since leaving Paris, Napoleon had recovered north-western Italy, and removed the Austrian troops without the need for a prolonged conflict besieging fortress after fortress. He thereby averted the invasion threat to southern France, stabilized public confidence, and secured a strong position from which to negotiate peace. Regaining France's lost territory in Italy was essential before Napoleon could secure an acceptable settlement, for no terms could endure if they left Austrian forces on the border with France. 'Peace lies in Italy,' wrote Berthier at the end of April. 'We must enter there decisively, and that requires taking great measures.'[54]

The key issue was therefore decided by Marengo; Hohenlinden simply nudged the Austrians to the peace table, and weakened their position. In fact, there would have been no need to fight Hohenlinden at all, if Moreau had previously complied with Napoleon's wishes and released a larger detachment to reinforce the Armée de réserve, for then Marengo could have been a truly crushing triumph.

Berthier, the nominal commander of the Armée de réserve.

Chapter 6

Commemorating a Legend

Napoleon was hardly the only commander in history to insist that everything had gone according to plan. To some extent, it was actually his duty to distort what had happened, to impose meaning and structure on the fear and chaos of battle, and to reassure his troops that they had achieved wonders, for actions are won or lost in the mind as much as on the actual ground.

Nor was it possible to write a balanced account of a battle in its immediate aftermath. Wellington's victory despatch after Waterloo notoriously failed to satisfy all his officers, many of whom criticised him for giving too little praise, and Napoleon encountered the same problem with Marengo. Within days of the battle, one of Desaix's subordinates, Général de brigade Louis-Charles Guénand, was writing a heartfelt protest that his deeds had been overlooked. 'I am tormented and distressed,' ran the opening line of his letter to Napoleon. 'I can barely tell myself that Bonaparte noticed me at the Battle of Maringo!' He then gave Napoleon the benefit of his own, detailed view of what had happened, and added the uncompromising assertion that it had been the bold thrust of his brigade that had caused the Austrian grenadiers to waver, thus creating the opportunity for Kellermann to charge. 'Yes, *mon général*,' he insisted, 'I say it from the bottom of my heart, the outcome of the battle was decided largely by this audacious and deliberate thrust.'[1]

Napoleon had a soothing reply sent to Guénand, explaining that he recalled perfectly his conduct at Marengo, and conveying his satisfaction with him. But Guénand was still aggrieved two years later, particularly at not having been mentioned in Berthier's reports on the battle. Berthier had pointed out, reasonably enough, that including him would have made it necessary to write about the whole of Desaix's corps. 'This reply is maddening', Guénand grumbled to a military historian of the time, Général de brigade Mathieu Dumas, 'and proves that the history of this battle has still to be written. I will supply whatever materials you want.'[2]

The widespread conceit of Napoleon's subordinates was experienced at first hand by a member of the Austrian staff, Major Adam, Graf von Neipperg. He angrily recalled what happened when Berthier and his officers came to arrange the armistice at Alessandria on the day after the battle:

> The conversation was just a pack of boastful lies, which grew more and more insulting. They all bragged about the brilliant role they had played in winning the battle. I have never had to steel myself with more coolness than on this occasion, so as not to let myself be carried away by the impetuosity of my blood, which I felt boiling with rage through all my veins. I believe that, if all [the Austrian officers'] minds had been so inflamed as mine, it would not have taken much to throw a whole bunch of contemptible men of this sort out of the windows. Since they owed their good fortune just to pure luck and our lack of energy, and not at all to their skill and bravery, they had absolutely no right, through their impudent claims, to insult an army that was so courageous and so worthy of the whole of Europe's admiration.[3]

A decade later, the hot-tempered Neipperg had the chance to vent his frustrations at Berthier himself. He met him while in Paris in the summer of 1810, and, as a fellow Austrian officer recorded:

> General Neipperg pressed [Berthier] into a fairly detailed conversation about the Battle of Marengo, and some of its incidents were keenly discussed. Berthier had described the

battle in a special publication [Napoleon's official history], but in doing so had made great errors by both concealing and falsifying information. Practically all of these had to be regarded as intentional, for the events were arranged to conform with the Emperor's retrospective views. It was widely said that many deeds had been attributed to General Desaix, who had fallen in the battle, even though they were really due to men who were still alive, but whom the Emperor did not think it convenient to acknowledge and reward. Berthier had a tough time of it with the well-informed Neipperg, but argued his case well, and was always able to produce fresh facts and arguments. Just as happened in the actual battle, where victory went to the French despite the Austrian advantages, so too did Berthier get the best of the conversation, even though his opponent's points were indisputably more justified.[4]

How was it possible, when faced with so egotistical and mendacious a set of Frenchmen, for anyone to combine all their contradictory claims into a balanced and comprehensive depiction of the battle? The obvious difficulties did not stop attempts to do just that, and in May 1801 a talented young artist called Capitaine Louis-François Lejeune exhibited a spectacular painting of Marengo in that year's exhibition at Paris.

It was the picture that made his reputation, and it managed to synthesize the roles of the key participants by compressing the whole of the battle's climax, with all its multitude of little incidents, into a single, frozen moment of time. The result was a canvas entirely filled with action in the minutest detail. Its apparent objectivity was strengthened by the knowledge that Lejeune had actually taken part in the battle, as an ADC to Berthier, yet this impression of accuracy was misleading, for in fact Lejeune carefully composed and sanitized his painting. Rather than show the fighting up close and from ground level, he chose to encompass the action as a whole by adopting an artificially elevated viewpoint, as if he had sketched the battle while perched in a tree-top. He glossed over the horror and butchery, painting instead a scene of colour and beauty set amidst an idyllic landscape. He also drew a veil over the disorder and fugitives, and indeed over the sheer narrowness of the victory. His Marengo is too neat and symmetrical, with the individual incidents assembled in a calculated manner at odds with the spontaneous and chaotic nature of the actual battle.

In the centre, for example, Lejeune shows the Austrian grenadiers under attack from three sides – by Desaix from the front, Marmont's artillery from the north, and Kellermann's cavalry from the south – yet it is clear from Kellermann's own report, supported by other eyewitnesses, that he struck the Austrians from the north. Lejeune may simply have forgotten what he witnessed during the battle, but is just as likely to have tampered with the facts in order to create a pleasing symmetry and avoid cluttering the foreground. He also omitted most of the vineyards, and showed the corn trampled flat so as to obscure none of the action. By making these subtle changes, he managed to produce one of the world's most spectacular battle paintings – harmonious, painstakingly detailed, and full of life, colour and drama – but as a record of what actually happened at Marengo, it was no more reliable than Napoleon's official account.

The very fact that Lejeune was personally present at the battle undermined his objectivity rather than ensuring his accuracy. He painted the picture for his superior, Berthier, whom he placed prominently in the right foreground, along with his retine of staff officers, who included Lejeune himself. Even Napoleon appeared no more prominently than Berthier – on the opposite side of the canvas, rather than in the central, dominant position traditionally accorded to kings and commanders-in-chief before the Revolution. Despite initial appearances, therefore, Lejeune arranged his painting in as meticulous and calculating a way as David had done for Napoleon crossing the Alps. Lejeune, of course, was more subtle, gently suffusing his canvas with patriotism and military glory, rather than aggressively thrusting a triumphalist message right into the viewer's face, but that merely disguised the underlying artificiality of his image.

So it was not just written accounts that distorted the story of Marengo. The myth was also spun on canvas, and Napoleon insisted on his artists following the new version of events set out in the official history. In March 1806, the painter Carle Vernet wrote that Napoleon had ordered him to finish his picture of the battle in time for the next exhibition. 'For the deployments of the battle', he added, 'I have conformed to the new plans that have been given to me at the Dépôt de la guerre'.[5] He had actually been commissioned by the Minister of the Interior as long ago as 1800, but found the government frustratingly slow in providing the historical information he needed, probably because the official account was still being revised. He painted a preliminary study, which was bought by Berthier and hung in his home outside Paris, the Château de Gros-Bois. As for the full-scale painting that the government had commissioned, it was finally completed only at the end of 1813, and not until 1815 could it be properly exhibited at the Louvre, though Napoleon felt it was worth the wait. 'Convey my pleasure to Vernet for his fine painting of the Battle of Marengo,' he directed, and awarded him a bonus of 6,000 francs.[6] But few critics have been so warm in their praise, for the massive painting lacked the life and sparkle of Vernet's smaller, informal scenes and caricatures, and was not even original, since its composition had obvious similarities with the earlier picture by Lejeune. The inescapable fact is that artists rarely manage to produce a masterpiece when obliged to conform to official requirements.

Attempts were made to capture the myth on an even grander scale, by erecting a massive monument on the battlefield itself. When Napoleon revisited Marengo in May 1805, he laid the first stone of a truncated pyramid intended to be 90 feet high, making it one-and-a-half times as large as the famous glass pyramid erected in 1989 outside the Louvre at Paris. The names of those who had fallen in the battle were to be inscribed in the interior, along with a plan of the action, and details of what had happened. Yet this ambitious project would never be completed.[7] Part of the problem lay with Napoleon's contradictory impulses. On the one hand, he wanted a memorial that would endure. 'I intend this monument to be a pyramid, made wholly with large blocks of stone, so as to with-stand the passage of time,' he explained, and he directed that the stone that he had personally laid was to be placed within a week under large blocks, 'so it cannot be dislodged, and so what has been done will not have to be redone'.[8] Yet at the same time, he was keen for the monument to be built cheaply and quickly, in just two or three years, which was hardly compatible with the aim of building something magnificent and durable. By 1808, almost one-third of the pyramid's volume had been completed, but the work then seems to have petered out.[9]

The slackening drive behind the pyramid of Marengo reflected the changing urgency of Napoleon's wider ambitions for the region, particularly for the fortress city of Alessandria just 2.75 miles to the north-west. At the time the pyramid was begun, the Austrians still possessed Venetia in the north-east of the Italian peninsula. That made Piedmont in the north-west a vital counter-balance to Austrian power in the region, and by annexing it, as he did in September 1802, Napoleon publicly committed the French nation to going to war, should that become necessary to ensure its preservation.[10]

Napoleon was intent on turning Alessandria into a powerful fortress that would become the central hub in the defence of north-western Italy. By demolishing lesser fortresses that were inconvenient to defend, he hoped to concentrate over 5,000 men to hold Alessandria, instead of dissipating troops among numerous garrisons as Melas had done in 1800. Alessandria had to be able to hold out long enough, in the event of another war, for Napoleon to bring an army from France and defeat the Austrians, so he could then use the artillery and ammunition stored in the fortress to capture the Austrian strongholds in Venetia. By strengthening Alessandria, therefore, and turning it into a major arsenal, he would avoid the predicament in which he had found himself in 1800, that of having too few guns as a result of the difficulties of crossing the Alps.[11]

At first, Napoleon hastened the work at Alessandria. In April 1803, he demanded it be accelerated, 'for it is on this fortress that I place all the hope of Italy'.[12] But towards the end of 1805 a renewed conflict broke out, and Napoleon changed the entire balance of power by crushing Austria at the Battle of Austerlitz in what is now the Czech Republic. Under the peace treaty, the Austrians lost Venetia, and their exclusion from Italy suddenly removed the urgency for strengthening Alessandria. Other fortresses, further to the east, now became more strategically significant, and so even at the end of 1813 the work at Alessandria remained incomplete.[13] Not surprisingly, therefore, the motivation for building the nearby pyramid of Marengo also dwindled.

Napoleon had mainly external opponents in mind when he developed Alessandria into a great, fortified base, but knew that its strength and reputation would also intimidate the inhabitants of Piedmont, and dissuade them from rising in revolt. The region around Marengo was notorious not only for drunkenness, but for smuggling, robbery, and murder.[14] Napoleon himself was partly responsible for the disorder, since the area had been pillaged and fought over during his Italian campaigns, but the lawlessness was also explained by the isolation of the inhabitants' homes, and the ease with which they could conceal their crimes in the woods. The core problem was the backward, almost feudal, system that concentrated power in the hands of a few major landowners residing in the city of Alessandria. Local farmers paid an annual rent for the land they cultivated, but their holdings were subdivided among their heirs, each of whom built a home on his particular plot, which was why the houses were so dispersed.[15]

If Napoleon was to restore order, and establish a firm grip on the newly annexed territory, he would have to address these underlying problems, and break the great landowners' domination of the rural inhabitants, for it was when local nobles loyal to the toppled Piedmontese monarchy provided leadership that the masses were a real threat to French control. The solution was clear to an officer of the Ingénieurs-géographes (the army's surveyors and map-makers), who reported in September 1802:

It would be wise policy, firstly to prevent the future construction of isolated houses, which facilitates brigandage and smuggling because of the lack of surveillance by neighbours; secondly to chose a place for building what would subsequently become a village; thirdly to detach from the municipality of Alessandria the whole region on the right of the Bormida, which would reduce its dependency and cause it to be better governed.[16]

This was the background to the idea of building a completely new settlement at Marengo. In the spring of 1803, a book was published in Paris under the title of *La Ville des victoires* ('The City of victories'). The author was J. Rivaud, one of Napoleon's commissaries – the administrative officers who supervised the army's logistical and support services. He wanted to build a city from scratch on the actual field of Marengo, as a reminder of the battle and a tribute to Napoleon. It was to be a modern city, with all the great status buildings of a metropolis, including a cathedral and a stock exchange, and with the main streets and squares lined with superb colonnades. The squares would have fountains, monuments, a triumphal column – there would even be a statue of Napoleon restoring France and Italy to bliss, located in the appropriately named place du Bonheur ('Happiness Square'). The Ville des victoires would be both the centre of French power in Italy, and the most important trading depot in the region, linked by a canal to the Po river. It was an idealistic dream, with everything about the octagonally shaped city mathematically arranged and slotted into the themes of military glory, hierarchy, and rational perfection. Each of the gates was to be decorated with a triumphal arch, while the streets radiating out from the centre would be named after Napoleon's battles, treaties, or other achievements.

But the grandiose scheme went beyond simply implanting a magnificent city in an empty, dusty plain; it had the altogether more radical aim of transforming society, of turning lawless peasants into loyal French citizens. Within his fantasy city, Rivaud set aside one of the buildings for a project to settle French veterans in the area in order to achieve this objective of taming the region. By establishing a settler colony at Marengo, Napoleon intended to solve an additional problem at the same time, for the question of how best to provide for France's retired or disabled veterans had become urgent as a result of a backlog of claims for new pensions that had built up before his seizure of power. Supplementing the veterans' inadequate pensions with a grant of land seemed a cost-effective way of enabling them to live in dignity and independence, and raise a family.[17] Napoleon hence decided to establish camps in recently annexed frontier territories, where wounded veterans could be given plots of land. 'The two-fold aim that the government has in mind is easy to grasp,' he wrote in September 1802. It was, he explained, 'to reward brave soldiers who are owed so much by the Republic, and, by means of marriages in these newly annexed regions, to strengthen the inhabitants' bond to the Fatherland, and to introduce the French language and mentality'.[18] In pursuit of this aim, he initially intended to select only men who were single and willing to marry a local woman and, although in the event he dropped this particular requirement, he still insisted on the veterans obtaining official permission if they wanted to marry.

The establishment of the first camp, outside Alessandria, was ordered in June 1803, and instructions for the formation of another, at Juliers on the west bank of the Rhine, followed in January 1804. Both camps lay close to key fortresses, so a body of Frenchmen with military experience was constantly at hand should they be required to help defend them. The twin camps were pilots for the project as a whole, for Napoleon envisaged the eventual establishment of as many as ten of them. It was not a new idea – the ancient Romans had established numerous veterans' colonies, partly to help control their frontier districts, and the Austrian Empire used settlements of soldier-peasants to defend its Military Border against the Ottoman Turks – but Napoleon soon ran into difficulties, the biggest of which was finding enough land. Houses, livestock, and farming tools were also in short supply, and the veterans themselves were part of the problem.[19] They were meant to be model citizens, whose presence would help pacify the conquered regions. 'It is necessary to win over the inhabitants of Alessandria, and Frenchify its population as much as possible,' Napoleon wrote in 1803, before emphasizing 'it is at Alessandria that everything must be done – everything at Alessandria'.[20] Yet the laziness and insubordination of some veterans had the opposite effect, by annoying the neighbouring farmers. Difficulties in obtaining land resulted in delays in the camps becoming fully functional, and thus many veterans were not peaceful and contented farmers, but soldiers living together in barrack-like buildings with nothing to do except make trouble.

At the very heart of the project lay an unresolved dilemma. Ultimately, were the veterans to be soldiers still subject to military discipline – a concept that many of them clearly resented – or farmers enjoying the independence of landowners as a reward for their past service? If they lived in houses concentrated to form a single, enclosed community of soldiers, they would be set apart from the local population, and too distant from the outlying fields to farm all their lands themselves. If, on the other hand, they were dispersed, they would be difficult to supervise, and slower to assemble as a unit in the event of an emergency. Napoleon's own ideas on this point seem to have changed. 'The word *camp* requires explanation,' he originally wrote in September 1802. 'It is not intended to mean that the individuals will be gathered into one and the same enclosure. Instead, *camp* is used to define any portion of lands given to veterans, and these [lands] must lie within the territory of communes less than 3 leagues away from each other.'[21] But when a subsequent order was issued in June 1803, it overturned that initial concept by ruling that the veterans' houses were to be contained within one, centrally located, walled enclosure.[22]

In the event, neither camp attained its target of 405 officers and men. In August 1810, Capitaine Mathurin Gajal, the *commandant* of the camp at Alessandria, described some of the obstacles he had encountered:

From its birth, our establishment has been the butt of acts of jealousy and persecutions of every sort. This is proven by the hindrances we experienced in taking up possession, despite the consent given by His Majesty the Emperor. Our enemies are constantly bent on our ruin, and do not cease intriguing; if ever they fulfil their designs, it will be only by means of lies and calumnies. They will not have neglected violently to attack the morality of individuals, or to dwell on imaginary acts of destruction caused by the veterans. The truth is that the majority are generally good, and that only a very small number of unruly men exist – these have already been reported several times and they alone have been able to put us in a bad light in the eyes of public opinion.[23]

Gajal had every reason to blame a conspiracy in order to fend off the accusations against his veterans, for he had heard rumours that the government intended to close down the camp. But the hard statistics suggest that the problems were more serious than he was prepared to admit. By the beginning of 1809, 9 per cent of the 308 veterans who had joined the camp since its formation had departed for good, mostly because they had been expelled or had left without permission.[24] The reasons for the expulsions ranged from insubordination and wild behaviour to murder, fraud, and running a brothel – which hardly reflected the idealistic vision that Napoleon had in mind. Almost one-third of the veterans were still bachelors, despite his hopes of marrying them to local women. Some of the men personally farmed their lands, while others had jobs as diverse as labourer, innkeeper, customs official, schoolmaster, hatter, wig-maker, tailor, second-hand clothes dealer, and orderly at the military hospital of Alessandria, yet three-fifths were listed as inactive.[25]

Napoleon had already written off the scheme. 'I abandon the idea of the veterans' camps,' he wrote in February 1806. 'However, I let the organization continue of the two that have been begun.'[26] The camps were not a total failure, but had clearly failed to live up to his expectations, and had proven too troublesome a solution to be expanded. By the time the Empire collapsed in 1814, the camp at Alessandria contained 253 veterans, with 534 women and children.[27] More than half of the veterans soon abandoned the camp, and the rest returned to France in 1815. Even the fortifications of Alessandria, on which Napoleon had expended so much money and effort, did not survive his fall, being demolished by the Austrians after they had evicted the French troops from Italy. The base of the incomplete pyramid was also destroyed at this time, and the stones appropriated by local inhabitants. For all Napoleon's desire to raise a monument that would endure, it has vanished so completely that historians are still unsure exactly where it stood.[28]

As for the Ville des victoires, it was never even begun, and remained just an idealistic vision, destined never to become reality. Yet the basic soundness of the concept was shown elsewhere, in two areas of western France where opposition to Napoleon was strong, and where he needed a central bastion and administrative centre from which to pacify the surrounding countryside. In 1802 and 1804, he ordered the construction of new towns at Pontivy in Brittany, and La Roche-sur-Yon in the Vendée. Both were designed on the same principles as the Ville des victoires, with everything arranged in a regular and centralised pattern and, although completed only after the end of the Empire, they still stand today as reminders of what might have been at Marengo.

Dreaming up designs for a permanent pyramid, for a network of hierarchical veterans' camps, or for a neat, octagonal Ville des victoires, were the counterpart of Napoleon's compulsion to rewrite the battle, and to impose ideals of glory and perfection on the messier reality of human life. Yet commemorating Marengo in such a grandiose manner went beyond mere vainglory. Underlying all these schemes was the altogether more practical and down-to-earth aim of tightening Napoleon's grip on Piedmont, and infusing a French character and mentality into these newly annexed territories. The pyramid would complement the nearby defences of Alessandria as a tangible, and impressively mighty, reminder to the local population of the hard reality of Napoleon's power. The veterans' camps would provide a permanent core of loyal and experienced men able to take up arms and help defend Alessandria in an emergency, while in peacetime they would marry local women and thus fuse the inhabitants inextricably into the new social order. The memories and monuments of Marengo would act as an inspiring and unifying force. They would not simply commemorate the battle and honour the fallen, but serve as uncompromising statements of French control, and – in the case of the pyramid – provide a landmark visible from afar by soldiers and civilians alike as they approached Alessandria.

These practical considerations help explain why Napoleon was so persistent in his efforts to produce a satisfactory account of the battle. He needed to stamp his own meaning on what had happened, in order to define and fix the victory, and co-opt its memory in support of his regime. Yet the supreme irony was that this quest for the perfect interpretation of the battle was itself disjointed, imperfect, and inconsistent. Neither the pyramid nor the Ville des victoires ever reached fruition, while Napoleon's official history simply underlined what had gone wrong in the battle, when his distortions eventually came to light. Indeed, the successive versions of the official history were actually published under the restored Bourbon monarchy, in order to undermine Napoleon's reputation by exposing the paper trail of his deceit. Trying to rewrite history, as Napoleon did so persistently with Marengo, ultimately resulted in history biting back.

❧ ♦ ☙

Had Napoleon's pyramid been completed, it might have become as great a tourist attraction as the Lion Mound at Waterloo. As it was, travellers in the three decades that followed his fall found little at Marengo to remind them of the battle. The German poet Heinrich Heine passed by one fine morning while travelling in Italy in 1828. 'We are on the battlefield of Marengo,' announced the postilion, and

Heine's heart bounded with joy. He loved this battlefield, since he believed that Napoleon at that stage in his career had been fighting in the cause of freedom. But his fellow-traveller was more down-to-earth. 'Who thinks of Marengo any more?' the man asked, pointing out that everyone's attention was focused instead on current events.[29]

Even at the adjacent city of Alessandria, the battle seemed to be practically forgotten, as a young American traveller, the Reverend Edmund D. Griffin, found in 1829:

> Being here in the neighbourhood of the village of Marengo, I hunted in all the print-shops and book-stores for a plan of the battle, but to my astonishment not only failed in the attempt, in a city containing thirty thousand inhabitants, and so near a scene so celebrated, but found that the name of the battle was hardly recognized. A lesson this for conquerors, from which they might derive salutary instruction.[30]

Even a modest column, erected outside Marengo for the first anniversary of the battle, had disappeared. At the end of April 1814, shortly after Napoleon's abdication, Austrian troops commanded by Generalmajor Laval, Graf Nugent von Westmeath reached the area of the battlefield, intent on occupying Piedmont in order to fill the power vacuum and restore order. As the reaction against Napoleon's rule set in, symbols of his regime were in danger of being destroyed by the angry population. Nugent decided to save the column at Marengo. He had it taken by cart to the nearest port, and then by sea to be deposited at Venice. Eventually it ended up at the home he bought on the far shores of the Adriatic, the old castle at Tersatto, near Fiume (now the Croatian city of Rijeka). There, the column joined his collection of antique statues, but for Nugent it was more than just another quaint garden ornament: it was also a trophy to soothe the bitterness of an old defeat, for he himself had served at Marengo as a staff officer. Of Irish descent, he enjoyed a remarkably long and distinguished military career, rising to become a *Feldmarschall*, and seeing action for the last time as an

81-year-old volunteer against the French and Piedmontese in 1859. He died three years later, revered as one of the grand old men of the Austrian army.[31]

The Marengo column remained at Tersatto, standing outside the mausoleum Nugent had built for himself and his wife, until the end of the First World War, when it was finally retrieved following the defeat and collapse of the Austro-Hungarian Empire. In 1922, it was replaced in its original location at Marengo, where it can be seen today at the roadside – but it is too small compared with the importance of the battle it is meant to commemorate to be anything more than a derisory substitute for the massive pyramid or the Ville des victoires.

Following the failure of Napoleon's great, official projects, the task of commemoration was left largely to private initiatives. These entailed problems of their own, for enthusiastic individuals were apt to be led astray by popular myths, as was shown by the extraordinary life story of a local inhabitant called Giovanni Delavo, a man who rivalled even Nugent in wealth and eccentricity. He was born soon after Marengo, into a rich family at Alessandria. As a child, he would accompany his father over the nearby battlefield, and would see the bones and other relics that labourers uncovered whilst ploughing the fields. He also remembered the French soldiers who were billeted in his family's home during the Empire, as they passed by on their way to join their units in southern Italy.

Delavo's father believed passionately in the cause of Italian freedom. After Napoleon's fall, much of the north of the chronically disunited country lay under the direct domination of the Austrians. But for Delavo's father, Marengo was the prelude to what he hoped would be Italy's eventual reunification as an independent nation, and this was why he so fervently admired Napoleon. Delavo himself became absorbed by these views. After his father's death in 1836, he invested the money he inherited, and rapidly became a millionaire. By the mid-1840s, he was in a position to carry out a grandiose ambition that had gradually taken shape in his mind. 'This idea – here is what it was,' he explained:

It was to buy the plain of Marengo, this hallowed land, this witness of so many glorious events that spoke ever more vividly to my imagination each day. It was to find and collect, on the terrain itself, all the items that could recall the First Consul's triumph and retell its glory. To turn Marengo into a museum, a trophy, a sanctuary. To surround with luxury and magnificence this impoverished hamlet where the destiny of the world was renewed. To build on the very plain of Marengo a splendid monument to Napoleon's glory and the dawn of the Empire, just as the English have raised a monument on the field of Waterloo to Bonaparte's defeat and the fall of his government.[32]

To house his museum, Delavo built a magnificent villa at Marengo. He wanted to preserve part of an old inn where Napoleon had supposedly stayed immediately after the battle, so he actually built his villa around it, and thus incorporated three of its rooms into the new building. Visitors were guided round the museum by an old Napoleonic veteran, and were taken on what amounted to a secular pilgrimage, which culminated in the sanctuary, the room reputedly used by Napoleon, whose walls and ceiling were completely covered with weapons and relics.[33]

It was ironic that Delavo should have gone to such time and trouble to preserve an incident that never happened. He had taken on trust the story that Napoleon had stayed at the inn after the battle, but it was too small, and too surrounded by carnage, to offer suitable accommodation, and Napoleon had actually returned to his headquarters at the Torre Garofoli. This was hardly a unique example of local traditions turning out to be fraudulent. At the village of Etroubles, on the Piedmontese side of the Grand Saint-Bernard, two rival inns tried to attract customers by claiming to have lodged Napoleon during his passage of the Alps in 1800, even though neither of them had even existed at the time.[34]

Delavo overlooked such details, blinded as he was by his veneration. In any case, his objective was never simply to com-

memorate the battle, but to fan the flames of Italian patriotism: he
saw Napoleon as a liberator, and Marengo as the great battle where
Italy was temporarily freed from Austrian oppression. The formal
inauguration of his museum on the anniversary of Marengo in 1847
became an anti-Austrian manifestation, attended by thousands of
people. Despite diplomatic pressure from Vienna, the Piedmontese
authorities were unable to prevent patriotic songs, cheers, and
shouts of 'Out with the Germans!'[35] This interpretation of Marengo
as practically an Italian victory, won by a commander who was largely
Italian by origin, was strengthened when Piedmont went to war with
Austria in 1848. Officers frequently used Marengo's history to exhort
their men, including Maggiore Generale Manfredo Fanti, the
commander of a brigade of volunteers, who reviewed them that
December in front of Napoleon's statue outside Delavo's villa.
'Soldiers, do you know this general?' he asked them, to cheers of
'Viva Italia!' 'He was a son of Italy; in our plains he more than once
trod under foot the enemy who now insults us, and more than once
passed as a conqueror through the cities. Cannot the land produce
a hero to resemble him?'[36]

Yet the truth about Marengo was more prosaic, as more level-
headed foreign tourists such as Charles MacFarlane realized. 'These
monuments seemed to me to be out of place in an Italian country',
he wrote in September 1848, 'for what did they commemorate but
the victory of one foreign people over another people of foreigners?'
For Italy, he pointed out, Marengo brought not freedom, but simply
a change in foreign masters. 'Yet the ultra-liberals of Piedmont were
now taking pride in these French monuments, and talking of the
battle of Marengo as if the Austrians had been defeated by a purely
Italian army.'[37]

The war of 1848–9 proved disastrous for the Italian cause. Austria
defeated Piedmont, and reasserted its control over Italy for the next
decade. Delavo himself soon faced financial ruin. He had spent
immense sums on his obsession, neglecting his business interests,
and saw his income reduced by the effects of Austrian occupation
during the recent conflict. He found himself in debt, but continued

to be carried away by ambition. 'I was mad,' he later admitted ruefully. 'I had lost a sense of proportion of the things of life. I no longer knew how to plan ahead.'

Delavo could have freed himself from his debts by selling Marengo, but was unable to face the break-up of all he had built. His troubles multiplied, and in 1855 he was stricken with grief at the death of both his wife and his only daughter. The following year, he was finally obliged to put Marengo up for sale.[38] A writer in a London political and literary review, *The Leader*, was unsympathetic to his plight. 'Inside this palace you perceive that Delavo has one religion, one thought, one capacity,' it sneered. 'He is the slave – the last, mortified, spellbound slave – of the First Consul's fame ... Was ever devotion more devout? And all this aggregate of triumphal trash is to be split by pieces by a notary's hammer.'[39]

In fact, the sale was cancelled, for Delavo was still deluded enough to believe that the French Emperor Napoleon III, the nephew of the victor of Marengo, would intervene to buy and preserve the site. But the end came in 1857, when Marengo was auctioned off in order to satisfy Delavo's creditors. The money raised was a fraction of what the domain was worth. Reduced to poverty, Delavo went into exile abroad, where he eked out an existence by teaching Italian. By his eighties, he had become too old and ill to continue working, but his last days were brightened by the help of charitable well-wishers and sympathetic press coverage, and he was granted some financial relief by both the French Republic and the Queen of Italy.

Delavo's tragic life reads like a fantastic, biblical tale of a rich man reduced to rags after becoming obsessed with the material things of the world, and spending his fortune with the reckless, compulsive drive of a gambler. Yet it is hard not to feel sympathy for his plight, and even a degree of admiration and gratitude for what he achieved. His herculean endeavours were not entirely wasted: his villa still stands, and now contains an altogether different museum, with the previous hero-worship replaced by a more objective version of events, retold using all the benefits of modern technology. Even so, when you visit Marengo today, you find the past and present jammed uncomfortably close together: to the north of the hamlet lies an expanse of open, unspoiled countryside, yet immediately to the south stands an industrial area, with a busy road, and a whole host of hotels, restaurants, and car showrooms. The dilemma confronting the local authorities is how best to commemorate and preserve Marengo's history without standing in the way of progress, and it is a task made all the more complex when even the basic facts of the battle are so elusive, and the interpretations so controversial. It is a challenge that has yet to be fully confronted, two centuries after the solution eluded Napoleon and destroyed Delavo.

French soldiers at the time of the Consulate.

Chapter 7

'It Smells of the Revolution'

Since chicken Marengo was so closely linked to one of Napoleon's victories, it might have been expected to follow the swings in his fortune. In fact, once launched into the world, it carved out a path of its own, and remained seemingly untroubled by the political upheavals surrounding his downfall.

The start of its trajectory is difficult to detect. Successive editions of cookery books make it possible to track the dish's growing popularity, but only on the broadest of terms. The eighth edition of Alexandre Viard's recipe book, *Le Cuisinier impérial*, contained no mention of any Marengo dish when it was published in 1814.[1] Nor did the ninth edition, published in 1817, and now entitled *Le Cuisinier royal* to reflect the change of regime. Not until the tenth edition, published in 1820, did recipes appear for not just *poularde à la Marengo* (fatted chicken), but even *lapereau à la Marengo* (young rabbit), and *ris de veau à la Marengo* (calf sweetbread).

But the inclusion of these Marengo dishes marked not the time when they were first created, but simply the year in which the publisher felt obliged to bring *Le Cuisinier royal* up to date. The first eight editions had been printed one after the other in less than ten years, and left out many dishes because the author had emigrated and was unable to edit the work while Napoleon was still in power. Only after the fall of the Empire could he return to France and add 150 recipes for the 1817 edition. Even then, the book remained so incomplete that it had to be revised in 1820 by a Monsieur Fouret, who contributed a further 850 recipes.

Le Cuisinier royal is a good example of just how belatedly cookery books might be updated, and how imprecise a guide they offer to the moment when a new dish became available. A time lag inevitably separates the birth of an idea from the period when it permeates the public consciousness, and chicken Marengo existed for several years before it gained sufficiently high a profile to merit automatic inclusion in cookery books. It is clear from other sources that the dish was known long before 1820. A German encyclopedia of 1817 described the delights of Paris, including the restaurants, 'where new dishes are often named after famous battlefields, such as *fricassée d'Austerlitz*, *poulet à la Marengo*, and the like.'[2] In the same year, a Pole called Antoni Wybranowski had a collection of poems published in Lublin, in one of which he mentioned *pasztety z Marengo*, or *pâtés à la Marengo*.[3]

It is possible to go even further back in time. A British tourist recorded that he ate *poulet à la Marengo* in Paris in August 1814, during the peace following Napoleon's first abdication.[4] A senior Russian officer, Ivan Stepanovitch Jirkevitch, also mentioned eating the dish in the spring of that same year, during the Allied occupation of Paris, and the fact that the dish was named after one of Napoleon's victories clearly did not bother him, since he wrote that he liked it very much.[5] The extent to which chicken Marengo had already conquered the restaurants of Paris by this time is clear from the pages of *Le Guide des dîneurs*, a survey published in 1814 and reissued the following year. It reprinted the menus of twenty-one respectable restaurants. Seven of them, or one-third of those surveyed, offered *poulet à la Marengo*, and an eighth offered rabbit Marengo instead.[6]

One of the restaurants that served chicken Marengo was the Trois frères provençaux, whose rise to fame may offer a clue to some of the reasons for the dish's growing popularity. The Trois frères provençaux became so fashionable partly because of the extravagant meals held by groups of Napoleon's high-spirited officers. Chief among them was the magnificent *déjeuner* given by Chef d'escadron Pierre Daumesnil of the Chasseurs à cheval of the Guard for all the officers of his regiment, featuring oysters washed down with countless bottles of expensive wine. By 1808, the restaurant was really beginning to make a fortune. It was at this time that Napoleon intervened in Spain and Portugal at the start of the Peninsular war and, as reinforcements based in central Europe passed through France, many of the officers took the opportunity to have a night out in Paris, and enjoy a dinner at the Trois frères provençaux. The restaurant's daily receipts at this time were said to have been at least 12,000 francs (about 800 times the daily pay of an infantry *colonel*). It saw a return of these profitable times when Napoleon fell from power, for thousands of foreign troops occupied Paris in 1814 and again in 1815, and peace reopened the capital to an influx of wealthy tourists, particularly from Britain.[7]

It was the tourists who ensured that chicken Marengo's existence now began to be recorded so frequently, since they were fascinated by all the novelties they discovered on their first visit to the Continent. But for the dish to be served after Napoleon's downfall, it must already have become common – so much so that it was too unremarkable to be specially documented by Parisians themselves. What is also clear is that the fame of chicken Marengo was a side-effect of the spectacular success enjoyed by the capital's restaurants. Originally, the word *restaurant* meant a restorative broth, served in the establishment of a *restaurateur*, but has come to refer to the establishment itself. The first of them had opened in Paris in 1766, and by the time of Napoleon's reign they had outgrown their original, limited function of serving health-cures for real or imagined invalids, and had evolved into fashionable places in which to dine in splendour. Restaurants were the height of sophistication: unlike inns and taverns, they provided individual tables, personalized service, a calm and relaxed atmosphere in luxurious surroundings, quality food at clearly defined prices, and a wide choice of what to eat, at a time of the diner's choosing. Chicken Marengo was a prestigious dish designed not for the communal table of a rowdy tavern, but for the discerning diner and the busy chef at a respectable restaurant, for while impressive it was also quick and easy to prepare in individual servings.

The restaurant was a distinctly Parisian institution that had yet to spread to the provinces, let alone the rest of the world. Few would be found outside the city until well into the second half of the nineteenth century, for Paris alone had the population, resources, and infrastructure to support large numbers of them. It was the growing size, wealth, and influence of the Parisian élite that spurred on the success of the restaurant during and after Napoleon's reign. Gastronomy expanded from being the preserve of the court and establishment to embrace an altogether broader section of society, and this surge was most marked during the three decades that followed Waterloo, which helps explain the parallel rise of chicken Marengo during that time.[8]

Not everyone welcomed the effects of the Revolution. Many despised the newly rich bankers, contractors, and speculators, scorning them as brash upstarts ignorant of the grace and polite manners that came so naturally to the old aristocracy. 'Four dishes of a deplorable vulgarity were then invented,' lamented a financial historian, Jean-Baptiste Capefigue. He listed them with obvious distaste: '*Sauce Robert*, truly a concoction for the guardroom; sautéd chicken, which has since been named Marengo, with its dressing of oil and garlic that turns even the strongest stomach; and *matelote normande* and *sauce en tortue*, which are copious and very coarse dishes.'[9] In Capefigue's jaundiced view, chicken Marengo was invented to satisfy men who had risen from the lower ranks of society, and who had acquired the trappings of nobility without being able to change their inner nature – men who demanded highly flavoured sauces because they lacked the finer sensibilities and were more used to eating round a bivouac fire than at a table.

It was a frequent complaint, but also an embittered and over-simplified one. The old, popular view that the Revolution saw the rise of bourgeois capitalists at the expense of aristocratic landowners has been discredited. The changes were political rather than social. Even those noble landowners who were dispossessed during the

Revolution often managed to buy back their confiscated estates. The bourgeoisie were more interested in gaining political power and public employment, along with all the status that came with an official position, rather than in becoming industrialists and making a fortune. Most entrepreneurs were not self-made men, yet those commoners who did strike it rich during the Revolution drew a disproportionate degree of attention. What was easier than for the envious to sneer that the parvenus were undermining standards by stuffing themselves with mediocre dishes and endlessly boasting about their cooks' skill in inventing new *ragoûts*? It did not take any skill to produce a *ragoût*, the jealous claimed. A second-rate cook could easily do so, secure in the knowledge that he simply needed to add a copious amount of garlic in order to win the diner's approval because of its enticing aroma and powerful flavour – not to mention its reputation as an aphrodisiac.[10] In the eyes of these cynics, chicken Marengo was not an invention of which to be proud, not one of the great triumphs in the art of cooking, but a symbol of all that was wrong with the Revolution. How ironic that so famous an emblem of elegant cuisine should have been disparaged in some quarters as a dish for gluttons rather than gourmets.

❧

We know from the menus reprinted in *Le Guide des dîneurs* that in 1815 the Trois frères provençaux was offering not just *poulet à la Marengo*, but also *poulet à l'Austerlitz*. Its mention is a reminder that Marengo was far from being Napoleon's only victory to be honoured at the dining table. Indeed, a provincial distiller produced a liqueur called Crème d'Austerlitz within two years of that battle.[11] Even sweets were named after Napoleon, and some actually bore his image. In 1807, the *Almanach des gourmands* described one shop's new confectionery:

> We must highlight the *boulets d'Jena* [Jena cannonballs], whose delicacy and pleasant taste make them worthy of note. All we

need now is to be given *bombes d'Austerlitz, balles de Marengo*, etc., and then we will have a sugary and uniquely glorious artillery, which cannot help but reconcile gastronomes with the art of war, so hostile as it is to the art of fine eating.[12]

The latter sentence was a typically barbed comment from the *Almanach*'s editor, Alexandre Grimod de la Reynière, a man instinctively hostile to the Empire, but one who had a lawyer's seemingly effortless knack of disguising his acid sarcasm, so it would be mistaken for just another innocuous tribute from a subservient courtier, or dismissed as the ramblings of an eccentric.

Why has chicken Marengo endured, whereas chicken Austerlitz vanished? That, surely, is the most intriguing question, for Austerlitz was an even more famous victory, and certainly more impressive. The lower profile of chicken Austerlitz was apparent as early as 1820, when a reviewer criticised the latest edition of *Le Cuisinier royal* for its choice of recipes. 'They have described very clearly *ris de veau à la Marengo, lapereau à la Marengo*, and *poularde à la Marengo*', he wrote, 'but were wrong to have remained silent about *poulet à l'Austerlitz*. Are these culinarians hostile to the nation's glory? Do they want to reduce us to just a single victory?'[13]

Even so, chicken Austerlitz enjoyed sufficient vogue in the 1820s and 1830s to appear in English fiction of the time. In 1838, William Makepeace Thackeray wrote a story seen through the eyes of a fictional hero whom he burdened with the improbable name of Major Goliah O'Grady Gahagan. Equally improbably, he made his unfortunate major dine with King Louis-Philippe of the French, and become the butt of such teasing that he fell into a state of confusion:

> I blushed, and stuttered, and murmured out a few incoherent words to explain – but it would not do – I could not recover my equanimity during the course of the dinner; and while endeavouring to help an English duke, my neighbour, to *poulet à l'Austerlitz*, fairly sent seven mushrooms and three large greasy *croûtes* over his whiskers and shirt-frill. Another laugh at my expense.[14]

It may well have been that chicken Austerlitz was created only after chicken Marengo, in which case it would have lacked the same novelty factor. Chicken Marengo would have had longer in which to become established, before Parisians grew bored with military victories, and before their disillusionment with the Empire was intensified by the defeats of its twilight years. Yet why should any dishes named after Napoleon's victories have remained on the menu after his fall? Chicken Marengo continued to thrive after the Bourbon restorations of 1814 and 1815, and was not even renamed, let alone banned. This was surprising given that Paris underwent a purge of politically incorrect names and symbols. Streets and bridges commemorating Napoleon and his battles were rebaptized, and the word 'imperial' in titles was replaced by 'royal'. The place de Marengo, immediately north of the Louvre, became the place de l'Oratoire, and the barrière de Marengo, the toll-gate on the south-eastern side of the city, through which Napoleon had entered on his return from Italy in 1800, received the less emotive name of the barrière de Charenton, after a nearby village.[15]

That locations honouring Marengo failed to escape this re-labelling process is significant, as it shows that the dish owed its political immunity to nothing inherent in the name of the battle. It has been suggested that chicken Marengo survived because Napoleon's opponents considered eating one of his victories to be a way of mocking him, and of rejoicing over his fall, but it is more likely that the dish's title was simply not thought important enough to merit concern. The great celebrity chef Marie-Antoine Carême even served it to the British Prince Regent at Brighton as early as 1817, after entering his employment.[16]

Chicken Marengo had simply become so familiar that its original meaning was ignored: rather than celebrating a Napoleonic victory, the term *à la Marengo* just described a method of cooking. Dishes were no longer seen as politically relevant. It had been different at the height of the Revolution, when citizens had eaten together in great, fraternal festivals, and when some *restaurateurs* had even changed the names of politically incorrect fruits. 'Good Christian' pears, for example, had abandoned their faith and become 'Good Republicans'.[17] But after the early years of the Revolution, food had become depoliticized, and this shift in attitudes owed much to the growing obsession with gastronomy, which was perceived as a harmless, apolitical pursuit. The pleasures of the table were now seen as a way of keeping the notoriously volatile Parisians distracted from politics and their lost freedoms.[18] If France was no longer blessed with liberty, equality, and fraternity, as least it had the consolations of glory and gastronomy. Dinner conversations tended to revolve around the meal itself, as the Duke of Wellington's friend, Frances, Lady Shelley, found when she dined with the French statesman Charles-Maurice de Talleyrand in August 1815. 'During the whole repast the general conversation was upon eating,' she recorded. 'Every dish was discussed, and the antiquity of every bottle of wine supplied the most eloquent annotations. Talleyrand himself analysed the dinner with as much interest, and seriousness, as if he had been discussing some political question of importance.'[19] For gourmets such as Talleyrand, food was a fascinating subject in its own right, and under Napoleon's autocractic regime it had become a safe topic, in a way that politics was not.[20]

Only one-third of the restaurant menus reprinted in *Le Guide des dîneurs* in 1815 included chicken Marengo. Its omission from the others was not necessarily due to political caution, since it had been ignored by some restaurants even during the Empire. Chicken Marengo seems to have escaped Napoleon's downfall lightly, although it did not remain wholly unscathed. In 1835, the *Revue de Paris* published a story by the novelist Léon Gozlan about the town of Ecouen, 12 miles north of Paris. It is unclear how much of Gozlan's story was based on fact, for he may well have drawn on his actual experiences, but he mentioned a Madame Dutocq, who had run an inn at Ecouen for the past thirty-five years, unmoved by the frequent changes of regime. 'Her only involvement in these political transformations consisted of some amendments that prudence compelled her to make to her menu of the day,' Gozlan explained. During the Revolutionary Terror, she had served *côtelettes à la Soubise* under the more politically correct title of *côtelettes à la Couthon*, named after a member of the powerful Committee of Public Safety. Similarly, after the Bourbons had been restored, she called chicken Marengo *volatile à la Condé* (Condé fowl), in honour of one of the most illustrious branches of the House of Bourbon.[21]

Was Madame Dutocq's action just an isolated, and perhaps wholly fictional, example of chicken Marengo being caught up in the deep divisions of French society at this time? Perhaps not, for some particularly touchy and frustrated officers of Napoleon's army seemed to regard the dish as a potent symbol of lost glory – or at least that was the conclusion that might be drawn from a dis-reputable little incident that occurred in Paris in 1814. Soon after the Bourbon Restoration, Colonel Jean-François Jacqueminot and a group of friends decided to have some fun ridiculing the pretensions of the royalists who had returned from exile. Having dressed up as *émigrés*, they went to have *déjeuner* at one of the leading cafés, and what ensued was later described by Captain Rees Gronow, a celebrated British dandy with an inexhaustible fund of anecdotes. According to Gronow, the friends called for the menu, and, glancing through it, spotted *poulet à la Marengo*. 'No, that won't do,' exclaimed Jacqueminot loudly, 'it smells too much of the Revolution.'

The reaction he provoked in the café was not the one he had expected, for a gentleman at the next table happened to have fought for Napoleon at Marengo, and now angrily jumped to his feet. 'What the devil do those *émigrés* know of our battles?' he protested, mistaking Jacqueminot and his friends for genuine royalists. 'They ran away from France when there was danger, but come back when it is over.'

Jacqueminot took this unexpected development in his stride. Continuing to act his part, he pretended to be equally irate, but

The two most famous portrayals of Napoleon crossing the Alps. David (*right*) shows him on a rearing charger, whereas Delaroche (*below right*) opts for a lowly mule. In fact, both interpretations are inaccurate.

Napoleon at the Hospice of the Grand Saint-Bernard on 20 May 1800. Note the soldiers hauling the gun barrel through the snow in a hollowed-out section of tree trunk. The dog is one of the famous Saint-Bernards.

The Hospice today.
The building on the right is the one shown in the picture at the top of the page.

The Torre Garofoli farmhouse, which served as Napoleon's quarters immediately before and after the battle. This, according to legend, was the birthplace of chicken Marengo.

As the French positions crumbled in the afternoon of Marengo, Napoleon personally intervened to try and rally the men. He was on the verge of defeat.

To San Giuliano

Church tower of
Cascina Grossa

Alessandria
and Marengo

W

Column of
Austrian
grenadiers

Kellermann's
charge

Desaix's infantry

Berthier with captured
Austrian officers

Austrian attack on Desaix

The scene of the decisive climax of the battle, as it is today. Note the flatness of the terrain. Kellermann advanced from behind the camera to launch his charge somewhere in this area (the exact location is unclear). At the time of the battle, the crops were taller, and much of the foreground was covered in vines, which helped conceal Kellermann's cavalrymen until the last moment.

Castel Ceriolo village

Napoleon

The climax of Marengo, as depicted by the artist Carle Vernet. His painting – similar in many respects to Lejeune's earlier, and more famous, picture – is equally inaccurate, not least in the direction of Kellermann's cavalry charge.

Desaix: the fallen hero.

Melas: the Austrian commander-in-chief.

Marmont: an expert gunner.

Kellermann: one of the most outstanding
cavalrymen of his generation.

An idealised interpretation of Desaix's last moments. In fact, his fall went almost un-noticed at the time, and he died without saying any of the flowery words attributed to him.

One of the monuments erected to Desaix in Paris. This fountain stood in the former place Dauphine, at the heart of the city.

The entrance gateway of the museum at Marengo today. The design was inspired by Napoleon's unfulfilled plan to honour the fallen with a massive stone pyramid.

Napoleon's statue outside the museum. Unveiled in 1847, it formed part of Giovanni Delavo's ambitious project to commemorate the battle.

went up to the gentleman to offer a quiet word of explanation. 'You are one of the right sort,' he told him in a low voice. 'I admire both your courage and frankness; and if all men of our party would follow your example, there would not be a Bourbon left in Paris twenty-four hours longer.'

Unfortunately, one of the waiters was a police informant. Overhearing Jacqueminot's words, he denounced the officers, who were subsequently court-martialled and condemned to lose their rank and pay in the army. The proceedings were interrupted when Jacqueminot angrily grabbed the informant, only to be stopped by the president of the court. 'You are too brave to hurt that villain,' the president exclaimed. 'All hail, Jacqueminot, as a hero!' It was then that Jacqueminot remembered that he had saved the president's life in Russia during the Battle of Borodino.[22]

Gronow had an eye for a good story, and his anecdote was unlikely to have lost anything in the telling. Yet the basic facts are confirmed by numerous other sources, including three who were particularly well-placed to know what happened. Mademoiselle Louise Cochelet, the *lectrice*, or reader, to Napoleon's stepdaughter Hortense, heard the details from one of Jacqueminot's fellow pranksters, Colonel Anatole-Charles-Alexis, marquis de Lawoëstine. The second source, Mademoiselle Georgette Ducrest, was related to Lawoëstine through her aunt, while the third, Claude-François Méneval, was one of his close friends.

It is unclear exactly when the incident occurred, but it would have been around the time of the former Empress Joséphine's death on 29 May.[23] Her daughter, Hortense, lived 12 miles north-west of Paris, in the Château de Saint-Leu. One day, some visitors from the city came to see her, including Lawoëstine, who excused his delay in paying his respects by saying that he had been placed under arrest. He then explained how he and some companions, including Jacqueminot and Chef d'escadron Charles-Emmanuel Lecouteulx de Canteleu, had dressed up like elderly *émigrés*, deliberately making themselves look ridiculous by exaggerating the foibles of the men who were derisively dubbed the *voltigeurs de Louis XIV* since they seemed so out-of-date and too old and unfit for any running around like *voltigeurs*, or skirmishers. Lawoëstine and his friends had powdered their hair, and put on old-fashioned coats, and large tricorne hats decorated with enormous white cockades. Mademoiselle Cochelet took up the story:

> Dressed like this, these gentlemen had gone to have *déjeuner* at the Café Hardy, near the *boulevard*, where they played their roles so well that, despite their youthful faces, they took people in for a time. But then they read the menu of dishes on offer, saw *poulets à la Marengo*, and exclaimed that they wanted nothing reminiscent of the usurper's regime. Peals of laughter broke out, and, as you can well imagine, the meal did not go short of champagne, jollity, and jokes.[24]

They then strolled round the Palais-Royal, each of them sporting an enormous Cross of Saint-Louis in his buttonhole and boasting of how the only fire he had seen in winning this decoration had been that of a kitchen. 'Ah, good day *marquis*!' they exclaimed whenever they met an *émigré*, as if they were greeting an old acquaintance. 'Good day *vicomte*! . . . There you are. . . . And how long have you been at Paris? . . . What are you going to do here?' They then conducted a loud and hilarious conversation in the midst of the crowd about the services they had performed while in exile, and about the rewards they anticipated for restoring the King to power. They even took their play-acting right up to the walls of the royal residence of the Tuileries. Standing outside, they put on simpering airs, and bowed to the ladies, who graciously returned their compliments from the upstairs windows.

According to Mademoiselle Cochelet, the prank was immediately known all over Paris. The culprits were placed under arrest, but there was a final, amusing sting to the story. On being released, Lawoëstine encountered an old *émigré* dressed as usual as a *voltigeur de Louis XIV*. 'You are very unwise to wear a costume like that,' Lawoëstine supposedly warned him with mock seriousness. 'Wearing something similar landed me in prison for a month.'[25]

In her heart, Hortense found the exploit hilarious, but could not be seen to condone it, for despite all her attempts to ban political discussions her *salon* was widely perceived as a nest for hotheaded Bonapartists. She therefore rebuked Lawoëstine, telling him that he had been wrong to mock old *émigrés* who had suffered years of exile and misfortune. Their adventure, she told him, might have been suitable for young pages, 'but *colonels* should have more gravity. You will give the impression that you earned your epaulettes through bravery alone, and that you are still only children.'

Her little sermon might have had more effect, if another young, Bonapartist officer had not been present. Colonel Charles Huchet de Labédoyère could not help bursting into laughter. 'Ah, here's the Queen delivering another scolding!' he exclaimed. (Hortense retained her title from when she had been Queen of Holland under Napoleon.) 'That doesn't worry me', he added, 'as I seem to be the only one who hasn't earned it.' But Labédoyère simply distracted Hortense from her original target, and made her turn on him:

> As for you – no, I don't scold you for being too childish. Quite the opposite: you take things too seriously, and must learn to resign yourself to events. All of you have risked your lives so often, and now you must enjoy the peace and all its benefits. I lose more than anyone from all these changes, but so what: I assure you that if my country is happy, I myself will be content at no longer having such a stormy life, constantly fearing for the lives of everyone dear to me.[26]

'But the humiliation, *madame!*' protested Labédoyère. 'Does Your Majesty think nothing, then, of seeing foreigners dictate laws to Paris?'

'Certainly', answered Hortense, 'we have been defeated by weight of numbers, despite all your courage, and so we must bear the full consequences. All the same, we have been conquerors for so long that a single defeat can grieve, but not humiliate, us.'

Then two Russian visitors were announced. Their arrival was nothing out of the ordinary, since Tsar Alexander had chivalrously taken Joséphine and Hortense under his protection following Napoleon's fall from power. One of them was the diplomat Carlo Pozzo di Borgo – born into an old Corsican noble family, he had been friends with Napoleon as a young man, until they had fallen out as a result of the political turmoil that beset their island during the French Revolution, and he had subsequently entered Russian service. Unfortunately, the sight of Pozzo di Borgo sparked off another outburst from the tempestuous Lawoëstine, who loudly ridiculed the Allies, and those exiled men who had so bravely returned to their country on the backs of the Cossacks. Pozzo di Borgo pretended not to hear, but was inwardly furious. 'What can I do about that?' was Hortense's comment when she heard of his anger. 'Who can prevent Frenchmen from opening their mouths without thinking? I can't, for I had just given them a scolding, and I can see it did not have much effect.'[27]

It is easy to sympathize with the perpetrators of the escapade, but many of the *émigrés* whom they ridiculed were old and defenceless victims, honourable men who had remained loyal to their King throughout the hardships of two decades of exile. One reason why some of them wore such old-fashioned clothes was simply because they were too impoverished to replace them with a more modern style. Nor was the incident a unique occurrence: in fact, similar taunts happened almost every day at the Palais-Royal. What made this particular event stand out was the seniority of the culprits. One royalist accepted that Jacqueminot had a most distinguished record, but asked pointedly: 'Was not his role in this clowning around in the worst taste for someone of his rank?'[28]

The problem was that, for *colonels*, they were remarkably young. Just 5 per cent of Napoleon's *colonels* were appointed to that rank before they were thirty, yet Jacqueminot was twenty-seven, while Lawoëstine and Labédoyère were a year older. They owed their accelerated promotion to the fact that they had all served as ADCs to prominent generals´or marshals, and also benefited from the dramatically increased demand for *colonels* in 1813–15 as a result of heavy losses among the officer corps. Labédoyère was promoted to that rank in May 1813, Jacqueminot in October, and Lawoëstine in April 1814. Bravery and brilliance on the battlefield were also vital. Lawoëstine, for example, won his promotion for his outstanding conduct at Saint-Dizier, Napoleon's final victory of the 1814 campaign.[29]

All were privileged young men. Labédoyère came from a noble family with origins in Brittany, and had begun his military career in the prestigious Gendarmes d'ordonnance, a unit created in 1806 to attract well-born youths into military service and prepare them for careers as officers. Lawoëstine was the son of a *marquis*, and related to several great European families. Lecouteulx de Canteleu (who, being three or four years younger than the others, was still a *chef d'escadron*) was the son of one of Napoleon's senators, and belonged to an old noble family from Normandy. Jacqueminot was also the son of a senator. 'He knew that he was a handsome man', noted a Saxon countess on whom he had been billeted during the 1813 campaign, 'and also that it is sounder to put yourself in the best light than to wait for someone else to come and notice you. It is clear that he is intent on making his own luck and forging his career, and it takes some time before you feel at ease with him.'[30]

They were devoted to the Empire, which was hardly surprising since they had enjoyed such spectacular benefits, and had known nothing other than Napoleon's rule for the whole of their adult lives, having been barely thirteen or fourteen at the time of his *coup d'état* and his victory at Marengo. They were all members of the Légion d'honneur, the prestigious order that Napoleon had established in 1802 to reward the most distinguished of his servants. Lawoëstine had been wounded at the Battle of Heilsberg in 1807, but emerged from the wars relatively unscathed compared to his comrades. Labédoyère was shot in the head in 1808, the foot the following year, and the leg in 1813. Chef d'escadron Lecouteulx de Canteleu received two wounds in 1809, was shot in the head in 1814, and mistakenly run through with a sabre by a French cavalryman during the chaos of a Cossack raid in 1812. As for Jacqueminot, he collected wounds with a frequency that suggested he was either blessed with a complete disdain for danger, or cursed by a permanent state of bad luck: he had been hit in no fewer than seven actions, the last three of them at the start of 1814 while defending France against invasion.[31]

It was a combustible mix: youth, privilege, ambition; the exuberance inculcated by starting their service as cavalry subalterns, the giddiness of reaching high rank at so early an age; and then the bitterness of defeat, the sudden release of tension after eight or nine years of campaigning, and the frustration of an apparently shattered career – emotions that were sharpened by the humiliation of seeing their status and future employment threatened by men from the other side of the political chasm in French society, royalists who had never seen a battle or suffered a punctured skin. Just months earlier, these young officers had been daily risking their lives and enduring untold discomforts as they defended their country from invasion during one of the bitterest winters on record. Small wonder that they now had difficulty in adjusting, and in settling down to the new order of things. 'Morals good; conduct unrestrained; very discontent' read the pithy comment on a report about Jacqueminot in 1820.[32]

Only Lecouteulx apparently regretted their antics, mainly as he was in love with a noblewoman, which made him ashamed at having acted so thoughtlessly. He switched his loyalties to the Bourbons, and continued to serve them after Waterloo, even becoming ADC to King Louis XVIII's nephew, the duc d'Angoulême, in 1822. Lawoëstine, in contrast, resigned from the army in 1816, and went to live in Belgium, where his family had its origins. Not until after the July 1830 revolution did he return from exile and resume his military career. Jacqueminot had remained in France, but in the absence of any active military employment established a factory at Bar-le-Duc.[33]

Lawoëstine and Jacqueminot's youth, and their previously accelerated promotion, mitigated the deadening effects of the decade-and-a-half of Bourbon rule that followed Waterloo. Finally able to resume their military service in 1830, they soon became generals. Jacqueminot entered politics as a deputy, was appointed a peer, and survived until he was seventy-seven. Lawoëstine became a senator, and died, aged eighty-three, as Governor of the Hôtel des Invalides, the national home for disabled soldiers.

They fared better than Labédoyère. Tragically, he ignored Hortense's advice to take life less seriously, and was dead in little more than a year. He had married in November 1813, but did not seem to become any less of a hothead. Ironically, his wife, a noble-woman called Georgine de Chastellux, was royalist, and her family used its influence to obtain him an appointment as *colonel* of the 7e régiment de ligne in October 1814, thinking that a return to army employment would distract and calm him down. In fact, this well-meant intervention had entirely the opposite effect, for it placed him directly in the way when Napoleon escaped from exile on Elba in the spring of 1815 and marched on Paris. Instead of trying to stop Napoleon, he defected, and led his regiment over to his side. For this crucial act, which helped ensure the success of Napoleon's bold gamble, Labédoyère was initially showered with rewards, being promoted to *général de brigade*, granted the title of *comte de l'empire*, and appointed both a peer and ADC to Napoleon. But the price he paid after the defeat of Waterloo was even higher. With France back under Bourbon rule, he was court-martialled on a charge of treason, and shot in August, aged just twenty-nine. When his wife died fifty-six years later, in 1871, she was found to be still wearing next to her heart a small silver locket, containing some of his blood-stained hair, and engraved with the words: 'No more happiness without him'.[34]

Chapter 8

Pinnacle of Fame

At first glance, the *colonels'* escapade seems to refute the notion that chicken Marengo had become a depoliticized dish. Yet, if anything, the incident simply confirms its banality – it was precisely because it was so ridiculous to take offence at the name chicken Marengo that the brash, young officers objected so loudly to it, as a way of mocking the foppish pretensions of the *émigrés*.

So banal was its title that the dish was eaten even by staunchly royalist gentlemen, such as Jean-Baptiste Mocquet. Known as the marquis de Montalet, he settled in the United States after fleeing from the Caribbean island of Saint-Domingue at the time of the slave revolt that established Haïti as an independent nation in 1804. Mocquet made no secret of his sympathies, attaching a white, Bourbon cockade to the rapier he hung on the wall of his home, and he died in June 1814, possibly from an excess of joy after learning of Napoleon's abdication. Yet his ideological hostility in no way prevented *poulet à la Marengo* from reportedly being one of his favourite dishes.[1]

Indeed, the supreme irony was that chicken Marengo enjoyed its heyday only after Napoleon's fall from power. His removal was, in fact, essential if the dish was to become internationally famous, since it was peace that opened Paris to a flood of British visitors. The onset of mass tourism was facilitated by the growth in middle-class prosperity, and the development of faster, cheaper, and more reliable means of transport, with railways making bad roads a distant memory, and steamboats replacing erratic sailing vessels. Curious tourists would visit a top Parisian restaurant at least once, in order to see how it operated, and to experience French cuisine for themselves. Chicken Marengo's growing popularity rapidly snowballed, for perplexed British tourists, confronted with a long list of unintelligible, foreign dishes, were likely to opt for one whose name, at least, was familiar. 'Most of our readers who have had a trip to the French metropolis have not returned without eating *poulet à la Marengo*, *tête de veau aux truffes*, or *turbot aux câpres*, and drinking a bottle of Champagne-Sillery, or Clos Vougeot at Very's in the Palais-Royal,' noted *The London magazine* in 1825.[2]

The British were blamed for undermining standards in many Parisian restaurants. It is true that the old cross-Channel rivalry was now seasoned with envy at Britain's financial wealth, yet much substance lay behind the complaints. In 1828, the novelist Edward Bulwer used his latest work, *Pelham*, to bemoan the tidal wave of low-born English visitors:

> What waiter – what cook *can* possibly respect men who take no soup, and begin with a *rôti*; who know neither what is good nor what is bad; who eat *rognons* [kidneys] at dinner instead of at breakfast, and fall into raptures over *sauce Robert* and *pieds de cochon* [pig's trotters]; who cannot tell, at the first taste, whether the beaune [wine] is *première qualité*, or the *fricassée* made of yesterday's chicken . . . ? O! English people, English people! Why can you not stay and perish of apoplexy and Yorkshire pudding at home?[3]

Grievances such as these were echoed by a US visitor, who pointed out that a *vol-au-vent de turbot à la Marengo* served at a restaurant that was frequented solely by Parisians was quite different from one cooked at an establishment patronized by tourists. It was not only the dishes that the British corrupted, but also the service, since their excessive tips gave the waiters exorbitant expectations, and they contaminated the relaxed atmosphere of the restaurants with their stiffness and silence. The root of the problem was that so many middle-class tourists lacked the inbred confidence of the aristocracy, their ability to speak French, and their knack of rewarding good service appropriately.[4]

❦

Food was seen as a symbol of national character. French cooking was widely decried in Britain as frivolous and pretentious, a triumph of style over substance, and fundamentally untrustworthy. For their part, the French disdained British food as tasteless and unsophisticated. Stereotypes such as these hid the fact that each country's cuisine had heavily influenced the other, but that did little to moderate the arguments, and Napoleon himself joined the great debate about their respective merits. While in exile on Saint Helena, he argued with his Irish physician, Dr Barry O'Meara, about the number of meals their countrymen ate. 'You English always eat four or five times a day,' he claimed. 'Your cookery is more healthy than ours. Your soup is, however, very bad: nothing but bread, pepper, and water.' On another occasion, he teased one of Saint Helena's residents, Betsy Balcombe, about the British fondness for *rosbif* and plum pudding. Betsy, a spirited teenager, promptly retorted that the French lived on frogs, causing Napoleon to laugh and pinch her ear.[5]

As Napoleon pointed out, roast beef and plum pudding were seen as uncompromisingly British dishes. Stout, traditional, and substantial, they were believed to epitomize the nation, for at the time corpulence was seen as a desirable characteristic associated with courage and determination. *The Roast beef of old England* was a patriotic song, performed at an opera as early as 1731, extolling the time when roast beef had ennobled Englishmen's brains and enriched their blood, and lamenting the decline caused by eating French *ragoûts*. A typical village celebration of the anniversary of Waterloo involved the inhabitants shooting at a stuffed effigy of Napoleon, drinking toasts, and eating beef and plum pudding, for these were national dishes, just as beer was perceived as the national beverage. A British orator was even heard claiming that it had been beer that defeated Napoleon. 'Beer and wine met at Waterloo,' he proclaimed, as he warmed to his theme. 'Wine red with fury, boiling over with enthusiasm, mad with audacity, rose thrice against that hill on which stood a wall of immovable men, the sons of beer. You have read history: beer gained the day.'[6]

Plum pudding evolved over the course of centuries, and has antecedents that can be traced right back to antiquity. Yet one legend – ludicrous, yet intriguingly similar to the myth of chicken Marengo – attributes its invention to a spur-of-the-moment improvisation on behalf of a hungry monarch. In the era before Anglo-Saxon England was unified under a single ruler, King Ethelbert of Kent was said to have become lost in a forest while out hunting. One of his retinue had the idea of picking some wild plums, grinding down their stones into a sort of flour, adding some wine, and cooking the mixed fruit and batter on a fire. So enchanted was Ethelbert that he supposedly insisted on the pudding being served every day.[7]

With their strong patriotic credentials, it is unsurprising that both plum pudding and a beefsteak encased in puff pastry were named in Wellington's honour. The origin of beef Wellington is disputed, but evidence of anything more than a nominal connection with him remains decidedly thin – in fact, if he favoured one particular type of meat, it was mutton rather than beef.[8] There is even a suspicion that beef Wellington was not British-born at all, but a classic French dish, *filet de bœuf en croûte*, which was simply given an unambiguously Anglo-Saxon title to make it more appetizing. Nonetheless, it proved remarkably successful, and was perceived as a solid, traditional dish that formed a stark contrast to the stylish but insubstantial French cooking. Beef Wellington is unlikely to have been created specifically as an answer to chicken Marengo, yet what better riposte could have been found? Moreover, the prestige of Wellington's name lent itself to variations on the basic theme of the puff pastry case, with the beef being replaced by perhaps salmon or sausage, in the same way that a whole range of core substances have been used for Marengo dishes.

Had the British tourists only realized it, chicken Marengo gave them a skewed impression of French cooking, and of the French way of life. Dining in a restaurant was an exceptional experience for all but an élite minority, and most French people in the mid-nineteenth century would never have eaten chicken Marengo. A vast gulf existed between *haute cuisine* and the food eaten by the bulk of the population on a daily basis. Chicken was too expensive to be an everyday food for the masses, for the birds were still generally reared by hand on a small scale, and many people did little more than hover above starvation.

Yet it was *haute cuisine* that tourists encountered when they dined in the top Parisian restaurants, and *haute cuisine* that was exported to other countries, partly by French chefs and entrepreneurs who went to seek their fortune abroad. By the second half of the nineteenth century, chicken Marengo had become a global phenomenon. While travelling through Russia in 1850, the writer Charles Henry Scott reached the city of Nizhny Novgorod, 250 miles east of Moscow, and found a French-run restaurant that served everything from *pâté de foie gras* to *poulet à la Marengo*. Similarly, Richard Monckton Milnes, 1st Lord Houghton, visited Egypt in 1882, where his daughter and her family were living. After a month, he yearned for a return to chips and stodgy omelettes, as a healthier alternative to the two daily dinners provided by his son-in-law's French cook, and noted sorrowfully that his servant was 'getting very fat on truffles and *poulet à la Marengo*'.[9]

The dish could generally be found in France's far-flung colonies. In the 1890s, railway passengers in Algeria who arrived at the un-promisingly remote station of Bouira could find a chicken Marengo fit for a first-rate restaurant. At the same time, Margaret Roy

Pember-Devereux ate the dish at a little café on the island of Nossi Bé, a French possession just off the coast of Madagascar. She was promised the best meal that the local resources could provide. 'The patron is better than his word', she added, 'and we dispute with the mosquitoes a *poulet à la Marengo* that would do credit to the Savoy itself. As we dined, a couple of French officers tripped in to drink *cognac* and play dominoes. I had some conversation with one who confessed that he was dreaming of Paris.'[10]

Yet while France's chefs and homesick colonists helped spread the dish abroad, it was also socially ambitious Britons and Americans who ensured its success. William Hardman, a well-connected man about town, invited three friends to dinner in London in April 1862. 'I had a very select dinner-party at the Club last night,' he wrote. Among his guests was Dante Gabriel Rossetti, one of the famous pre-Raphaelite Brotherhood of painters. Besides cigars and several different wines, the dinner featured oysters, salmon, fillets of beef, *fricassée de poulet à la Marengo*, and *omelette aux fraises*. 'I flatter myself they never sat down to a better selected meal in their lives,' Hardman boasted. 'They were enthusiastic, and I have added fresh laurels to my fame as a dinner giver. An enviable notoriety, but expensive.'[11]

Versions of chicken Marengo are still served around the world today, in homes, in restaurants, and at state banquets and wedding receptions, as far afield as Australia, the United States, Chile, and the Philippines. Yet its rise was not as smooth as might be supposed. Even as early as the 1840s, indications were beginning to appear that the dish had become too ubiquitous. William Makepeace Thackeray described a dinner in 1841 that consisted of eighteen dishes, starting with oysters, and ending with macaroni. Dish number seven was *poulet à la Marengo*, which provoked him to grumble: 'very fair, but why the deuce is one always to be pestered by it?'[12]

Another popular novelist, James Fenimore Cooper, made the same complaint in *The Redskins* (1846). He wrote about the Little-pages, an uncle and nephew who were travelling the world. They had reached Paris after being away from the United States for five years, and the uncle was vainly longing for clam soup, or some other

New York food to assuage his homesickness. 'Shall I send you some of this eternal *poulet à la Marengo?*' he asked his nephew. 'I wish it were honest American boiled fowl, with a delicate bit of shoat-pork alongside of it. I feel amazingly *homeish* this evening, Hugh!'[13]

Boredom with chicken Marengo was a symptom of a far broader problem, namely the deep-rooted wariness that many foreigners felt about French cooking. When a tourist called James Mitchell stopped to eat one evening on his way to Paris in 1816, he was loathe to try the countless alternatives on offer. 'Every thing was as far as possible from nature,' he wrote, 'boiled, broiled, fried, roasted, five times more than was necessary, and all floating in sauces of some sort or other. Not even potatoes could be had as nature produced them. They must be cut each into ten or twelve pieces, and be brought on covered with sauce, or butter about them, [so] that I could make no use of them.' Mitchell knew of one gentleman who was so curious about French cuisine that he gradually worked his way through the entire menu of a Parisian restaurant, by ordering four or five new dishes every evening. 'In the course of a month, he made his way to the end of the bill,' Mitchell wrote, and then added tartly: 'I would sooner be induced to take a draught from every bottle in an apothecary's shop.'[14]

Prestigious names conferred an aura of sophistication on a dish, but did precious little to enlighten diners. Grand, purely honorific titles, such as *à la Marengo*, provided no guidance about the actual ingredients. The problem haunted foreign visitors, including the dramatist August von Kotzebue who was bewildered by the vast range of dishes available at the best Parisian restaurants in 1804. 'The choice is difficult', he wrote, 'and all the more so since bizarre and technical terms are often incomprehensible. Who, for example, could guess what a *mayonnaise de poulets* was, or a *galantine de volaille*, a *côtelette à la minute*, or indeed an *epigramme d'agneau?* Often, misled by a fine name, you order a dish that does not satisfy the demanding palate at all.'[15]

Thomas Raffles, a nonconformist minister from Liverpool, was similarly puzzled by the menu in 1817, but found his appetite whetted by curiosity, 'and many things were tasted for the sake of ascertaining what could be contained beneath the disguise of names and forms that had never saluted the eye or the ear before'. Whereas a sense of the unknown spurred Raffles to experiment, it provoked passive resignation from an American called John Sanderson in 1835. The best option when confronted with the menu, Sanderson advised, 'is to call the *garçon*, and leave all to him, and sit still like a good child, and take what is given to you'.[16]

The restaurant naturally benefited, whether the diner adopted either the Raffles or the Sanderson approach. More problematic were stubbornly cautious customers like Isaac Appleton Jewett from the United States. 'Your great governing principle should be this,' he argued in 1838. 'Never select very compounded dishes. No cooks compound alimentary elements so much as the French. Nine dishes out of ten are described by one or other of those terms of art, *à la*, or *sauté*, – that is to say, *got up*.' He had found on several occasions that the central substance was completely lost in the finished dish, and so he went instead for the simplest options, such as a fried sole, in order to avoid the risk of eating an elaborately camouflaged stray cat. 'Exercise *great* caution in selecting the *à la*s, and the *sauté*s,' he warned. 'The *à la* was there, and that *à la* enshrouds mysteries.'[17]

🐓🐔🐓

So what lurked behind the compound mystery of *poulet à la Marengo*? What were its basic ingredients? The answer might seem obvious: chicken, garlic, olive oil, tomatoes, onions, wine, mushrooms, truffles, crayfish, aromatic herbs, and a fried egg. Of course, none of these individual substances was unique to chicken Marengo – it was the unorthodox combination of them all in the same dish that proved so memorable. Each ingredient added something to please the diner's senses. The egg was a colourful and humorous touch that enabled him to eat the two life stages of the chicken at the same time. The crayfish had an obvious decorative role, and added another dimension to the complex flavours. (Combining food from land and sea is less bizarre that it might seem, and can be found in *paella* and several other popular dishes from around the world.) Truffles, which grow naturally amid the roots of some trees, were highly prized for their flavour. 'The truffle can be said to be at the height of its glory,' explained the gastromic writer Jean-Anthelme Brillat-Savarin in 1825. 'However good an *entrée* may be in itself, it is poorly regarded unless enriched with truffles.' They were also supposed, like garlic, to have aphrodisiac properties. One of the greatest Italian composers, Gioachino Rossini, claimed that he had wept just three times in his life: when his first opera failed; the first time he heard Niccolò Paganini play the violin; and that traumatic moment when a truffled turkey fell overboard while he was out boating with some friends.[18]

Chicken Marengo was more than the sum of all these parts, yet there has never been a single, agreed recipe, and many of the classic embellishments tend to be left out today, starting with the truffles, which have become prohibitively expensive following a drastic drop in cultivation. Crayfish, too, are more difficult to obtain, following the devastation of the native European varieties by a plague introduced from North America. The *croûtons* – fried pieces of bread – that were normally served with the dish are often replaced nowadays by rice or pasta. Tomatoes are nearly always included, but are actually absent from many early recipes, having been slow to become popular in Europe following their arrival from the New World. Lemon juice is sometimes used to enhance the flavour, and even oysters, pineapple, or a slice of ham occasionally find their way into the dish.

It comes as a jolt to realize that there are practically no essential components at all. Not even the chicken is required, since veal, pork, beef, rabbit, or another core ingredient can be used instead. Tuna, shrimp, or sausage are sometimes substituted – or flatfish, as in the fantastically elaborate *vol-au-vent de turbot à la Marengo*, whose title alone is a mouthful. There is even a dish called *bouillabaisse à la Marengo*, containing a variety of fish and lobsters.[19] The only constants seem to be that some description of meat, poultry, or seafood is fried in oil, combined with a sauce, and enhanced with some description of garnish.

Even this extremely loose and generalized rule can be broken, for the oil is occasionally replaced by butter or dripping, and the central ingredient might consist of practically anything, as in eggs Marengo.[20] The key, transferable element that bestowed the *à la Marengo* title on this ever-increasing collection of dishes would therefore appear to be the sauce, and yet it, too, defied precise definition: everything in the sauce was designed to heighten and add to the rich blend of flavours, and this constant quest for perfection caused its colour, taste, texture, and contents to vary widely. Wine was often included, but by no means always – some British recipes substituted sherry, one of the nation's favourite drinks – and since tomatoes were also optional the final colour could range from a light brown to a deep russet. The sauce, therefore, was neither defined nor unique to chicken Marengo.

In short, the title *à la Marengo* became almost empty and mean-ingless, or rather a catch-all concept, a loose and ambiguous phrase that could be roped around a whole spectrum of more-or-less embellished dishes to give them cachet and attract patrons. This was not altogether a bad thing, for it encouraged culinary boldness, and gave imaginative chefs the scope to indulge their creativity. This was why chicken Marengo differed in quality and style between different restaurants and different years. 'The fund of invention in a Parisian *chef de cuisine* is inexhaustible,' wrote an anonymous author in 1839. 'His gravies and his sauces are as various as the tastes of his customers; to-day you may at Véry's partake of a *poulet à la Marengo*, and to-morrow the same dish at the Trois Frères Provençaux will be as different as a wild from a tame duck.'[21] Much depended on the quality of the ingredients, and the way they were used, as the writer William Makepeace Thackeray found to his disappointment when he had dinner in 1841:

> The *poulet à la Marengo aux truffes* is bad, – too oily by far; the truffles are not of this year as they should be, for there are cart-

loads in town . . . They do not flavor the meat in the least; some faint trufflesque savor you may get as you are crunching each individual root, but that is all, and that all not worth having; for as nothing is finer than a good truffle, in like manner nothing is meaner than a bad one.[22]

Elastic though the epithet *à la Marengo* may have been, it has undoubtedly been overstretched, and often bestowed on dishes whose qualifications for the title have been tenuous at best. In fact, the basic recipes for chicken Marengo have been manipulated as shamelessly as Napoleon progressively distorted the official account of Marengo, yet the development of so many different versions did at least prevent the dish from dying out as a result of becoming too familiar. Complaints from Thackeray or James Fenimore Cooper about the eternal *poulet à la Marengo* were mitigated by the existence of an almost inexhaustible range of different interpretations. Nowhere was the extent of that variability clearer than at the Palais-Royal – that great, glittering, and often scandalous collection of shops, cafés, brothels, restaurants, and gambling dens, offering every imaginable human pleasure, all crammed into a single precinct at the heart of Paris. A British journalist called George Sala vividly captured these stark contrasts in 1864:

> He who writes these lines was, many years since, dining in a cheap restaurant in the Palais-Royal. He liked to dine in state; but, being poor, was forced to put up with the second-floor splendour of the great Palace of Gormandising. The glass is as glittering, and the gilding as gaudy in the attic as in the basement of this place, only there is a diminution of price correspondent to the ascent you make, and, by an odd paradox, you lose caste as you mount. What matters it? If that which they call a *poulet à la Marengo* on the first floor be, as they assert, a nasty mess hashed up from the scourings and leavings of better cook-shops, and the *poulet* downstairs be a triumph of the art in which Carême and Ude excelled, it must come to the same thing in the long run. Abate a little for the difference

in flavour – and what is flavour? Is there anything nastier than an olive, or caviar, or the trail of a woodcock, at first tasting? You will find both dishes equally rich in colour, multifarious in ingredients, rich and sloppy. And both will make you equally bilious the next morning. He of whom I write, then, being pinched in purse, dined, not at Véfour's below, but at the humbler Richard's above.[23]

The potential rewards for restaurant owners were immense. In the 1820s, it could take under five years to make a fortune in the business in Paris, but the number of fashionable establishments made competition intense. 'They are under the continual necessity of employing every resource of art to attract customers, and secure a continuance of them,' noted an English visitor in December 1801.[24] Parisians constantly craved novelty. Incorporating new ingredients or ideas into chicken Marengo was not a superfluous gesture, but a vital necessity in a fiercely aggressive business, where restaurants had to accentuate their dishes if they wanted to remain distinctive, and not vanish into the sea of blander rivals. In 1880, a French writer described the idiosyncracies that made the *poulet à la Marengo* so memorable at one establishment: 'We found the restaurant's cooking excellent, with its unfamiliar, dark-coloured sauces, and with its flourishes of lemon slices, of *croûtons* in the shape of stars, and of crayfish jabbing their tails so they looked like acrobatic crustaceans.' Even calf's brains were sometimes used, partly for decorative purposes, since they were added in small, white slices, each studded with a piece of black truffle.[25]

The need continually to produce new sensations such as these was underlined by the brutal vagaries of fashion. Véry's, one of the most prominent restaurants of Paris, was mercilessly skewered by the *Nouvel almanach des gourmands* in 1825:

Monsieur Véry is, at it were, the patriarch of caterers: his fame has spread through Europe, and his cooking is mentioned from one pole of the earth to the other. Yet his great reputation has been unable to preserve the popularity he previously enjoyed, and his magnificent *salons* contain only a handful of regulars. Monsieur Véry's food is nevertheless always good, and his wines especially are excellent in quality, but who can explain people's fickleness? The crowd goes elsewhere; the tables and bar remain deserted. To this old sanctuary of cookery it can truly be said: 'You are no longer what you were!'[26]

It was difficult for a restaurant to stand out from its numerous competitors. Sumptuous furnishings were common, including marble floors, rich gilding, and immense mirrors, and hence many leading establishments also boasted of a unique feature. One café during Napoleon's time was called the Mont Saint-Bernard, and contained a model of the Alpine pass in one of its rooms in order to exploit public interest in the Marengo campaign. Similarly, a truly great restaurant might be known for a particular speciality: the Rocher de Cancale, for example, was famed for its oysters.[27]

Chicken Marengo was an obvious choice to serve as a flagship dish, for it was convenient as well as elegant. The sauce, for example, did not have to be made from scratch specifically for the dish: chefs might instead use a basic sauce that had been prepared in advance, such as the classic *espagnole*. The actual process of making *espagnole* was costly and complicated, involving the production of a stock; the addition of seasoning, some clarified soup, and a *roux* (a paste of flour and fat to thicken the sauce); and then a prolonged period of simmering. All this took several hours, yet the great advantage of *roux*-based sauces was that they could be reheated without losing their flavour. Once made, therefore, the *espagnole* was handy and versatile, and enabled chicken Marengo to be produced remarkably easily. The dish appeared to be sophisticated, yet even its *haute cuisine* version was quick and simple. The chicken could be fried, covered with a sauce speedily made by combining some *espagnole*, mushrooms, and concentrated stock, and then garnished. The convenience of the dish lay in the ease with which its various components could be produced by a team of specialized cooks, before being quickly assembled: the only complex and time-consuming elements were the *espagnole* and the stock, and they could both be prepared in advance. This made chicken Marengo ideal for busy restaurants, and for diners who did not want to be kept waiting. Indeed, haste had always been associated with the dish, and lay at the heart of the myth about its invention by Napoleon's cook racing to produce a meal for his hungry master.

It was also moderately priced. It is difficult to compare precisely the cost of dishes, since they varied with the size of the serving, the quality of the ingredients, and the method of preparation. The addition of truffles, for example, added considerably to the bill: in 1814, the Trois frères provençaux was charging 1 franc 15 for a quarter of chicken Marengo, but 2 francs 10 with truffles included.[28] What is clear is that chicken Marengo was neither the cheapest nor the most expensive meat or poultry dish on a menu. It was not an élitist or exclusive option, even if its title retained a certain cachet, as the novelist Léon Allard vividly described in 1880 in *L'Impasse des couronnes*:

> In order to run swiftly through the menu, the waiter adopted the tone of an omnibus driver announcing connections. Almost all you heard were word-endings: *sauce vreuil-pin sauté* . . . His voice rose at the final dish: *poulet marengo*!
>
> 'Marengo, eh? *Poulet marengo!*'
>
> 'Yes, yes, *poulet marengo!*'
>
> The prestige of the epithet 'Marengo' persuaded everyone to opt for the chicken.[29]

Though the passage of time dulled the initial lustre of chicken Marengo's title, it was quickly reburnished whenever its patriotic connotations were rediscovered. When France went to war in 1870, the frenzied atmosphere in Paris was captured in special menus that quickly appeared in the restaurants. The dishes they listed evoked either past French victories, or areas of Germany that were intended for conquest:

> *Potage Solferino* [soup named after a battle of 1859]
> *Jambon de Mayence* [Mainz ham]
> *Poulet à la Marengo*
> *Vin du Rhin* [Rhineland wine]
> *Kirschenwasser de la Forêt Noire* [Kirsch from the Black Forest][30]

A similarly themed menu is even said to have helped spark one of the great love affairs of the 1840s. Among the many admirers of the famous French actress, Mademoiselle Rachel, was Alexandre Colonna, comte Walewski, the illegitimate son of Napoleon and his Polish mistress. Rachel reputedly won his heart by serving him an unmistakably Bonapartist dinner:

> *Saucisson à l'ail de Toulon* [garlic sausage]
> *Omelette au jambon de Mayence* [omelette with Mainz ham]
> *Andouilles à la Bonaparte* [smoked pork sausages]
> *Poulet à la Marengo*
> *Bombe glacée à la Moskowa* [ice-cream in the shape of a sphere][31]

Every one of these dishes was connected with Napoleon in some way. He had helped recapture Toulon in 1793, while some of his troops had been besieged inside Mainz in 1814, and La Moskowa was the alternative name for the Battle of Borodino in 1812.

Even today, the last remnants of Napoleon's mystique continue to linger over chicken Marengo. To learn the full truth behind this legendary dish, we must therefore turn to the perpetually controversial, and surprisingly elusive, figure of Napoleon himself, and try to discover the man who hid his real identity so carefully behind the mask of the military commander and the imperial trappings of power.

Chapter 9

Napoleon and his Meals

Today's custom of having three meals a day is based on habit and convenience rather than on any biological imperative. In Napoleon's time, the number and timing of meals varied by social class, occupation, and personal habits. He himself normally ate just twice a day, although both his meals – *déjeuner* and *dîner* – were hot and substantial. His only breakfast was a cup of tea or orange blossom water, drunk before he had his bath and got dressed.

While in exile on Saint Helena, Napoleon did occasionally experiment with changes to the number and times of his meals. Towards the end of 1817, he decided that he wanted only one regular meal a day, in the middle of the afternoon. His physician, Dr O'Meara, thought that illness was causing a loss of appetite, but the changes also seem to have indicated Napoleon's boredom, and frustration at his unaccustomed lack of power over his life. In any case, he decided that he disliked the change, and reverted to his usual, convenient format of two meals. Similarly, when he tried having three meals a day, he abandoned the idea after only a fortnight.[1]

Déjeuner was meant to be at 9.30 am, but was often delayed until 11.00 if Napoleon's audiences with ministers and other individuals overran. Since he woke no later than 7.00 am, this meant he frequently spent most of the morning on an empty stomach. The meal was served on a small pedestal table of mahogany, with bowls of hot water under the silver plates keeping them warm until

Napoleon was ready to eat. The bowls were regularly replaced as the water cooled, and the plates were kept covered by lids.[2]

Napoleon's *déjeuner* normally lasted just seven to ten minutes. 'The Emperor ate quickly', wrote his Master of the Horse, Armand-Augustin, marquis de Caulaincourt, 'and swallowed so fast that you would think he chewed little, or even not at all.' He frequently used his fingers, as the prefect of the Seine-et-Marne recorded after finding him at *déjeuner* one morning in April 1814: 'The Emperor was holding a joint in his right hand, and removing, with a knife grasped in his left, all the bits that encased it.' Not surprisingly, Napoleon often managed to stain his uniform coat.[3]

Déjeuner was served for him alone. For a brief period after his second marriage in 1810, he ate with his wife, the Empress Marie-Louise, but returned to his former habits after she became pregnant. He found it more convenient to eat on his own, rather than try and conform to a fixed time, and this was nothing unusual, for *déjeuner* was an informal meal, and members of respectable French families tended to eat it separately, when and where they pleased. Yet, although the table was laid just for him, Napoleon often admitted children from his extended family, for *déjeuner* was a brief interlude in his working day, a time to relax and receive visitors. He liked to see his nephews and nieces, to hug and tease them, and to ask what they had learned since he had last seen them. Chef de bataillon Louis-François Lejeune – the talented, young artist who had painted the Battle of Marengo – reached Paris in February 1809, bringing news from Spain, and found Napoleon holding a nephew on his knees, and sharing his *déjeuner* with him, using the same fork. While talking to Lejeune, Napoleon caressed the child with obvious tenderness, and then drank some coffee, which was unsweetened. 'The child held out his thin, little arms to grab the cup and drink the coffee as well', recalled Lejeune, 'but was surprised by the bitter-ness of the liquid, and pushed the cup away with a sharp grimace.' Napoleon laughed at his nephew's reaction. 'Ah!' he told him. 'You've not yet completed your education, for you have still to learn how to hide your feelings.'[4]

Napoleon teased the children mercilessly, but with the best of motives. 'He liked to mock,' noted his secretary Méneval, 'never in a harsh or unpleasant way, but with a benevolent heart and a roar of laughter.' Sometimes his targets hit back, as happened when he distracted a nephew and stole a boiled egg from him. 'Give me back my egg, or I'll kill you,' the three-year-old demanded as he grabbed a knife. Napoleon called him a rascal, and asked if he would really kill his uncle, but could not persuade him to back down. 'You'll be a fine, strapping fellow,' he assured him as he returned his loot.

On another occasion, he was joined at *déjeuner* by Napoléone, the daughter of his sister Elisa. 'Well, *mademoiselle*,' he said mockingly. 'I've heard some fine stories. You wet the bed last night.' It was untrue, but had an hilarious effect on his niece. Sitting up very straight on her chair, she looked at him with all the imperiousness of a five-year-old girl. 'Uncle', she announced, 'if you have only silly things to say, I shall leave the room.'[5]

Napoleon was particularly fond of the eldest son of his step-daughter Hortense, Napoléon-Charles. Their mutual affection survived Napoleon's habit of pinching his cheek, or hugging him too hard, and even the teasing way in which he would feed him lentils, tantalisingly, one by one, until his face grew red with vexation. Napoleon later tried the same trick with his own infant son, the King of Rome, who was regularly brought to his *déjeuners*. But the little king was less tolerant of such teasing. Napoleon held out a piece of food enticingly, only to withdraw it just as the child opened his mouth. The third time Napoleon tried this, his son turned his head away. Napoleon promptly abandoned the game, but was amazed to find that the boy then obstinately refused the food at all. The child's governess, Françoise, comtesse de Montesquiou – known affectionately as *Maman Quiou* – had to explain that he did not like people trying to deceive him, and she added that he was proud and sensitive. 'He is proud and sensitive', Napoleon repeated, as he tenderly embraced him. 'That's very good, that's the way I like him.'[6]

On other mornings, Napoleon might take his son on his knees, and even give him some of his diluted wine to taste, ignoring *Maman*

Quiou's horrified protests. Alternatively, he would dip his finger in a sauce for his son to suck, and would then smear some over his little face, to the delight of them both. Yet sometimes – just occasionally – Napoleon was actually better behaved than his young guests: when the children of the Grand Marshal of the Palace, Henri-Gratien, comte Bertrand, attended his *déjeuner* one morning on Saint Helena, they started throwing meatballs at each other.[7]

It was not just children who enlivened Napoleon's *déjeuners*. He took the opportunity to receive some of the most prominent men of the age from the arts and sciences, and particularly enjoyed conversing with scientists who had accompanied his expedition to Egypt in 1798. He might discuss plans for beautifying Paris with his architects, the latest books with his librarian, or drama with the great actor, François-Joseph Talma. Less frequently, he admitted painters or sculptors to make sketches of him. Using his *déjeuner* for this purpose was an efficient use of Napoleon's time, for he was notoriously impatient and unwilling to waste hours giving formal sittings.[8]

Staff officers, too, might report during Napoleon's *déjeuner*. In August 1803, Lieutenant Philippe-Paul de Ségur was sent on a three-week tour of inspection of the Channel coast, and on his return found Napoleon having *déjeuner* at the palace of Saint-Cloud outside Paris. 'Never before had I been greeted so warmly and cheerfully,' Ségur recalled. 'After a hundred questions, he grumbled that he had spoiled his fine uniform, for while listening to my replies, he had spilt his coffee on the white lapels of his coat. He then asked me if I had had *déjeuner*, and I truly believe that, pleased with my reports and replies, he was about to pour me a cup of coffee.'[9]

Ségur was privileged to witness this scene, for as his account suggests, *déjeuner* was the most fascinating time of the day, since it was so revealing of Napoleon's character. 'No man was ever a hero in the eyes of his valet,' ran the popular saying, yet Constant, who spent fifteen years as Napoleon's valet practically without a break, denied the truth of the remark. 'However near you saw him, the Emperor was always a *hero*,' he explained, 'but you also gained much from seeing the *man* close up and in detail. From afar, you felt only the prestige of his power and glory, but as you approached you were surprised to find yourself enjoying, too, all the charm of his conversation, all the simplicity of his family life, and – I do not hesitate to say it – the ingrained benevolence of his character.'[10]

It was at *déjeuner* that Napoleon dropped the emperor's mask and was the most human. A close servant, Louis-Etienne Saint-Denis, known as Mameluke Ali, particularly liked serving at this meal, because of the interesting conversations he heard. Often, when Napoleon had no visitors, he chatted with the men of his household who were in attendance, perhaps asking what they had done the previous evening. Best of all were the rare occasions when Napoleon prolonged his *déjeuner* in order to have a proper break from his work. One of his prefects of the palace, Louis-François, baron de Bausset, treasured such times: 'Nothing equalled the agreeable light-heartedness and charm of his conversation. He spoke rapidly, and in a positive and picturesque way, and it was these moments in my service that constituted the most delightful times of my life.'[11]

Dîner was Napoleon's main meal of the day, and an altogether more formal and elaborate affair than his *déjeuner*. When he was in Paris, Napoleon normally ate with just the Empress, although he did sometimes invite guests, such as a family member, or ministers with whom he had worked earlier in the day. He relieved himself of too many social duties by entrusting the Grand Marshal of the Palace with the task of receiving dignitaries and diplomats, and of presiding over ceremonial *dîners*.[12]

Napoleon could vary between charm, rudeness, and simple absent-mindedness. He sometimes remained silent throughout the meal, for he never really stopped working in his mind. At one *dîner* at Mainz in the summer of 1813, he was so absorbed in his thoughts that he reacted purely mechanically to what was happening around him. He did speak to one guest, but only about trivial matters, and without paying any attention to the replies, so they seemed to the others at table to be playing an amusing game of exchanging unconnected comments. In contrast, the playwright Antoine-Vincent Arnault fondly recalled the *dîners* Napoleon had given whilst a young general living in Paris, before he had grown more aloof after becoming head of state: 'These *dîners*, where the food was more elegant than with the Armée [d'Italie], were delightful when the general made the effort to be polite, which happened fairly often during this interval between the campaigns of Italy and Egypt.' At this stage in his life, Napoleon liked to provoke an open conversation among his guests, many of whom were accomplished scientists and intellectuals, and willingly joined in, partly as he found it a convenient way of broadening his education.[13]

Dîner was meant to be at 6.00 pm. That was the time that the prefect of the palace came to let Napoleon know that the meal was served. But his first wife, the Empress Joséphine, usually found herself obliged to wait, since Napoleon would be so preoccupied by his work that he forgot that *dîner* was ready. It was often gone 7.00, and sometimes 8.00 pm, before he arrived. One evening, he forgot completely, and finally left his office after 11.00. 'It is a little late, I think?' he remarked to Joséphine, before explaining that he had thought he had already dined.[14]

Napoleon's unpredictability meant that a chicken had to be put on the spit to roast every quarter-of-an-hour, so that an edible one was always ready, whatever time he emerged from his office. On that exceptional occasion when he finally had *dîner* after 11.00 pm, no fewer than twenty-three chickens had been cooked one after the other. All the other dishes had to stand on the table for up to five hours, kept warm by continually having fresh bowls of boiling water put under them.[15]

Napoleon could be breathtakingly inconsistent, and oblivious to how his criticisms of other people's lack of punctuality could apply to himself. '*Madame*, it is not good, nor polite, for you to make people wait,' he scolded the wife of Bertrand, his Grand Marshal of the Palace, when she arrived late for Sunday *dîner* on the island of

Elba. Yet he made an effort to please his second wife, Marie-Louise, for she was just eighteen at the time of their marriage in 1810, and he was conscious of their twenty-two-year age gap. Since she liked to eat at a regular hour, he tried to be on time for *dîner*, and in fact, she often kept him waiting rather than the other way round. Instead of complaining, he would greet her with a compliment: 'Ah! I see you have been making yourself smart.'[16]

Napoleon's *dîners* could hardly be called modest, but neither were they extravagant. He was often served as many as sixteen dishes, besides dessert – these included soups, appetizers, and also the four *entrées*, two roasts, and several side dishes that constituted the core of the meal. But this was fewer than in many bourgeois households, and some of the options might be left untouched, for the whole point of serving a large number was to enable people to pick and choose what they wanted while they were sitting at the table with the actual food before their eyes. (The so-called Russian service, in which each person was served an individual helping that had already been carved and placed on a plate, as happens today, had yet to gain widespread acceptance.) The structure of Napoleon's *dîners* was simpler than was customary at the time, for instead of being served in several courses, his dishes were all brought to the table at once, except for dessert, which arrived once the rest of the meal had been cleared. As a result, Napoleon often followed an illogical order, absent-mindedly starting with whatever dish lay in front of him.[17]

Dîner lasted only twelve to twenty minutes – barely longer than *déjeuner*. During the Consulate, Napoleon actually extended the time he spent at table by a few moments, after being told it was too short. When one of his guests commented on the change, Napoleon joked that he was becoming lazy. 'Power is already beginning to corrupt,' he remarked. It was partly because of his haste that his table manners left much to be desired. Even when he had company, he might dunk his bread in the sauce of one of the dishes on the table, although his guests hid any disgust they may have felt, and several of them actually seemed to regard having a serving from the same dish as a way of paying court. Of course, dining with the Emperor was more of an honour than a pleasure, and a common complaint was that the meal began too late and ended too early. On one occasion, as Napoleon rose from the table, he saw his stepson, Eugène, do the same, and told him he could stay, only to be informed that Eugène had already eaten – he had wisely taken the precaution of having a more leisurely *dîner* of his own beforehand.[18]

Napoleon sometimes ended the meal abruptly, especially during those occasions when his mind was still focused on his work. Hortense, his stepdaughter, recalled how the silence would be broken as Napoleon stood up to leave. He tended to do so in a startling manner, suddenly pushing his chair away and rising as if he had received an electric shock. When reminded that dessert had yet to be served, he would smile, sit down again for a moment, but then leave without a word.[19]

Not surprisingly, the Empress Marie-Louise had difficulty adapting to Napoleon's habits. A guest who had *dîner* with the imperial couple in June 1810, less than three months after their wedding ceremony, noticed that she seemed irritated at the speed with which the dishes followed each other. Towards the end of the meal, Napoleon got up without giving her time to finish, and she actually complained to her uncle, who was eating with them.[20]

❧ ⚘ ❧

Dîner was generally followed by coffee in another room, but Napoleon often cut the evening short in order to return to work, or to hold a council meeting he had been obliged to postpone from earlier in the day. He did not have a fixed bedtime, but was generally in bed before 10.00 pm. He had the priceless gift of being able to sleep at will, so although he needed six hours' sleep a day, he did not have to take it in a single stretch. At night, after three or four hours' rest, he frequently rose around 2.00 am, went into his office to work in his dressing gown, and sometimes had his secretary awoken to take dictation. Towards 5.00 am, he might return to bed for another couple of hours' sleep.[21]

When working at night, Napoleon occasionally had a light refreshment brought. Less frequently, he would call for something more substantial, and so a basket was prepared each evening, just in case, containing plates and a variety of food, along with some water and wine. Later, during the Empire, Napoleon lost the habit of having this nocturnal snack, yet the basket was still prepared each evening, as had become customary, and the provisions were normally disposed of the next morning.[22]

One night, disaster struck. Napoleon's valet, Constant, had returned from hunting, feeling hungry and exhausted. After putting Napoleon to bed, he decided to take some of the food from the basket, since it was bound to remain untouched, and he then went happily to sleep. As luck would have it, Napoleon chose that particular night to ask for his snack, and there was no way of disguising its half-eaten state, let alone of replacing it at that early hour. 'It's you, isn't it, you fat ___,' he exclaimed, looking accusingly at his Mameluke servant, Roustam. 'You're the one who's eaten my chicken?' Roustam denied it, and blamed the absent Constant. 'That ___ should go and eat his own food,' came Napoleon's angry retort.

Unsurprisingly, Constant himself told a different story in his memoirs, and shifted the blame on to Roustam. The incident apparently occurred in 1809, at Schönbrunn palace outside Vienna. In Constant's version, Roustam was exhausted after a long day, and talked him into letting him have a chicken wing. Constant claimed that Roustam confessed when Napoleon demanded to know who had eaten it. 'So, it was you, funny fellow?' Napoleon chided him. 'Don't let me catch you doing that again.' Next morning, Napoleon told the Grand Marshal of the Palace the story, but more in amusement than anger, and when Roustam entered, he threatened to make him pay if it happened again, and tugged his ears affectionately.[23]

Napoleon's paternal and tolerant approach helps explain how he retained the devotion of most of his servants, even if Constant and Roustam both abandoned him after his abdication in 1814. Despite his mania for running his household as economically as possible, he treated his servants with respect and affection. A chamberlain, Auxonne de Thiard, remembered him warmly, even after falling out of favour and leaving his service in 1807. 'The Emperor is generally said to have had a rigid and despotic character', he noted, 'tolerating neither objections nor annoyances, and ready at any moment to respond with an unpleasant word to the slightest remark.' Yet this image was at odds with Thiard's own experiences: 'I saw nothing in him that resembled this depiction.'[24]

Claude-François Méneval began working as Napoleon's secretary in April 1802. 'I had expected moments of abruptness, and changes of mood,' he later admitted:

> Instead, I found him patient, indulgent, easy to get along with, not demanding at all, quite often cheerful in a noisy and mocking way, and sometimes charmingly jovial. But this familiarity on his part did not give you any ideas of responding in the same fashion. Napoleon played with men without mixing with them. He wanted me to be wholly at ease with him, and so, from the first days, I no longer felt the least awkwardness in his presence. He could of course impose on me a bit, but I was no longer afraid of him.[25]

Napoleon took an interest in his servants, asking them about their families and hobbies. According to the memoirs of Marie-Jeanne-Pierrette Avrillion, the Empress Joséphine's *lectrice*, he was neither hard nor quick-tempered. 'He was actually very easy to serve, provided you were punctual, and he was even very indulgent of little mistakes that the servants made.' His bad moods soon passed, and if he felt he had treated someone unjustly in a moment of anger, he soon came and pulled the person's ear, and said something affectionate.[26]

The confidence Napoleon placed in his servants was one reason why he seemed so unconcerned about the possibility of being poisoned. His best protection was the well-ordered running of the household. 'The Grand Marshal of the Palace was alert to everything,' noted a secretary, Agathon-Jean-François, baron Fain. 'As for Napoleon, he trusted his servants completely, and placed his life in their hands, as if not even the thought of danger had occurred to him.' The food was delivered from patented and sworn suppliers, and was examined, weighed, and measured as a check against fraud, before being handed over to the *maître d'hôtel*, who personally supervised the preparation of the meals. Daily inspections were ordered of the kitchens and stores. The areas where Napoleon's meals were prepared were placed strictly off-limits to anyone who had no duties there, and not even the lowliest member of staff could be appointed without the Grand Marshal of the Palace being informed.[27]

Yet there was a surprising gap in these arrangements, in that the Tuileries palace lacked a room set aside exclusively for Napoleon's everyday meals. Instead, he decided where the table should be laid, and this might be in either his apartments or those of the Empress. The absence of a dining room, combined with Napoleon's habit of eating on the spur of the moment, made him vulnerable. In the morning, for example, the table could not be laid for his *déjeuner* until he had finished giving audiences in the room where he would eat. As a result, the food waited in an antechamber, sometimes for hours on end, alongside people who were waiting to be admitted to see him.[28]

Napoleon commented that he was too much of a fatalist to take precautions against assassination. In general, he seemed to disregard the possibility of an attempt on his life, and appeared bored or incredulous when informed of plots. 'No, it not as easy as you think to kill me,' he reportedly replied when told of concerns about his safety. 'I have no fixed habits or regular hours. All my periods of exercise are abruptly broken off, and my departures are on the spur of the moment. It's the same with the table: no preferences for the dishes, I eat sometimes from one thing, sometimes from another, and it might be from the furthest plate as from the closest.'[29]

Yet this lack of concern was partly an act. Napoleon did adopt some basic safeguards, such as following the advice of his doctors to spit or vomit anything he drank should he find a bitter or unpleasant taste. Shortly after arriving on Saint Helena, for example, he found his cup of coffee so bad he threw it away, and drank that of one of his companions instead. He also insisted on certain procedures. When Louis-Joseph Marchand was on duty for the first time as his head valet on the island of Elba, he found that Napoleon wanted some tea, and so he had a servant bring the necessary items on a tray. Napoleon was about to drink the tea when he asked: 'Where does this cup come from?', and on being told that it was from the pantry, he instantly hurled it against the wall, and told Marchand only ever to use items from his *nécessaire*, or personal kit.[30]

Napoleon's wariness gave rise to some amusing situations. When he asked for tea one day, it was made by the valet who happened to be on duty on that particular occasion. But Napoleon found the taste revolting, summoned Constant, the valet who usually served him, and complained that an attempt had been made to poison him. 'That was the word he used', explained Constant, 'when he found that something tasted bad.' The truth was that Napoleon was used to being served by Constant, and did not like change. Constant went away, poured a cup from the very same teapot, and on his return used a spoon to taste the tea himself to show it was fine. This time, Napoleon found it excellent. 'Teach them how to make tea,' he told Constant. 'They're hopeless at it.'[31]

🐦🕊🐦

For such a prominent figure, Napoleon led a remarkably isolated life while in Paris. Except when he held meetings of ministers or councillors, he spent most of the week secluded in his private apartments, surrounded only by close servants and members of his family. Sundays were exceptional, in being a day on which to show himself to his people as their Emperor. After having *déjeuner* as usual in his private apartments, he emerged at noon for a series of public appearances, beginning with mass, followed by an audience attended by the court and foreign ambassadors. A stiff, formal étiquette prevailed, designed to impress those around him with his authority and prestige. A grand military parade might be held in the courtyard of the Tuileries, with Napoleon himself reviewing the troops. In the evening, instead of eating alone with the Empress, he regularly had a large *dîner* attended by those members of the Bonaparte clan who were in Paris. Apart from the presence of Napoleon's wider family, and the fact that he remained slightly longer at table, the only differences from a *dîner* during the week were minor. Even though the meal included a few more dishes, it could hardly be called a lavish feast.

To mark exceptional occasions – such as his coronation as Emperor in 1804, and his marriage to Marie-Louise in 1810 – Napoleon followed the old royal custom of dining in state, or having *dîner en grand couvert* as it was known. His table was set up on a platform, in one of the large state rooms of the palace, with an ornate canopy overhead. Other tables in the rest of the room might seat as many as 250 guests. These public meals were grand and pompous occasions, designed to outshine the other courts of Europe. They were also opportunities for Napoleon's pastry chef, Hubert Lebeau, to draw gasps of astonishment with his spectacular *pièces montées* – edible decorative showpieces enhanced with delicate strands of spun sugar – depicting such triumphant scenes as the assault on the bridge at Lodi in 1796. Napoleon never lost sight of the potential for these formal meals to be a tool of power and patronage, yet undermined their effectiveness by his habit of eating so fast, which set the tone for the proceedings as a whole. Some guests were left feeling distinctly underwhelmed by the experience. 'You eat marvellously well there, but far too quickly,' complained a Russian aristocrat, Elisabeth Petrovna Divova, who attended several of these *grands dîners* during the Consulate.[32]

Napoleon considered having *dîner* in public not just to mark exceptional events, but on every Sunday, as the Bourbons had done during the *ancien régime*, with admission being granted not just to courtiers and invited guests, but to any respectably dressed people who wanted to witness the occasion. But he decided that the ceremony had become outdated, and that it had a touch of the ridiculous, since the onlookers were liable to gawp.[33]

❧ 𝕚 ❧

Napoleon's popular image is that of the legendary battlefield commander, yet he actually spent most of his time dealing with paperwork. 'The Emperor lived his life in his office,' explained his secretary, baron Fain. 'Only there was he at home and free to be himself. You could say that all the other situations of his life were no more than digressions.'[34] Two-thirds of his time as head of state, from 1799 until his first abdication in 1814, were spent in Paris or its vicinity.[35] Even on campaign, Napoleon continued to carry out the ordinary business of ruling a vast empire, with his office able to function equally well from magnificent palaces, half-wrecked cottages, or his campaign tent.

While travelling long distances, Napoleon used his coach as a mobile command post, so he could work or even sleep while on the move. A relay of supporting vehicles and servants preceded him by at least twelve hours, and a second relay followed behind at a similar interval. These two relays repeatedly relieved each other, taking it in turns to lead the way. This system ensured that Napoleon always found a household waiting for him when he arrived at his day's destination, and he was able to leave servants behind to clear up afterwards.[36]

The efficiency of his travelling arrangements enabled Napoleon to race across Europe without having to forego his usual comfort. The Grand Marshal of the Palace would identify a suitable place for him to have *déjeuner*, possibly a local town hall, or the residence of an archbishop or administrative official. The meal was cooked ready for Napoleon's arrival, and the vehicles restocked to replace the consumed provisions. In fact, it was perfectly possible for him to be served *déjeuner* in a deserted expanse of countryside. A leather sheet would be laid on the ground, and the provisions placed on top.

Napoleon would sit at the foot of a tree, surrounded by his entourage, and everyone, from lowly pages to the grandest dignitaries, would help themselves. Coffee was then heated on a fire, and within half-an-hour everything had disappeared, and they were on their way. On one unforgettable occasion, Napoleon even had his *déjeuner* on the seawall while visiting Cherbourg in 1811. The weather was fine, and after he sat down at the table, a squadron of ships left the harbour and sailed around him, forming a spectacular backdrop for his meal.[37]

The speed with which Napoleon ate had its advantages on campaign. As soon as he finished his *déjeuner* in the morning, he often exclaimed 'Mount up!', and set off. Sometimes, he did not even bother to sit down to eat. Constant recalled him standing with his staff as he ate *déjeuner* inside the Hospice of the Grand Saint-Bernard on the day that he crossed the pass at the start of the Marengo campaign. On another morning, during the retreat from Moscow in November 1812, while he was busy supervising the building of bridges over the Beresina river, he was served a cutlet for *déjeuner* at the headquarters of a corps commander, and ate it standing up. He was also seen one day during the 1814 campaign, standing with a handful of senior subordinates as he ate *déjeuner* outdoors.[38]

While on campaign, Napoleon normally had both *déjeuner* and *dîner* with Berthier, his chief of staff. They were occasionally joined by other senior figures, such as his stepson Eugène, or a marshal or two. Shared meals gave Napoleon a chance to study the character of his subordinates, and gauge their abilities. A newly appointed ADC joining his headquarters in Italy in 1796 found himself seated beside him at *dîner*, and questioned in detail throughout the meal about his previous service. Similarly, if Napoleon spent more than a single night in a town while travelling, he would have the local authorities assembled so he could meet them, and might invite the mayor, bishop, or administrative prefect to *dîner*. Napoleon was in the habit of bombarding his guests with questions about the local area and its history, their family and past services, the condition of the peasantry, and a host of other matters. This also happened on Saint Helena when a British naval surgeon, William Warden, was invited to *dîner*. For an hour, Napoleon fired all sorts of questions at him, on topics ranging from how to cure illnesses to the time when the soul entered and left the body. 'So frequent were the questions of my host', recalled Warden ruefully, 'that from the perplexity I suffered in conjuring up answers to them, I scarce knew what I [ate], or what I drank.' At the end of the evening, one of Napoleon's companions-in-exile, Las Cases, reassured him apologetically: 'Well, this has been a day of questions; indeed, I fear it must be a punishment for you to dine with us, it is so like undergoing an examination; but you may be assured, that your answers afford satisfaction, or you would not be troubled with so many questions.'[39]

A group of companions at *dîner* was also a way of relaxing. When a battle was imminent, Napoleon habitually admitted officers of his entourage to his table, although some were so intimidated in his presence that they preferred to move aside, and eat standing up in the background. On the eve of Austerlitz in 1805, Napoleon had *dîner* with a group of key subordinates, and apparently enjoyed the conversation so much that he remained at the table unusually long, and discussed such abstract topics as the work of Pierre Corneille and other dramatists.[40] Pre-battle meals such as these also had a more serious purpose. On the morning of Waterloo, Napoleon assembled some of his top generals at his headquarters for *déjeuner*, and tried to invigorate them by disparaging Wellington's ability as a commander. These discussions reached a far wider audience, since the generals were likely to repeat the main points to their staff officers, who in turn would cascade the message to the various formations. By inviting subordinates to share his meals, Napoleon could therefore communicate his will throughout the army, and this was particularly evident during his occupation of Moscow in 1812. Three or four times a week, he gathered some of his marshals and divisional commanders for *dîner*. 'During the conversations that followed the meal', noted Caulaincourt, the Master of the Horse, 'the Emperor shaped opinion in the way that suited him, and put a spin on his actions just as he wanted the army to understand and discuss them.'[41]

When fighting a battle, Napoleon generally waited until he had returned to his quarters at the end of the day before he had *dîner*, but if the action dragged on too long, he would be brought a snack, consisting of a small piece of toast and a little wine. For Napoleon's servants, these trips from the safety of the rear could be a distinctly unsettling experience, since shells were sometimes exploding around the command post. Nor did Napoleon always take kindly to being interrupted if he was absorbed in the progress of the fighting. At Borodino, which had begun early in the morning, a prefect of the palace, Louis-François, baron de Bausset, asked Napoleon at noon if he wanted to have *déjeuner*. 'The battle had yet to be won, and he gestured in the negative,' recalled Bausset. 'I was unwise enough to tell him that there was no reason in the world why he should not take *déjeuner* when he could. He then dismissed me in quite a brusque manner.'[42]

The sight of Napoleon eating on the battlefield had a mixed effect on his less fortunate soldiers. On the morning of Wagram in 1809, a Saxon infantryman watched him at his command post:

> Two loaded mules, led by French soldiers, brought his *déjeuner*, and even if we had empty stomachs after eating nothing for twenty-four hours, we nevertheless observed these preparations without envy. We saw how a rug was spread on the ground, and dishes placed on it, and how the Emperor helped himself and drank wine from a silver cup. We wholeheartedly wished him a good appetite, and yet the scene did something to stir our ravenous hunger. It also gave us an idea, and we sent a couple of men with empty bottles into the nearby village to find some bread and water.[43]

Napoleon occasionally used the prospect of food as a way of motivating his troops, by appealing to their bellies as much as their hearts. As he moved through his army's bivouacs on the night before Austerlitz, he is said to have seen some infantrymen busy cooking, asked if they were content with the unappetizing contents of their pots, and then – pointing to the enemy campfires – promised them a real celebratory feast in Vienna if they helped him to get rid of those b___ over there.[44]

For ordinary soldiers, life on campaign was a lottery that could veer abruptly between extremes. Some of the thousands of French prisoners taken at Leipzig in 1813 were so destitute that they were reduced to eating rotting cabbage leaves, raw horsemeat, and even human flesh sliced from the bodies of dead comrades. Yet hunger could make even the most improvised and unpromising of meals seem delightful. Chef de bataillon Louis-François Lejeune never forgot that freezing, pitch-black night in December 1806 when he became lost while carrying orders to a division. Exhausted, he eventually stumbled across some Imperial Guardsmen, who had thrown all the food they could find into a pot that was now bubbling merrily away on their bivouac fire. They welcomed Lejeune, and gave him a share of their meal. 'The heaps of rice, fowl, and geese in their mess tins formed a delicious soup', he recalled, 'seasoned by an appetite that the bigwigs of this world will never know.'[45]

♥♠♥

Napoleon's troops were expert foragers, yet the fact they had to plunder in order to survive was liable to alienate the local population, and cause problems with straggling and indiscipline. Napoleon remained acutely conscious of these drawbacks, but was unable to supply all the needs of his vast armies in an age when supplies had to be found locally, or else transported by animals that themselves required feeding.

The famous saying that 'an army marches on its stomach' has often been attributed to Napoleon, but also to the Prussian King Frederick the Great. Napoleon may never have made the remark in so precise a form, but it captures one of his major concerns as a commander. While in exile on Saint Helena, he discussed the logistical challenge of feeding an army, and commented that the great advance in war would be to accustom soldiers to living on rice and meat, which were easier to transport than bulky loaves of bread. They would carry their own supplies, and thereby enable the army to dispense with a large and bureaucratic administrative machine. The men would grind their own flour from wheat requisitioned locally, using small, portable mills, and could then cook pancakes on metal sheets, instead of requiring ovens for baking bread. To illustrate the concept, he ordered a pancake made for him that evening from flour and boiled rice.[46] But Napoleon knew that his proposals would amount to a revolution in the habits and attitudes of the soldiers, and would require a long period of peace to become established. Changes so fundamental in nature could not be implemented simply by issuing an order of the day to an army that was on a war footing. Napoleon added that he had experimented in 1812 by issuing hand-mills for the invasion of Russia, only to find that the troops threw them away as they were too heavy.[47]

The idea of the self-sufficient soldier was hardly a new one. Napoleon himself said that he based the concept on the Roman method of issuing troops with grain instead of bread. In fact, he was only partly right: grain was just one element in Roman military rations, even if the most important, and was supplemented by meat, lentils, beans, cheese, wine, vinegar, salt, and olive oil. Despite burdening their legionaries with heavy packs, the Romans still needed mules, and, far from dispensing with a logistical tail altogether, owed much of their success to a flexible balance between exploiting local resources and setting up supply lines. Besides, the Roman army was well disciplined; its foraging expeditions were properly organized, and its logistical system would not have worked for Napoleon's army, where pillaging was so rampant, individualized, and wasteful.[48]

Other civilizations habitually carried dried foodstuffs on campaign: the Mongols, for example, took dehydrated milk with them, which they could reconstitute with water. A more modern solution to the problem had actually been developed during Napoleon's reign. A French chef and entrepreneur called Nicolas Appert conducted a series of experiments to develop a way of preserving food without loss of flavour and without requiring large amounts of sugar, which was expensive as a result of the British naval blockade. In 1810, he was awarded a 12,000-franc prize for his work, in return for agreeing to publish the details, which he did later that year in the form of a book. His method – sealing food in jars and then heating them in a water-bath – was not, in fact, a new concept, but he systematically ascertained the correct heating times for different foodstuffs. This allowed a wide range of substances to be preserved for years, and, unlike salted, dried, or smoked foods, reduced the risk of scurvy. Appert's work had far-reaching implications not only for naval power and the health of sailors on long voyages, but also for the emergence of a global trade in perishable foods. His method was developed by others, who replaced his fragile glass preserving bottles with metal tins, and by 1830 canned food could be bought in shops in Europe and the United States.[49] Napoleon's logistical revolution did happen, there-fore, but in technology rather than attitudes, and involved not simply the introduction of canned food in armies, but the develop-ment of railways and motor transport, and the improvement of roads.

Apart from feeding his army, Napoleon's other great concern was feeding Paris. Ever sensitive to anything that might threaten a return to the popular unrest of the Revolution, he used food as a way of keeping the population content. He held *fêtes* to mark special occasions such as his coronation as Emperor in December 1804, featuring fountains of wine and a lottery with 13,000 poultry as prizes.[50] At times of food shortages, he intervened to prevent the poor of Paris from being starved into revolt. He regulated bread prices, and in November 1801 tried to introduce a cheap, but good quality, brown bread for the lower classes. Unfortunately, in Paris even the workers insisted on having white bread – it was actually less nutritious, but was regarded as finer. In the face of their obstinacy, Napoleon was forced to think again, but being reluctant to abandon his idea altogether, he now focused on the underclass – those inhabitants who were so poor that they depended on charities to survive. He ordered one baker in every neighbourhood to produce the cheap brown bread, and had the poor issued with ration cards to use at these bakeries. To give the brown bread a fashionable allure, Napoleon had it served at a grand official *dîner* in December 1801 to 180 guests, who according to press reports found it very tasty. Yet all his efforts ended in failure. Even people dependent on charity were so reluctant to eat brown bread that they wanted to pay the difference in order to have the more expensive white loaves.[51]

Napoleon also championed the potato, one of his favourite vegetables. Potatoes had not been widely used in France during the eighteenth century, except as animal fodder. Napoleon referred to them as *parmentières*, after their leading advocate, Antoine Parmentier, who had written an *Examen chimique des pommes de terre* in 1773 to demonstrate just how nutritious they were. Indeed, they were so packed with calories that they offered a potential solution to the threat of famine, and that gave them political significance as a means of preventing a revolt.[52]

Potatoes were one of the ingredients in soups specially developed for feeding the poor. They were popularly known as Rumford soups, after their creator, Sir Benjamin Thompson, Count Rumford. He was multi-talented, outstanding as both a physicist and a philanthropist, but was also a complex and abrasive man, and as apt to make enemies as scientific discoveries. Born in Massachusetts in 1753, he remained loyal to Britain during the American Revolution, emigrated, and in 1784 entered the service of Karl Theodor, the Prince-Elector and Duke of Bavaria. Granted wide-ranging powers to alleviate Bavaria's widespread social problems, he established a workhouse in the capital, Munich, in 1789, and cleared the streets of beggars. The workhouse gave him a setting in which to develop his ideas on how to feed the masses, especially when bread – their core foodstuff – became too expensive in times of hardship. He devised not only a kitchen range, which was more fuel-efficient than an open fire, but vegetable soups based on barley, potatoes, dried peas, and beer or vinegar, as a cheap but nutritious alternative to meat and bread.

Rumford's work earned him an international reputation, and while visiting France in 1802 he not only met Napoleon, but even dined with him at the Tuileries. Rumford's soups proved their worth in Paris during the food shortages of 1801–2, and again during the subsequent crisis of 1810–12. Napoleon insisted on them being sold cheaply, as well as simply distributed free, since he knew that some workers would be too proud to seek charity.[53] Rumford's concepts have been used around the world, and he has often been described as the father of the soup kitchen, although he was not, in fact, the first to provide nourishing food to the poor on a large-scale basis. What did distinguish him – and here the parallels with Appert's work on food conservation are striking – was the modern, scientific approach he adopted to crack an age-old problem.

The lesson is an austere one. A golden age of gastronomy Napoleon's rule may have been, but even in Paris much of the population went hungry.[54] For all the fame acquired by chicken Marengo, and the other fanciful creations of *haute cuisine*, it was Rumford's down-to-earth soups, and the methodical experiments by the largely forgotten Appert, that proved infinitely more practical and truly world-changing.

The cavalry of Napoleon's Consular Guard on the evening of Marengo.

Chapter 10

The Belly of an Emperor

What foods did Napoleon like best? Chicken, certainly, was one of his favourites, and we know from the testimony of Jacques Chandelier, one of his cooks on Saint Helena, that he ate it in a whole variety of styles, including not just as a plain roast, but also *à la Marengo*, *à la provençale*, *à l'italienne*, and *à la tartare*.[1]

As for red meat, Napoleon liked beef, veal, or mutton – perhaps coated in breadcrumbs and grilled. In terms of fish, he was fond of the red mullet of the Mediterranean, which was probably a legacy of his Corsican childhood, and while in exile on Elba he was invited to attend the raising of the nets used to catch tuna as they swam along the coast – he accepted on condition that he would be fed some fish stew, or *bouillabaisse de pêcheur*, on the shore. He is also known to have eaten with evident relish part of a turbot, a flatfish prized for its flavour, while a prisoner on HMS *Bellerophon* after Waterloo.[2] A couple of months later, he even ate a dolphin. By that time, he was on his way to Saint Helena on board HMS *Northumberland*, and when the sailors managed to harpoon one, he asked to try some of the meat, and actually enjoyed it.[3] On the other hand, he found sharks inedible. Hearing a noise on deck, he found that one had been caught, but in his eagerness went too close. Suddenly flinging aside four or five sailors, the shark brought Napoleon crashing down on to his side, leaving his companions aghast until they realized that none of the blood covering him was his, and that he had escaped without breaking a leg. At least, that was the story given by Las

Cases, who probably exaggerated the danger in order to portray Napoleon in a heroic light. It is true that another of his companions, Louis-Joseph Marchand, wrote that Napoleon was nearly injured by the thrashing tail, but three others – Mameluke Ali, Gaspard, baron Gourgaud, and Charles-Tristan, comte de Montholon, recorded nothing about him being knocked over, while a British eyewitness merely described him scrambling on to the poop like a schoolboy in order to see what was happening.[4]

As for more conventional dishes, Napoleon welcomed macaroni in any form, including macaroni cheese and *timbales de macaroni à la milanaise* (arranged artistically in a mould and then held together with a sauce). He was also partial to pastry dishes, such as *vol-au-vents* or the smaller but similar *bouchées à la reine* (bite-sized pastries filled with a purée of poultry meat). In terms of vegetables, Napoleon enjoyed lentils and broad beans; he was also keen on potato, whether it was boiled, fried, baked under the ashes of a fire, or served in a salad.[5] Napoleon liked eggs, perhaps hard-boiled, cooked *sur le plat* (baked in an oven), or made into an omelette. On Elba, when he found himself too busy one day to break off for a full-scale *déjeuner*, he asked instead for an *œuf à la mouillette*, which was an egg served with fried sticks of bread for dipping into the yolk. Stews or soups were frequently served to him, and he might finish his *dîner* with a piece of cheese.[6] He did eat fruit, but only in limited amounts, taking only a quarter from an apple or pear, or just a small handful from a bunch of grapes. Cherries were a lifelong passion: just a few weeks before he died, he recalled his childhood on Corsica, and spoke of the Genoese cherries his family had grown. 'I think I have never eaten anything so good,' he said. After Waterloo, while travelling to Rochefort on the western coast of France in the hope of escaping to the United States, he ordered his carriage to stop in a small town, and sent a servant to buy some cherries. He and his companions clearly enjoyed them, for as they resumed the journey, a succession of cherry stones were thrown out of the window, leaving a long trail on the road.[7]

Napoleon also loved *glaces*, which are best translated as ices, for instead of having dairy products whipped in to make ice-cream, they might be just a frozen mixture of water, sugar, and puréed fruit. Napoleon tended to have them as a refreshment while working at night. His secretary Méneval recalled these moments well, for he would be summoned to take dictation in the early hours of the morning: 'When the work was finished, and sometimes while it was still in progress, he used to have *glaces* or *sorbets* brought. He would ask me what I preferred, and extended his concern so far as to advise me what he thought would be the best for my health.'[8] One of Napoleon's tribulations on Saint Helena was the absence of ice. In Europe, ice could be collected in the winter, and stored underground for use during the rest of the year, but this was impossible in the perpetually mild climate of the island. In August 1816, a primitive ice-making machine arrived, sent to Napoleon by a British admirer, Elizabeth Fox, Baroness Holland. The results were disappointing. Admittedly, the machine, which relied on an air pump to cool the water, managed to freeze a cupful in fifteen minutes, and this was an historic moment, for it was the first ice ever seen on Saint Helena. But Napoleon managed to break the thermometer in one of the frozen cups by trying to pull it out by brute force, and attempts to freeze lemonade and milk both failed. The machine produced too little ice to be useful, for it took a day to create enough to make just five or six *glaces*.[9]

❦

Napoleon's servants agreed that he ate sparingly, and preferred simple dishes to rich or highly seasoned food. Guests, too, were struck by the apparent plainness of his tastes. A Polish admirer, Anna, comtesse Potocka, saw Napoleon served some peppered artichokes at a *dîner* in June 1810. He extolled the virtues of the ascetic dish, and laughingly offered to share it, but found no one was tempted, and finished the whole plate himself.[10]

Yet the fact that Napoleon was deceitful so systematically makes it unwise to accept anything connected with him at face value. Too often, historians have taken on trust the traditional stories that were later circulated about his austere lifestyle. He is known to have been particular about the quality of his bread, and yet his mother supposedly claimed that when he went to the local school on the island of Corsica, he used to exchange the white bread he brought from home for the rougher type of a soldier. On being scolded, he explained that he wanted to be a soldier, so he ought to get used to eating ration bread, and that he preferred it in any case. This tale, too neat and convenient to be credible, was surely dreamed up with the benefit of hindsight, in order to portray Napoleon as a pre-destined hero who willingly shared the hardships of his men.[11]

Napoleon was hardly unique in making so much of his preference for straightforward food. Indeed, one of his favourite writers as a teenager, before his youthful idealism had given way to a harder and altogether more cynical view of the world, had been Jean-Jacques Rousseau, one of the great philosophers of eighteenth-century Europe. Rousseau advocated a return to a simpler lifestyle, one closer in tune with nature, and favoured plain, wholesome, and unprocessed food. He was not the first man to champion the quest for the good life, nor would he be the last, but he was remarkably influential. The idyllic image he spun ignored the harsh reality of life for most rural inhabitants, who often eked out an existence on the verge of starvation, yet the misconceptions he popularized were so fashionable that Queen Marie-Antoinette, the wife of Louis XVI, had a replica hamlet built in the grounds of Versailles palace, as a congenial retreat where she could shed the formal étiquette of the court.

This was the context of Napoleon's desire to portray himself as an ordinary soldier and as a man of the people, but in his case, the charade of simplicity went beyond the mere flattering of a naïve, idealistic whim. In his eyes, even food was a leadership tool, since it offered a way to establish a link with his men, and project a certain image of himself. At the Battle of Friedland in 1807, for example, he was seen eating some of the coarse black bread, liberally filled with straw, that his soldiers had to live on at that time, as a way of ostentatiously demonstrating to them, just before they went into action, that he shared their discomforts.[12]

The reality of Napoleon's daily life belied such posturing. After gaining power, he ate only the best food, as is clear from a contract of November 1804, which listed the amount of poultry and game that an entrepreneur undertook to provide for his kitchens. Every line in the list – from chickens to red partridges, and from ducks to quails – ended with the stipulation *'tout ce qu'il y a de plus beau'* ('all of the best quality').[13] Furthermore, a strict sense of hierarchy prevailed within Napoleon's household, and extended to the food that was served. In May 1807, when the Empress Joséphine was staying in Brussels while Napoleon was away on campaign, 36 francs were spent on each person who had *dîner* at her table, compared to just 4 francs for the footmen and others of similar, lowly status.[14]

The truth is that Napoleon was a man of habit, rather than of invariably simple tastes. For example, he retained a liking for foods that he had eaten during his expedition to Egypt: for a long time afterwards his favourites were dates and pilaf, the latter being a dish, made from rice, wheat, or other grains, that was widely consumed in the Middle East.[15] Napoleon's preference for the familiar helps explain the contradictions in his lifestyle, for he grew fond of a number of sophisticated dishes. *Quenelles de volaille au consommé*, for instance, could hardly be called simple food. They were elegant, poultry meatballs, and the *consommé* with which they were served was a clarified soup, simmered to intensify the flavour and extract the fat. *Consommé* was simple only in the sense that it was thin and healthy; the actual process of making it was complex and wasteful. It was not a soup that could be produced quickly, cheaply, or easily, and would hardly have been seen at any of his soldiers' campfires. Nor would his men have eaten another of his regular dishes, *boudins à la Richelieu*, which were ovals of chicken meat paste that were poached, before having their centres filled with a truffle-flavoured sauce. And what would Napoleon's soldiers have thought of his partiality for sweet desserts, such as *nougat* cakes or *petites pâtisseries* (small, often cream-filled delicacies)? 'What he liked very much were almonds, freshly picked from the tree,' added Mameluke Ali. 'He was so fond of them that he would eat almost the entire plateful. He liked waffles as well, rolled up with a bit of cream inside.'[16]

Ali added, by way of excuse, that Napoleon was served these various titbits only at *dîner*, and that the only sweets he took were two or three *pastilles*. He did carry a *bonbonnière*, or sweet box, in the pockets of his coat, but it contained just aniseed-flavoured liquorice, cut into very thin pieces, and intended simply as a mouth-freshener. Yet the fact remained that Napoleon's supposed preference for plain food was a sham, despite the occasional, well-publicized acts he put on to try and prove the contrary. On Saint Helena, for example, he once asked his cook, Jacques Chandelier, for a thick, soldier's soup. Since Chandelier did not dare to give him literally what a soldier would have eaten, he produced a refined version that seemed more suitable for his august master. But Napoleon was dissatisfied. 'You've been a soldier,' he told Chandelier. 'You know perfectly well this is not a soldier's soup, so make me a better one for tomorrow.' Next day, Chandelier served a real military soup, stuffed with so much bread and beans that a spoon would have stood up in the middle of it.[17]

The menu for one of Napoleon's *dîners* underlines just how exceptional it was for him to eat a soldier's soup, or even a spartan dish of peppered artichokes. The menu began with two genteel soups (chestnut and macaroni), and two dishes known as *relevés* (rump steak of beef, and pike *à la Chambord*), followed by four *entrées* (duck, young partridge, mutton chops *à la Soubise*, and an elaborate chicken *fricassée* known as *à la chevalière*), then two roasts (lamb, and cock served with watercress), and six side dishes – four of them sweet (orange jelly, a *génoise* sponge cake, German-style waffles, and a coffee-flavoured custard), and the other two consisting of vegetables (cauliflower in a crusty-topped sauce, and celery-and-turnips with gravy). Dessert would have followed.[18]

Yet Napoleon was so successful in portraying himself as a robust, down-to-earth, and hyperactive commander that it has become entrenched in the way he is perceived. He was supposedly at home with the discomforts of the bivouac, and able to thrive on a lack of sleep, yet in reality, he not only liked his creature comforts, but was extremely sensitive to touch, taste, and smell. 'His body was subject to the slightest influences,' recorded Las Cases on Saint Helena. 'The smell of paint was enough to make him ill, and certain dishes, or the least humidity, had an immediate effect on him.'[19] So sensitive were his feet that he had new boots and shoes broken in by a servant with the same foot size. Similarly, he disliked new hats, and kept old ones for as long as possible; the new ones were padded, and broken in by his valet, Constant, who would wear them himself for a few days in the privacy of his room.[20]

Napoleon was also surprisingly squeamish for a soldier. On one occasion, deciding that he wanted a basic understanding of anatomy, he had his doctor, Jean-Nicolas, baron Corvisart, bring some wax models of parts of the heart and stomach. But he had unwisely scheduled this lesson for immediately after his *déjeuner*, and was so revolted that he vomited. Somehow, this queasiness did not prevent him from riding through the carnage of a battlefield unaffected by its sights and smells. He would even dismount, check if a wounded man was still alive, and give him some *eau-de-vie* to drink from the flask that his Mameluke servant always carried. It was willpower, and the ability to concentrate intently on the matter at hand, that enabled him to suppress his physical weaknesses.[21]

The acuteness of Napoleon's senses was also revealed by how he ate. On the one hand, he did so hurriedly, without appearing to take much interest in the food, yet at the same time, he had definite dislikes, and quirks to his personality. 'The simplest dishes were those that he preferred,' Constant insisted, before admitting that 'he was fussy about the quality of the bread'.[22] In addition, he liked his soup to be boiling hot, generally drank only Chambertin wine, and was physically revolted by anything unhygienic. 'More than anyone else I have known', explained a prefect of the palace, the baron de Bausset, 'he was extremely disgusted by anything that was not very clean. The idea of a hair on a dish would have been enough to turn his stomach and make him leave the table.'[23] That was why

Napoleon hardly ever ate green beans, even though he liked them, for the stringy ones gave him the nauseating impression of chewing on hair. Once, whilst inspecting Cherbourg in 1811, he asked to taste the soup of some soldiers. Taking a spoon, he filled it, and was about to put it to his mouth when he noticed a long hair. Normally, this would have repulsed him, but he did not want to upset the soldiers, so he hid his disgust, quietly removed the hair, and swallowed the soup.[24]

Napoleon's stomach also turned over if he encountered fishbones or undercooked meat. He insisted on having his meat well done, and immediately had fish removed if he found too many bones. 'I don't like the spines,' he explained, for that was what he called them. He feared that a bone might lodge in his throat and make him throw up, for vomiting came easily to him, and might be triggered by a mere cough after a meal.[25]

Not only did Napoleon eat fine dishes in addition to the plain food he claimed to prefer, he also did so in a remarkably grand and luxurious manner. He ate off ornate silverware, even while in exile on Saint Helena, where British guests were impressed by the way he continued to be served formally as if he were still a ruling monarch. 'It was a most superb dinner,' wrote Colonel Sir George Bingham of the 53rd (or the Shropshire) Regiment of Foot after dining with Napoleon in 1816. 'The dessert service was Sèvres china, with gold knives, forks, and spoons. The coffee-cups were the most beautiful I ever saw.' For all the complaints from Napoleon's entourage about the ingredients supplied by his British captors, his table had a certain splendour, which was enhanced by elaborate representations of palaces and triumphal arches made from *pâtisserie* and strands of spun sugar.[26]

A whole household waited on Napoleon's every want. In January 1813, the monthly wages of 211 of the employees came to a staggering total of over 20,600 francs, and yet they were only some of the people who worked in the household.[27] Those responsible for preparing and serving Napoleon's food, under the direction of the Grand Marshal of the Palace and his prefects, included *maîtres d'hôtel*, various *chefs* and their assistants, specialists for roast dishes and *pâtisserie*, stewards, table-layers, and young pages, besides personnel to look after the silver and tableware, others entrusted with the wine, and even five or six carvers.[28] It was all designed to impress outsiders, but had the effect of distancing Napoleon from a soldier's life, rather than enabling him to share it. Soon after arriving on Saint Helena, he is reported to have carved a chicken, and was pleased to find he could do it so well for, as he pointed out, it was a long time since he had last had a chance to carve.[29]

Napoleon was not a good cook, which was hardly surprising given that he had neither the time nor the inclination to practise, yet his incompetence did nothing to restrain his innate urge to take charge of everything. The Empress Marie-Louise decided one day that she wanted to make an omelette herself, and had the necessary ingredients brought to her apartments. She was interrupted when Napoleon suddenly entered, and tried to hide what she was doing, but forgot just how acute a sense of smell he had. 'What, you are making an omelette?' he exclaimed. 'Bah! You know nothing about this; I'll show you how it's done.' He then set to work, only to find that he was trying to teach someone considerably more skilled than himself. As a child, Marie-Louise had helped her parents with household chores when they relaxed by staying in a rustic dwelling in one of the Habsburg parks. Yet for all his inexperience, Napoleon managed to make something that at least resembled an omelette, until, that is, he tried to flip it over to cook on the other side. Sure enough, he managed to drop it on the floor, and then, finally forced to admit his ineptitude, he left Marie-Louise to start again on her own.[30]

Napoleon continued to live in luxury even while on campaign. The popular image of him visiting the bivouacs, and asking his soldiers for a potato, was one that he carefully fostered, yet such occasions were in fact exceptional. Indeed, it was their rarity that made them so effective in boosting morale on the eve of a battle. The stark reality is that he shared few of his soldiers' hardships, least of all during his notorious retreat from Moscow in 1812. Caulaincourt, the Master of the Horse, who accompanied him during that campaign, recorded that Napoleon continued to enjoy his usual meals every day. 'Only the Emperor had always been well fed during the retreat,' he wrote. 'He had always had table linen, white bread, his Chambertin wine, some good oil, some beef or mutton, rice, and broad beans or lentils, his favourite vegetables.'[31]

Caulaincourt was right that Napoleon continued to be served his usual fare, but was misleading in his implication that the household went hungry. A staff officer, Capitaine Boniface de Castellane, noted as early as 9 September, during the advance on Moscow, that the troops were already badly off, yet at the same time he and the others in the household always had bread, half-a-bottle of wine, some soup, and a *ragoût*. 'It's a lot', he wrote, 'and I do not know how they manage to feed us in this country.'[32] It was all the more challenging a feat in that Napoleon's headquarters were preceded by thousands of his troops, who swept the region clear like a plague of locusts. Supplies, therefore, had to be either brought with the headquarters, sent after it all the way from France, or found by sending out foraging parties a long distance. 'We did not lack food even during the retreat,' confessed another member of the household, Roman, comte Soltyk, 'although admittedly it was both less abundant and poorer in quality at that time.'[33]

Napoleon's aloofness from the deprivations of the retreat helps explain his remarkable ability to keep his nerve and save the remnants of the army, yet his insulation from reality also meant that he only gradually realized the full severity of the unfolding catastrophe. Food, therefore, fortified his resolve, but also clouded his judgement as a commander. He himself realized the drawbacks of being so well served on campaign: apart from the risk of alienating his hungry soldiers, it made his headquarters too cumbersome as a result of all the vehicles needed to carry the supplies and servants. It was essential, he decided, to make some changes after his experience in Russia. 'I intend to put my baggage on an altogether different footing from that of the past campaign,' he instructed the Grand Marshal of the Palace in February 1813:

> I want to have many fewer people, fewer cooks, fewer bowls and plates, no large *nécessaire* [kit of essential items] – in order both to set an example and to lessen the encumbrance. While on campaign and on the march, the tables, even my own, will be served with a soup, a stew, a roast, and vegetables – no dessert. While staying in large towns, people can do as they wish.

Austerity was an appropriate response to disaster. Napoleon had to be seen to be sharing the general sacrifices, although it is unknown just how long he stuck to this self-imposed rationing.[34]

Towards the end of his life, Napoleon recalled how his mother had instilled in him a sense of the vital importance of outward impressions. It was better, she would say, to cut back and eat only bread in the privacy of their home, so they could afford to wear fine clothes in public.[35] Napoleon implied that he had taken the lesson to heart, not least as a hungry and impoverished young officer when his family was plunged into debt by his father's premature death. '*Monsieur*,' he once rebuked a public servant who complained about his meagre salary, 'when I had the honour of being a *lieutenant en second*, I used to eat stale bread for *déjeuner*, but hid my poverty behind my bolted door.'[36] In fact, this was yet another distortion of the truth, for the reality was that at the time Napoleon had done the exact opposite, and had actually boasted of his hardships. 'I have nothing else I can do here except work,' he bragged in a letter in 1789. 'I change my clothes only once a week, and since my illness I get very little sleep. This is incredible. I go to bed at 10.00 pm, and rise at 4.00 am. I have just one meal a day, and this does my health much good.'[37]

For all his claims about maintaining a dignified silence, therefore, Napoleon actually advertised his deprivations. In any case, his poverty was no more than a passing episode. His childhood on Corsica had been frugal rather than spartan. His family was largely self-sufficient, produced its own wine, and owned an olive grove, along with a mill and an oven that it would allow villagers to use in exchange for some flour, milk, or goats' cheese. Although Napoleon may have eaten little meat, he had plenty of fresh fish, and sometimes pillaged figs from his family's enclosures. What he ate as a child was, in fact, a healthy, balanced, Mediterranean diet. Similarly, the meals at the military school he attended at Brienne in Champagne were full and nourishing, even for teenage boys, and could be supplemented with provisions bought from a local woman. At the École militaire in Paris, where Napoleon completed his formal military education, the cadets were fed and served magnificently, just as if they were wealthy officers – wealthier, in fact, than most of their families.[38]

The reality was that Napoleon liked comfort for its own sake, and not merely because he knew that wealth and luxury were indispensable in overawing people. This love of comfort was obscured by his insistence on running his household as cost-effectively as possible. He was even said to quiz his servants about the food they were serving him for *déjeuner*. 'How much did that cost?' he might ask.[39] He had a similar attitude to clothes. Apart from ceremonial occasions, when he appeared in the spectacular robes of a sovereign, he gave the outward appearance of dressing simply, in a familiar, grey overcoat on top of a uniform that would be worn until it was almost threadbare. Yet at the same time, he insisted on having clothes made from the finest material, including waistcoats and breeches of white cashmere, and stockings of silk. He had himself dressed by his valets like a child, and often changed his clothes during the course of the day, not least when he absent-mindedly spilt food on them. A paradox therefore lay at the very heart of the way Napoleon presented himself. Even the apparent lack of ostentation of his attire was deceptive, for one of the reasons he dressed simply was to stand out amidst the glittering uniforms of his entourage.[40]

♦ ♦ ♦

Napoleon's reputation was for eating not just simply, but moderately. During the Consulate, Parisians never tired of repeating a droll remark comparing him to his fellow consuls. 'If you want to eat moderately, come to me,' he was reported to have joked, 'but if you want to eat well and fully, go to Cambacérès' – before adding, in a mischievous aside, 'with Lebrun, you don't eat at all.'[41]

Those servants who lived closest to Napoleon agreed that he ate little. 'Napoleon ate without eating much,' insisted one of his prefects of the palace, Louis, marquis de Cussy. 'Above all, he did so without selecting [particular dishes], since he ate for sustenance and not for taste, although he did understand the taste for gastronomy. Sensual life would have been incompatible with his so active cerebral life.'[42] If he thought his table was overloaded, Napoleon would reportedly grumble to his valet: '*Monsieur*, you can see that you are making me eat too much, and I don't like that. It causes me discomfort. I want to be served only two dishes.' He pointed out that it was possible to have a stomach-ache from eating too much, but not from eating too little, although he overlooked the unwisdom of wolfing down his food.[43]

Assertions that Napoleon ate little were repeated until they became a mantra, yet can his servants' memoirs be trusted? Too many of them were ghost-written, and the temptation for ghost-writers seeking to capitalize on a famous name was to pad out an account by drawing information from elsewhere. The potential existed for a supposed fact to be repeated in a whole raft of ostensibly reliable accounts by well-placed eyewitnesses.

Indeed, some men from outside the household thought that Napoleon was actually a hearty eater. 'He eats very quickly and abundantly, especially of *pâtisserie*,' wrote Chef de brigade Jean-

Baptiste Dubois-Crancé of the 1er Chasseurs à cheval after having *dîner* with Napoleon in February 1800. The inescapable fact is that Napoleon progressively put on weight. As a young man, he had been thin to the point of emaciation, but became stouter during the Empire, and developed a pot-belly. Capitaine Boniface de Castellane, who had seen him at close quarters while on campaign in 1809, was struck by the difference three years later. 'I follow the Emperor on his walk', he recorded in July 1812, 'we have always been at a stroll. His Majesty now goes more slowly. He has put on a lot of weight, and mounts his horse with more difficulty. The Master of the Horse has to give him his arm to get him into the saddle.' By 1816, Napoleon had become obese. He had man-boobs, or, as Las Cases put it more delicately, 'a certain plumpness that is not of our sex, as he sometimes commented light-heartedly'.[44]

Some commentators have suggested that Napoleon had a rare medical condition called adiposogenital dystrophy, caused by a tumour affecting part of the brain called the hypothalamus. The condition takes years to develop, and would explain the gradual but relentless increase in Napoleon's weight, yet the theory is controversial, and impossible to prove without any clinical tests. Napoleon's obesity may actually have been due to a combination of more straightforward reasons, and insufficient exercise was certainly one of them, for despite his reputation for relentless activity he spent too much of his time secluded in his office. It could be difficult, especially at the Tuileries in the heart of Paris, to go for a proper walk outside the palace without being recognized by the public. Imperial dignity also caused Napoleon to become less active, for after he became Emperor he restricted himself to horse riding, rather than the games in which he had indulged during the Consulate.[45] Even on campaign, his physical activity was more limited than might be thought. Riding a horse, or travelling in a carriage, could clock up an impressive tally of distance travelled without expending much energy; nor do spectacularly long hours of work in the office demonstrate more than mental stamina. On Saint Helena, where Napoleon's weight problem grew most acute, he became reclusive, partly as a result of illness and dejection, and partly as he revolted against the idea of being seen outside his residence by the British sentries, or escorted during longer excursions by a British officer.

Even so, one of Napoleon's secretaries, baron Fain, suspected that his stoutness was the result of relaxing in too many long hot baths, more than any other reason. 'At any rate', he insisted, 'it cannot be attributed to eating too much, for he was certainly not fond of the table.' Napoleon himself protested that he was physically unable to over-eat, even if he had wanted to. He used to refer to his *tirant d'eau*, a phrase that literally means the draught of a ship, and one that can be taken in this context to mean his capacity, or physical needs. 'If I exceeded even by the smallest amount my *tirant d'eau*', he would say, 'my stomach would immediately throw up the excess.' This, he added, was one of the two priceless advantages with which nature had endowed him, the other being the ability to sleep at will.[46]

Yet British officers guarding Napoleon during his captivity after Waterloo flatly contradicted this image of moderation. 'Buonaparte ate a great deal, and generally of strong solid food,' stated Captain Frederick Maitland of HMS *Bellerophon*. He was supported by one of his officers, Lieutenant John Bowerbank, who observed Napoleon eating very heartily at dinner. It was the same story on board HMS *Northumberland* during the ten-week voyage that took Napoleon to Saint Helena. Colonel Sir George Bingham of the 53rd Regiment was on the ship, and recorded in his diary that Napoleon 'ate heartily, taking up both fish and meat frequently with his fingers'. Another eyewitness, Rear-Admiral Sir George Cockburn, wrote that 'at dinner he generally eats and drinks a good deal, and talks but little'. Napoleon also seemed to like well-seasoned, rather than plain, food, or at least food that seemed well-seasoned by British standards. 'General Bonaparte ate of every dish at table', noted Cockburn's secretary, John Glover, 'using his fingers instead of a fork, seeming to prefer the rich dishes to the plain dressed food, and not even tasting vegetables.'[47]

At the same time, British observers were surprised that Napoleon took so little exercise while on HMS *Northumberland*. He sometimes dispensed with his stroll before dinner, and even when he did go on deck, he spent much of the time leaning against a cannon; his evening walks were also curtailed by the shorter days as the ship sailed south. In fact, Cockburn was surprised that Napoleon's health remained so good. 'Such a life of inactivity, with the quantity and description of his food, makes me fear that he will not retain his health throughout the voyage; he, however, as yet, does not appear to suffer any inconvenience from it.'[48]

Yet a man in captivity is unlikely to preserve the same habits as when he had been a head of state. It was hardly surprising that Napoleon seemed lethargic, since he suddenly found himself confined on a ship with so little to do. His demoralization was obvious to observers. Lieutenant Henry Smith had been impressed by his bearing when he first came aboard HMS *Bellerophon* in July. 'He is very affable and pleasing in his manners,' Smith wrote. 'He speaks to anyone he comes athwart and is always in a good humour, he bears his misfortunes with a great deal of fortitude which to me is astonishing.'[49] Yet this did not last, and Napoleon became visibly crushed in spirit once he realized that he faced the prospect of spending the rest of his life not in a comfortable place of exile, but as a prisoner on the remote, tropical island of Saint Helena. By 7 August, when Napoleon left the *Bellerophon* to transfer to the *Northumberland*, Midshipman George Home saw that he was sadly changed from the last time he had appeared on deck: 'His clothes were ill put on, his beard unshaved, and his countenance pale and haggard. There was a want of firmness in his gait; his brow was overcast, and his whole visage bespoke the deepest melancholy; and it needed but a glance to convince the most careless observer that Napoleon considered himself a doomed man.'[50] During this time, Napoleon's sociability and appetite varied as much as his morale. He sometimes talked throughout a meal, but on other occasions remained aloof, hiding his thoughts and rarely speaking, which was, in fact, understandable since anything he said was likely to be reported home by his hosts. Occasionally, when the swell was particularly high, he suffered from sea-sickness, and ate and conversed little. Occasionally, he even remained in his cabin, and completely skipped dinner.[51]

Hence the truth about Napoleon's attitude to food was altogether more complex and interesting than the superficial impressions that emerge from the memoirs written by either friend or foe. His appetite, like his charm and attentiveness at table, depended on his mood and circumstances, while the speed with which he ate, and his penchant for skipping rapidly between different dishes with scant regard to the order, could easily mislead observers. Such habits could be interpreted equally readily as showing that he ate either remarkably little or too much. 'Napoleon ate of a vast variety of dishes, but drank very little,' recorded Mrs Younghusband, the wife of a British infantry captain, after she dined with him on Saint Helena, yet it does not necessarily follow that he ate a vast amount. Even when he did take a big helping, it might be through sheer absent-mindedness.[52]

Often, those who met Napoleon saw simply what they expected to see, with hostile British witnesses describing him in disdainful terms as fat, greedy, cowardly, uncultured, and decidedly not a gentleman. Some were shocked when the defeated and demoralized Emperor in his years of physical decline failed to match the inflated, heroic image of him that had previously formed in their mind. 'I felt very much disappointed, as I believe everybody else did, in his appearance', wrote Captain Bayne Ross of HMS *Northumberland*, 'as I have never seen a picture of him that conveys any likeness to what he really is. He appears by no means that active man he is said to be.' A similar disappointment filled the officers of the 66th (or the Berkshire) Regiment of Foot when they met Napoleon on Saint Helena in September 1817. 'The great Napoleon had merged in an unsightly and obese individual', wrote the regiment's surgeon, Dr Walter Henry, 'and we looked in vain for that overwhelming power of eye and force of expression, which we had been taught to expect by a delusive imagination.' Napoleon's overall appearance, he thought, was more like that of an obese Spanish friar than the hero of modern times. The same comparison had occurred to Captain Ross, who thought that Napoleon, with his pot-belly, sallow skin, and greasy-looking brown hair, seemed 'altogether a very nasty, priestlike-looking fellow'.[53]

This was the exact opposite of the image that Napoleon sought to project. He wanted to be contrasted favourably with other monarchs of the time, such as the monumentally obese King Friedrich I of Württemberg. It was in Napoleon's political interests to portray himself as a fit and energetic ruler, who preferred simple food and shared the concerns of his people. The Revolution, sparked partly by the perceived gluttony of the Bourbons at a time of food shortages, was a stark reminder of the need for a ruler to project a careful image even of what he ate. Supposedly frugal habits, and a well publicized disinclination to remain long at table, were politically useful as a way of reinforcing Napoleon's identity as the people's Emperor, a monarch chosen by the will of the French nation, rather than one who ruled by divine right. This was particularly evident during the upheavals of 1814–15, at the end of his reign, when he was depicted in favourable French caricatures as the antithesis of his main rival, the fat Bourbon King, Louis XVIII.

Ironically, this misperception of Napoleon as a thin and moderate eater was actually reinforced by hostile British caricaturists. The great, satirical artists of the age, such as James Gillray and George Cruikshank, persistently portrayed him as a small, slender person. Indeed, the whole point of drawing a tiny figure in a grotesquely large hat was to make him look ridiculous. Stoutness was regarded in Britain not as a health hazard, but as an indication of prosperity and of robustness of character. The slight Napoleon was therefore an insubstantial figure, to be contrasted unfavourably with the solid bulk of John Bull. One caricature emphasized the effects of the Royal Navy's blockade, by showing Napoleon eating a meagre soup, whilst John Bull enjoyed a full table of roast beef. Even in the final years of the Empire, Napoleon continued to be portrayed as a little man, sometimes so that he could be threatened by a gigantic Cossack. Such caricatures were out of date, as they failed to reflect his increasing obesity, and this helps to explain the disappointment of British officers when they finally met him in the flesh. Their reaction suggests that the caricaturists actually missed an opportunity to undermine Napoleon in the final years of his reign, but little 'Boney' had become too familiar a figure to be suddenly transformed into a pot-bellied glutton.[54]

Even if the myth of Napoleon's frugal habits had been true, his household as a whole incurred a massive expenditure on food. During the eleven weeks of the 1814 campaign, for example, it spent more than 17,800 francs just on alcohol from local suppliers.[55] By way of comparison, Dunant's monthly wages as Napoleon's *maître d'hôtel* amounted to just 250 francs.[56] Stark statistics such as these could have been politically damaging, and so it is hardly surprising that Napoleon proved so assiduous in spinning stories about how little he ate. He later claimed, for example, that when he was First Consul he had wanted to moderate his *dîners* – along with everyone else's. 'I wanted three main dishes,' he said, 'which would be standard for everyone.' This rationing, he explained, was a republican idea, one of those ideals that come readily to men when they are young, but he abandoned the plan, supposedly after Joséphine pointed out how ridiculous it would be to try and introduce such frugality in Paris, the city of luxury and fine dining.[57]

❧ ⚲ ☙

Largely because of an undeserved reputation of being able to do without sleep, Napoleon was widely believed to be a heavy coffee drinker. In fact, he generally took just two cups a day, one at the end of each meal, and tended to leave much of it undrunk. He liked his coffee quite strong, without milk, and preferred mocha, which was a fine quality coffee. The Empress personally added sugar to Napoleon's cup before handing it to him, for otherwise he tended to forget to do so.[58]

Equally surprisingly, he drank little alcohol. 'He rarely drank as much as half a bottle, and always added as much water as wine,' recorded Mameluke Ali. 'Almost never fine wines. During the day, he sometimes used to drink a glass of champagne, but always diluted it by at least as much water.'[59] In fact, Napoleon did not really drink wine, but rather water disinfected and flavoured with wine. Water taken from wells or rivers was often dubious in quality, or unpleasant in taste, and Napoleon believed that the small amount of wine he did drink was vital for his health. His habit of diluting what he drank seems to have been a legacy of his schooldays at Brienne and the École militaire in Paris, where the pupils had drunk wine mixed with up to an equal amount of water. Another reason for Napoleon's abstemiousness was that he needed a clear head, so he could go straight back to work after a meal, for his body was so sensitive that alcohol had an unusually strong effect, with a single glass of Madeira making him talkative. While reminiscing one evening on Saint Helena, he called, unusually, for a glass of champagne, which was enough to flush his face and induce him to remain more than two hours at the dinner table, until he was astonished to realize just how late it was.[60]

This low tolerance did not prevent Napoleon from boasting about his wholly imaginary capacity to absorb alcohol. At a *dîner* in July 1800, he sat a politician called Pierre-Louis Rœderer at his side, and asked if he had a strong head. He then poured him a tumbler of wine, and mischievously moved the carafe of water out of his reach. 'I can drink four bottles like that without becoming tipsy,' he claimed. Trying to get his companions drunk seems to have been a favourite game. His physician, Dr O'Meara, described a meal on Saint Helena, when Napoleon had a bottle of champagne brought, took one glass himself, and made him finish the rest.[61]

Napoleon normally stuck to a dry red Burgundy called Chambertin, which he had drunk ever since his expedition to Egypt in 1798. Not everyone thought much of his taste. He once had a glassful served to Maréchal Pierre-François-Charles Augereau, and asked with an air of pride what he thought of it. Augereau, a rough diamond who had risen from the ranks, tasted it for some time, slapping his tongue against his palate, and finally pronounced, with his usual bluntness: 'There are some better ones.' It was hardly the answer Napoleon had expected, but he had to smile at its frankness.[62]

Supplies of his beloved Chambertin accompanied Napoleon wherever he went on campaign, even as far as Moscow. Only occasionally did he have to forego it. In October 1805, he stopped one evening at the Bavarian village of Oberfallheim with just his escort and a few officers, for his headquarters was still in the rear, along with his servants and supplies. An ADC did his best to cook a meal, and Napoleon remarked on the irony of being able to find only warm beer when they were in so fertile a country. 'The conversation was not very lively', recalled one of his company, 'for the plain water we had to drink and the rain that had fallen on us the entire day always affect a soldier's morale, be he an emperor or a drummer.'[63] Napoleon's long attachment to Chambertin posed even more of a problem while he was in exile. Towards the end of his stay on Elba, he was obliged to drink the local wine as he cut back on his expenditure, while on Saint Helena he had to resort to Constantia imported from the Cape of Good Hope.[64]

Napoleon's close servants noted that he rarely consumed any spirits. It is true that a Mameluke carried a silver flask full of *eau-de-vie* whenever they were out riding, supposedly for Napoleon's personal use. In fact, he almost never drank any, but frequently ordered it to be used to revive wounded soldiers on a battlefield. Otherwise, his main use for spirits was as medicine or mouthwash; on Saint Helena he used diluted *eau-de-vie* when he ran out of opiate with which to keep his teeth shiny.[65]

Captain Frederick Maitland of HMS *Bellerophon* confirmed just how little alcohol Napoleon drank. 'He was extremely abstemious', Maitland stated, 'confining himself almost entirely to claret, and seldom taking more than half-a-pint at a meal.' This testimony throws doubt on the startling claim by a British officer on board HMS *Northumberland*, Colonel Sir George Bingham, that after one dinner Napoleon was 'quite loquacious, having, besides his usual allowance of wine (two tumblers of claret) drank one of champagne, and some bottled beer.' The allegation probably reflected Bingham's own consumption, for although Napoleon was offered a small glass of liqueur at his dinners on board the ship, he rarely put it to his lips, and apparently preferred simply to inhale its aroma.[66]

If Napoleon had an addiction at all, it was not to alcohol or coffee, but to snuff – powdered, smokeless tobacco sniffed into the nose – which he took compulsively throughout the day. It was a fashionable habit, and Napoleon had numerous snuffboxes, typically oval in shape, lined with gold, and decorated with a cameo or medallion. But Napoleon did not really take snuff in the usual sense. He got through several boxes every day, but often mislaid them, and discarded most of the snuff. Frequently taking a large pinch, he would bring the snuff to his nostrils, but then throw it away without actually sniffing it into them. Sometimes, he simply passed the open box under his nose to savour the smell. 'I can affirm that he lost more than he took,' wrote his prefect of the palace, Bausset. 'It was a sort of absent-minded habit rather than a real need.' Even when his snuffbox was empty, he still compulsively went to take a pinch.[67]

When Napoleon ran out of snuff during a session of the Council of State, another box was slipped to him by a chamberlain, but this was not enough. According to one of the councillors, if Napoleon heard the sound of a snuffbox being opened somewhere in the room, his eyes immediately swivelled in that direction, and he gestured for an usher to go and bring it to him. After taking a couple of pinches, he would cast the confiscated box on his desk, and often into its drawer, in which case the owner lost it for good. Snuffboxes could be precious items, enriched with portraits and jewels, but the councillors soon learned to bring only cheap versions that were little more than cardboard boxes.[68] Equally amusing was Napoleon's penchant for feeding snuff to the gazelles that lived in the grounds of one of his palaces. They seemed inordinately fond of it, probably because of the oils that were added to provide an alluring flavour, and they became so tame that Napoleon is said to have been able to place a nephew on the back of one of them, as if on a horse. It is an incongruous image, and one that highlights the gulf that frequently separates reality and popular perception, for it was hardly what people would expect a gazelle to tolerate, any more than they would think of Napoleon as a doting uncle or compulsive snuff-taker.[69]

Chapter 11

Saint Helena

If anything, the myths and controversies that pervaded Napoleon's life intensified during his final years, which he spent in British captivity on the remote South Atlantic island of Saint Helena. He was soon locked in a bitter feud with Lieutenant General Sir Hudson Lowe, who became the governor of the island in April 1816. It was in the interests of Napoleon and his companions to exaggerate the physical conditions they endured, in the hope of swinging public opinion and forcing the British government to move them to a more congenial place of exile.

Food became a central point of friction in these escalating disputes. From Napoleon's retinue came complaints about both the quality and quantity of the provisions supplied to his household. In September 1816, he even ordered some of his personal silverware to be broken up and sold, so he could afford to run his household in the style that he expected.[1] It was yet another attempt to win the public relations war, by portraying himself as a persecuted victim, but in Lowe's view the amount of food sent to Napoleon's residence at Longwood was perfectly adequate, and was being wasted. It simply was not possible to provide items of the highest quality on such an isolated island. 'It is true that the meat is tough, the fowl very lean, the vegetables watery, all the provisions bad,' admitted the Russian commissioner on the island in 1817. 'But there are no others, and Longwood, as always, has the best procurable.'[2]

It was Napoleon's own presence that caused the biggest problems, for the British garrison had to be increased to guard him, and that led to food shortages and price inflation. Soldiers and civilians alike had to put up with monotonous and poor quality meals. Dr Walter Henry, surgeon with the 66th Regiment of Foot, noted that, even in 1818, after more supply routes to the island had been opened, the officers commented bitterly about the standard of their food:

> Notwithstanding this improvement in our living, the superior quality of every thing used at Longwood at this time was notorious. The purveyor for that establishment found means always to monopolise the best meat; and his daily cart conveying provisions to Longwood often underwent the envious scrutiny of our officers, as they met it in the course of their rides; when the peevish exclamation, 'We can't get any thing like that for the mess,' was generally the result.[3]

Dr Henry's complaints were echoed by the French royal commissioner, Claude-Marie-Henri, marquis de Montchenu, who noted how rare beef and mutton had become on the island by November 1817. 'If this continues', he wrote, 'I know not what will become of us, for the poultry will soon run out.' Despite the shortages, Napoleon's household continued to receive regular supplies of meat, and continued to express its dissatisfaction. 'They complain that without any butter they are deprived of pastry', Montchenu explained, 'yet we are unable to obtain essentials, even by paying their weight in gold.'[4]

One of the cooks who served Napoleon, Jacques Chandelier, exaggerated the hardships in order to emphasize his own sacrifices in going to Saint Helena. Some of his complaints were applicable only to Longwood, rather than to the island as a whole, while others were simply untrue. He claimed, for example, that the sea yielded no oysters or lobsters, and just a couple of reasonably good types of fish. In reality, as many as seventy-six different kinds of fish swam in the surrounding waters, some of them large and excellent in quality. The real problems were the islanders' laziness, and the regulations put in place to restrict the activities of fishing boats in order to minimize the risk of Napoleon escaping.[5]

Chandelier described the local turkeys, chickens, and geese as scrawny. Yet John Glover, who was on board HMS *Northumberland* when it took Napoleon to Saint Helena, thought that 'the interior of the island abounds with vegetables of the best quality, and the poultry is superior in flavour to any I have ever met with'.[6] For beef, veal, and mutton, livestock usually had to be imported from Brazil and the Cape of Good Hope and then slaughtered. Chandelier asserted that the animals arrived emaciated after three or four weeks at sea, and that, since three days' supply was sent to Napoleon's household at a time, meat sometimes had to be thrown away in the absence of any ice. Yet Chandelier added that the Chinese pigs reared on Saint Helena made excellent cutlets, sausages, and *boudins* (meat puddings).

As for fruit, Chandelier claimed it did not ripen properly, was bitter or flavourless, and often had to be imported from the Cape of Good Hope. Again, this was only partly true. The island actually produced many excellent apples, although it was true that some trees, such as the cherry and pear, did not thrive. Much depended on the conditions in specific parts of the island, and although the bleakness of the Trade wind made the heights of the interior unsuitable, there were many sheltered locations. Bananas, as even Chandelier had to admit, were plentiful: marinaded in rum, and fried after being dipped in batter, they made a tasty side dish known as banana rum fritters. Napoleon was one of a small minority of Frenchmen at this time to have eaten bananas, since in the age of sailing ships they could not be brought quickly enough to Europe before they went off.[7]

❧❦❧

During his earlier exile on Elba, Napoleon had established himself as a pioneering advocate of grow-your-own fruit and vegetables. He had even imported nurseries of mulberry trees, being convinced that they would help boost the island's economy, along with cuttings of chestnut and olive trees, and encouraged the landowners to grow them. But his efforts on Saint Helena were less successful. Towards the end of 1819, he began to take an active interest in gardening at his Longwood residence, an interest that would last for almost a year. The project kept him active, and involved extending the grounds, which deterred British officers from approaching his windows in their attempts to keep him under surveillance. Yet as an effort in grow-your-own, his gardens proved disappointing because of the unsuitable soil, the often scorching sun, and the rats gnawing at the plants. They provided Napoleon with peaches, some radishes and salad, and some reasonable cabbages, but the peas and broad beans were hard, the cauliflowers failed to grow proper heads, and the strawberry plants produced more flowers than berries.[8]

It was a meagre return for the effort invested, but that did not stop Napoleon from taking a drastic approach to garden pests. He was liable to shoot any animals that strayed on to his property, and in January 1820 even managed to kill the favourite goat of the wife of his Grand Marshal of the Palace, under the mistaken belief that it belonged to a British officer. The following month, he potted a hen belonging to one of his servants, and his shooting sprees sometimes degenerated into mere murderous sport. 'Blood is flowing at Longwood,' noted the Russian commissioner ominously. 'Bonaparte has just bought a flock of goats and is doing considerable execution. It amuses him to fire on them one after another.' In April, he found some cattle in the gardens, and killed one of them, but they belonged to the East India Company, and were so rare on the island that anyone else would have been prosecuted for the deed. Despite his blunders, Napoleon's enthusiasm for shooting remained undiminished, and in August he was still blazing away at goats.[9]

Napoleon's dependence on food constituted a weak point in his defences, for it enabled Sir Hudson Lowe to insert a couple of informants in the very heart of his household. In June 1816, Michel

Lepage, the first in the series of cooks who served Napoleon during his exile, injured his thumb and became temporarily unable to work. To fill in for him, Lowe sent a 32-year-old Belgian woman called Catherine Sablon, who had been in his own service. She was a reasonably good cook, and remained at Longwood even after Lepage recovered; they actually fell in love, married, and had a baby girl in September 1817. Then, in May 1818, they abruptly left Napoleon's service. It seems that Catherine had been deliberately planted on Longwood to report on what happened there, and she and Lepage were expelled when Napoleon found out about these secret links. Three days before they embarked, the couple were questioned by Lowe, and supplied information about Napoleon and his health, intelligence that was immediately shared with the British government.[10]

♦ ⚲ ♦

Until a couple of years into his exile on Saint Helena, Napoleon enjoyed good health – or so it seemed. In fact, he was not particularly robust, for he suffered throughout his life from minor ailments, and frequently caught colds, including one a couple of days before Marengo. The hot baths of which he was so fond may actually have been a remedy for constipation and dysuria (difficult, painful urination). Nevertheless, he liked to project the impression of being active and healthy, and largely succeeded, partly because he was known to be able to work such long hours.[11]

Napoleon's health had political implications. That was one reason why he was so keen to refute any suggestion of illness. When he issued a bulletin in December 1812 to break the news to the public about what had happened during the disastrous retreat from Moscow, he ended with the words: 'His Majesty's health has never been better'.[12] The phrase became notorious, for his enemies alleged that it showed his colossal egotism, but it was essential for him to reassure the world that he was alive and well – especially as there had been an abortive *coup* during his absence from Paris, when conspirators claimed that he had perished in Russia.

Napoleon's servants loyally repeated the line about his health. 'I never saw Napoleon ill,' his secretary, Méneval, wrote. 'He was merely prone, on the odd occasion, to vomiting bile, which did not cause him to feel unwell, and which he regarded as just a natural and healthy process of purging his system.'[13] Others also mentioned the vomiting, and it has been attributed either to indigestion caused by Napoleon's habit of eating too fast, or chronic gastritis, an inflammation of the stomach lining, perhaps caused by a bacterial infection.[14]

Napoleon's defeats have sometimes been blamed on these incidents. His Prefect of Police recorded one such episode, as told to him by Pierre, comte Daru, the head of the State Secretariat. It occurred in August 1813, when Napoleon set out from the city of Dresden after winning a victory, in order to supervise the pursuit. But to Daru's astonishment, he suddenly turned round and headed back the way the way he had come; only later did it emerge that his return had been caused by a violent stomach-ache. 'It was no more than indigestion,' Napoleon told Daru, 'the result of a wretched *ragoût* containing some garlic, which I cannot tolerate, but I feared it was something more serious.'[15]

Some versions of this tale identify the malignant *ragoût* as chicken Marengo, while others – based on a favourite anecdote of Napoleon's Foreign Minister, Hugues-Bernard Maret, duc de Bassano – blame *pâté de foie gras*. Napoleon himself is said to have identified the culprit as a garlic-flavoured joint, and he may well have had a garlic allergy, which can cause heartburn, flatulence, or nausea.[16] Yet the solution to the puzzle could be an altogether simpler one. According to Las Cases, one of his companions on Saint Helena, Napoleon remarked that as head of state he had been advised by doctors to take precautions against any attempt to poison him. He should be particularly wary, they had said, of wine or coffee, which he should reject 'if he detected the slightest odour of garlic, and – particularly in the case of wine – to spit it out immediately, if he felt even the slightest bit taken aback by its taste'.[17] The suspicion grows that it was not garlic in itself that made Napoleon vomit, but simply the taste of garlic, as it might indicate the presence of poison. That may well explain the incident after the Battle of Dresden, with Napoleon deliberately vomiting as a result of detecting garlic, only to pretend later that he had genuinely been ill as an excuse to absolve himself of any blame when he learned that one of his corps had been trapped and destroyed a couple of days later at Kulm. Had Napoleon actually been suffering from indigestion, he would surely have halted at a local town rather than travel more than 10 miles back to Dresden.

None of this prevented the popular story Napoleon had spun from being endlessly repeated, for at its core lay a pitiful thought: a crucial battle lost because of a simple clove of garlic, and an empire destroyed by so common an ailment as indigestion. The details became progressively more confused, and by 1877 a US writer called William Mathews was even claiming that 'Napoleon lost a battle one day because his *poulet à la Marengo* was inconsiderably scorched by his *chef-de-cuisine*.' Other writers misidentified the battle in question as Waterloo, making Napoleon's legendary dish a scapegoat for his most famous defeat.[18]

ᴥ🕴ᴥ

Napoleon did not believe in medicines, and enjoyed teasing physicians about their ineffectiveness. 'There you are, you great charlatan!', he jocularly addressed his doctor, Jean-Nicolas, baron Corvisart. 'Have you killed many people today?'[19] Napoleon preferred to rely on natural remedies for illnesses, namely abstaining from most food, drinking plenty of fluids, and taking warm baths. He would also change his level of activity suddenly and drastically, to try and restore his body's balance by giving it an unexpected shock.

Napoleon initially enjoyed reasonably good health on Saint Helena, despite his obesity and lack of exercise, and the dispiriting circumstances of his captivity. But he then deteriorated, notably from October 1820. He was in pain, lost weight, and for the most part remained lying down on a sofa or in bed. The cause of his death has long been disputed, partly because it was politically so emotive a subject. It was in the interests of Bonapartists to portray him as a martyr, whereas the British were acutely sensitive that they would be blamed if his death could be linked to the climate of Saint Helena. Allegations that he was poisoned are dubious and controversial. The overwhelming weight of medical opinion suggests that he died from stomach cancer, as did his father, Carlo, in 1785, and possibly other close relatives. Napoleon himself suspected a genetic predisposition to the disease, and gave instructions for a postmortem in case the findings would help his son.

The trigger for Napoleon's fatal illness could have been a longstanding bacterial infection of the stomach, which caused first a benign ulcer, and then a cancerous tumour. His diet may have been a contributing factor, for he preferred meat to be well cooked, and according to some accounts ate little fruit and vegetables – in fact, he may even have suffered from mild scurvy on Saint Helena, for his gums became spongy and prone to bleed. Whether or not Napoleon's food was partly to blame for his illness, the cancer certainly changed his diet. He lost his appetite, and ended up eating mostly soft foods that were easier to digest, such as soups and meatjellies, toast dunked in juice, waffles, puréed pheasant meat, baked apple, creamed rice, and *œufs à la neige* (poached meringues floating in a vanilla custard). In February 1821, the British orderly officer at Longwood, Captain Engelbert Lutyens, learned that the ailing Napoleon had eaten some turtle soup, and had 'relished it very much'. Ironically, Lutyens added, the soup 'was so good the damned Doctor would not let [him] eat much of it'.[20]

Napoleon became delirious as death approached. In the early hours of 5 May, he murmured a half-incoherent string of words. 'France – army – head of the army – Joséphine' were what one of his retinue heard, or at least thought he heard. But Napoleon's last words were politically potent, and, as with the rest of his life, were easily distorted to fit a writer's own, particular agenda. According to one version, Napoleon's mind even wandered back to Marengo, and what he supposedly uttered was: 'My son – the army – France – Desaix!'[21] Later that morning, he lapsed into a coma. His breathing grew weaker and more laboured, yet without any sign of pain. Release finally came shortly after sunset.

A French gun team.

Chapter 12

Rebranding a Legend

As Napoleon passed into legend, he was embraced by an extraordinary array of causes, and interpreted in numerous different guises. From the bogeyman of a British nursery rhyme, to the strong-man hero of tycoons and dictators, or a champion of the *Risorgimento* in the eyes of Italian patriots, he has probably been reinvented more often than any other man in history. It was inevitable that such an iconic figure should also have become commercialized, and used to promote a whole variety of products from clocks to cigars.[1] Mounted on a dazzling grey horse, and encased in his famous overcoat and cocked hat, he is instantly recognizable around the world, and, in contrast to living celebrities, is a safe brand, unlikely to become a toxic asset for the advertiser by suddenly making the news headlines for all the wrong reasons.

Just as chicken Marengo's title was stretched to cover a whole spectrum of variations on the basic dish, Napoleon's own name has been bestowed on a remarkable range of foods and drinks, including a cocktail, a brandy, a cherry, a pear, and a type of Irish potato.[2] Most bizarrely of all, a 'napoleon' may be a cream-filled pastry – although in France itself it is instead called a *mille-feuille* ('thousand sheets'), a vivid description of its countless, crusty leaves of puff pastry sandwiched between layers of cream.[3] It has been claimed that *mille-feuilles* were dubbed napoleons because he liked them so much, and they have even been blamed for his defeat at Waterloo after he supposedly ate too many of them, which served as a useful cautionary tale for children with a sweet tooth. In reality, *mille-feuilles* probably acquired his name simply through a corruption of the adjective 'Neapolitan', which referred to a block of different layers of ice-cream. Later, the term 'napoleon' moved beyond the narrow definition of a cream-and-pastry *mille-feuille*, and embraced a multitude of other layered dishes – combining perhaps potato and mushrooms, salmon and goat's cheese, or even peppers, polenta, and aubergines.

The use of Napoleon's brand name for such items has had an interesting side-effect – that of softening his image. After all, it is difficult to regard as a bloodthirsty tyrant someone who has given his name to a cream-filled pastry. Through his association with food, he has become a warm, homely figure, like an alley cat improbably domesticated after years of disturbing the neighbourhood with blood-curdling shrieks and vicious scraps with other strays amid the dustbins. His name is even used to market *cognac*, and to help classify the age of brandies, so much so that most people would be surprised to learn that he almost never drank spirits. Commercialization has therefore reinforced certain myths, and the popular image of Napoleon today – even the Napoleon described in many history books – is an often comic parody based largely on his own propaganda, the hostile caricatures produced at the time, and the subsequent inventions of literary hacks.

❧ 🧍 ❧

Chicken Marengo has undergone a series of reinterpretations of its own, and over the decades its evolving identity has been captured in the pages of popular fiction. Indeed, novelists have not merely recorded the ways in which the dish has been perceived, but have actually helped shape those shifting perceptions.

The dish appeared in fiction as early as 1833, when the French dramatist Etienne de Jouy wrote a play set against the background of the Revolution. He invented a character called the baron de Bouchencour, and gave him a love of fine food and a career at the heart of these tumultuous events. The most interesting moment comes at the end of a scene when Bouchencour leaves the room with the explanation: 'I have to give some advice to the *chef* about a new chicken *fricassée* that I have invented. I am calling it *poulet à la Marengo*, in the *Cuisinier impérial*, [a recipe book] that I edit in collaboration with my old friend Grimaud [*sic*] de la Reynière.'[4] Jouy's story was historical fiction, and should be treated no more seriously than that, yet is worthy of note since it indicates that the legend about chicken Marengo's invention by Dunant on the battlefield was not universally believed in the 1830s, however dominant it later became.[5]

In Anglo-Saxon fiction, chicken Marengo was soon being used to symbolize French cuisine as a whole. In 1855, for example, a US naval officer, Henry Augustus Wise, produced a sometimes hilarious novel of derring-do called *Tales for the marines*. He set one scene on board a US frigate during the 1830s, and described how the officers' grumbles about their mess food provoked the caterer to hint that some of them could not recognize a good meal when they saw one. Half-a-dozen disgruntled diners immediately begged him to have a go at serving up even the hint of a good meal, and so he announced the menu he would provide, sardonically picking the most sophisticated dishes he could think of. 'Well, then, gentlemen, to begin, I'd give you oysters with lemon juice, – Julienne soup – then *poulet à la Marengo* – ' At that point, he was interrupted by a sarcastic protest that this was bound to be followed by 'islands of moonshine in syllabub lakes', to which he responded by resigning.[6]

Tales for the marines was typical of such fictional references to chicken Marengo. First came the casual mention of the dish, artfully slipped into the conversation as the obvious embodiment of all fine, fashionable cuisine, and this then unleashed a barrage of patronizing comments, with the disdain thinly veiled by a gentle, mocking humour. Some writers continued to poke fun at chicken Marengo early in the twentieth century. In *From place to place* (1913), Irvin S. Cobb mentioned chicken Marengo being served in a restaurant in New York City, and added that it was an appropriate name for the dish, since Marengo had been a tough battle, and his fictional character had an equally tough battle trying to cut the sinews of that particular chicken. Another writer, Frank Richardson, pointed out how common it was to find a Marengo dish without any chicken in it. In his novel *There and back* (1904), he joked that at the French town of Lourdes, 'we lunched on *poulet à la Marengo*, not, oddly enough, made of rabbit, as is the prevailing custom'. Similarly, in an early example of chick lit, *A Girl capitalist* (1902), Florence Bright described the chicken Marengo served at a lodging house in London, supposedly made from two chickens, but containing only three legs, two wings, and one breast. It was the old complaint resurfacing, about how French cooking was able to disguise dubious methods.[7]

The derision was also apparent in 1928, when the humorist Stephen Leacock satirized the predictable format of detective stories. The detective, he wrote, was always thin, inscrutable, and described as having the face of a hawk. (He clearly overlooked Agatha Christie's podgy creation, Hercule Poirot.) In the past, added Leacock, the great detective never seemed to eat or sleep, but in more recent stories had become a connoisseur of food, and to illustrate his point, he invented a dialogue in which a detective tells his companions about a restaurant where – and here Leacock dreamed up a ludicrously sophisticated dish – they could eat the best frogs' legs *à la Marengo* in London.[8]

Beneath these jibes about French cookery lurked an uncomfortable awareness of Anglo-Saxon inferiority in that art. Hence the mockery of chicken Marengo has often been replaced with respect, and the dish has been used – not just in fiction, but in real life – as an example to aspire to. In 1884, one of Queen Victoria's sons, Prince Leopold, Duke of Albany, made a speech expressing the hope that the poor would have better dinners. His idea that cookery should be taught in every school was promptly lampooned by the satirical magazine *Punch*. Just let working-class men taste all kinds of fishes, it prophesied in a specially composed poem, and such dainty dishes would surely end all marital frays. The verses hardly constituted one of Mr Punch's finer efforts, but he pressed on regardless:

> Little wonder that poor men go
> Out upon the 'spree' to roam,
> When no chicken of Marengo
> Greets them when they dine at home.[9]

In the most recent fictional references, Marengo dishes are used more as a tool of humour than as an object of derision, and, indeed, they have a rich comic potential, partly since, however tasty, they are just a smelly mess if they end up anywhere other than on a plate. Elinor Lipman's romantic comedy, *The Ladies' man* (1999) examines the impact on three single sisters living in the US city of Boston when the former fiancé of one of them turns up thirty years after deserting her. One of the sisters soon smashes a casserole of veal Marengo over his head, splattering his jacket with the contents.[10]

For another author, Captain Hugh Kennedy, writing in the 1860s, chicken Marengo offered an unmissable chance to set two of his characters talking at cross-purposes. They have had dinner in the French colony of Pondicherry in India, and while one of them is in raptures about the chicken Marengo he has eaten, the other is thinking solely about their host's charming daughter:

'She is, indeed, a most delightful girl.'

   'I say, did you taste that *poulet à la Marengo*? The most exquisite thing that ever crossed my palate.'

   'Such a foot and ankle.'

   'Gad, I should enjoy a bit of it now – grilled.'

   'A charming figure – I certainly admire a gown with a stomacher when the figure is good.'

   'A Burdwan stew dressed that way would be divine. I'll try it to-morrow.'

   'What an eloquent eye! how full of soul, feeling, and expression.'

   'But, I think, a thought more of chili vinegar in it would be an improvement.'

   'Chili vinegar! Good heavens, my dear sir, what do you mean?'[11]

For novelists, Marengo dishes are invaluable scene-setters, since they are so well-known to their readers – along with such other favourites as minestrone soup and baked Alaska. This was particularly the case after the Second World War, when chicken Marengo enjoyed a renewed burst of popularity, especially in the United States. The *New York Times* conducted an unofficial poll at the end of each year, based on the number of letters that had been received by its food editor, and found that chicken Marengo was the recipe third most requested by its readers in 1957, while shrimp Marengo was the favourite in 1964.[12]

These dishes were popular in the United States partly because of their convenience and versatility, since they could be served with a wide variety of accompaniments, including pasta, rice, or polenta, and thus constituted a whole meal in themselves. But the crucial reason for chicken Marengo's heightened profile was the dramatic growth in the availability of cheap chicken, as traditional farming methods gave way to mass production. This was an extraordinary change, for chickens had previously been expensive – indeed, before the Second World War they had actually been a symbol of prosperity, with the Republican Party boasting in 1928 of having put a 'chicken in every pot' and a 'car in every backyard'.

It was around the 1920s that chicken began its rise to become one of the United States' favourite foods, and demand was boosted during the Second World War by the shortages of beef. The upward trend continued after the war, with the development of more efficient methods of production and distribution, including factory farms, and the use of the latest scientific research in rearing the birds. Chicken was now cheap, classy, and convenient. It remained available throughout the year, whatever the season, was welcomed as a healthier alternative to red, fatty meat, and could be turned into hundreds of interesting dishes. Chicken Marengo enjoyed its heyday in the United States during the decades after chicken had been transformed into a food for the masses, but before more processed forms of the meat, such as chicken nuggets, became increasingly popular from the 1980s.[13]

Despite this background trend, chicken Marengo would not have become popular in the home kitchen unless it had existed in simpler versions than those enshrined in classic *haute cuisine*. Recipe books written by professional cooks gave instructions for preparing the sauce that could take as long as three hours. That was feasible in a large restaurant, where a handful of basic sauces, the so-called *grandes sauces*, could be prepared in advance and then quickly used to make a whole range of derivatives for different dishes, but it was hardly practicable for busy housewives cooking a single meal for a few guests without a team of assistants. Simplified recipes for chicken Marengo, intended for use in domestic kitchens, had been published within the first decades of its creation. They made it possible to prepare the sauce both quickly and at the same time as the rest of the dish. By forming a *roux* from flour and fat, to serve as a thickening agent, and then adding wine and stock, a cook simply had to simmer the blended mixture to complete the cooking of both the chicken and the sauce. An alternative to using a *roux* was to rely on reduction alone, first deglazing the pan after frying the chicken – that is, adding liquid to incorporate the rich deposits – before simmering to evaporate half the water content, thereby reducing the mixture to a thickened, intensely flavoured sauce.

The recipes grew even simpler in the twentieth century. Some of the traditional ingredients, such as truffles, gave way to cheaper and more readily available alternatives, even if this resulted in the dish being toned down to the point of blandness. It was possible to make the sauce simply by mixing tins of tomato and mushroom soups, and adding a dash of lemon juice. Growing numbers of domestic freezers made chicken Marengo more convenient than ever. It was easily prepared in advance and frozen, and could then be reheated and garnished, making it ideal for a family meal, a buffet lunch, or a dinner party. It could even be made entirely in a microwave oven, sauce and all, thus halving the cooking time.

Such was the popularity of Marengo dishes that they inevitably became stereotyped in popular fiction. They were a safe, reassuring choice – even if hardly an original one – and while evoking a sense of elegance they also conveyed an informal atmosphere laden with a hint of intimacy. Veal Marengo was therefore an obvious dish for a couple at a romantic dinner, as Christiane Heggan demonstrated in her thriller, *The Search* (2005). Her heroine, Sydney Cooper, grows close to Jake Sloan, invites him to dinner, and ponders what to serve. She does not want the meal to be too fancy, as Jake is down-to-earth and her cooking skills are limited, but it has to be sophisticated enough to impress him, so she opts for veal Marengo.[14]

The dish strikes the right note: impressive, but not over-ambitious; endowed with a touch of class, and yet reasonably easy to prepare. As a symbol of sophistication, it offers novelists a useful contrast with junk food. In his humorous story, *Miss Undine's living room* (1987), James Wilcox describes a man being promised veal Marengo for dinner by his former mother-in-law, only to end up eating a pizza-burger when she is unable to find the recipe.[15] Another author, Mary Wesley, uses the dish in *The Vacillations of Poppy Carew* (1986) as a revelation of just how skilled one of her characters has become in the kitchen: when Victor's former wife learns that he can now produce veal Marengo, having previously struggled to boil an egg, she wonders uneasily whether he has found another woman.[16]

Novelists have not always regarded the dish so positively. Its very prevalence, which ensured that readers would recognize it, could also make it seem boring and old-fashioned. For Mary Braddon in 1871, chicken Marengo epitomized a lack of imagination. Her character, Lady Laura, is preparing to receive visitors, and discusses the menu with her cook in a typically haughty style:

> 'My good Volavent,' she would say, tossing the poor man's list aside, with a despairing shrug of her shoulders, 'all these *entrées* are as old as the hills. I am sure Adam [the father of mankind] must have had stewed pigeons with green peas, and chicken *à la Marengo* – they are the very ABC of cookery. Do, pray, strike out something a little newer.'

Lady Laura then hands her cook the menu for a dinner served in Saint Petersburg, which she has copied from the published diary of a count. 'There really are some ideas in it,' she tells him condescendingly. 'Do look it over, Volavent, and see if it will inspire you. We must try to rise above the level of a West-end hotel.'[17]

For other novelists, Marengo dishes were altogether too complex, and symbolized the artificiality of city life compared with simple, rural pleasures. In a light-hearted collection of sketches published in 1937, Stephen Leacock wrote of his longing to leave for the countryside at the start of summer. He realized that most of those living in the cities of North America felt the same way. Even while staying in palatial hotels, they were dreaming of morning mists rising from river valleys. As they looked through the menu, they searched not for *pâté bourguignon à la Marengo*, which the chef included because he was French and pining for France, but for solid, familiar, American comfort food, such as liver-and-bacon, or pancakes drizzled with honey.[18]

Chicken Marengo could frequently be found in the dining cars of US trains. In 1903, the writer Simeon Ford wrote ironically that whenever he visited Boston, he had a long, tiresome trip by train from New York, during which he would pay 'seven dollars for the privilege of sitting in a stuffy palace car of the vintage of 1843, and eat for lunch *Chicken à la Marengo* canned in the same year'.[19] Yet the way that railway travellers regarded chicken Marengo varied according to their social background and the scenes they happened to see through the train window. On the one hand, when wealthy businessmen passed through prosperous communities, they admired the splendid houses that reminded them of their own homes, and as a result they regretted having to eat on the train, where the options were limited to chicken Marengo, mutton stew, or pork-and-beans. On the other hand, at least one person deliberately left a mining town in the sparsely populated western state of Montana at Christmas time, in order to ride on the railway and enjoy the atmosphere of the dining car while he ate his chicken Marengo, solely because of a sentimental yearning for a more refined sort of

Christmas – one closer to what others were having over 1,500 miles away on the East Coast.[20]

The bored or indifferent reaction of many diners when confronted yet again with chicken Marengo was symptomatic of wider problems. During the nineteenth century, French *haute cuisine* had enjoyed a predominant reputation, partly because the concept of the restaurant was exported from Paris to other countries, and because French cooks who found work abroad acted as ambassadors for their nation's cooking. In the 1880s and 1890s, a series of great internationally famous hotels opened, such as the Savoy in London, and the Waldorf-Astoria in New York City, which not only attracted prestigious chefs to cater for their guests, but gave them the means to promote *haute cuisine*. Celebrity chefs, guests, and establishments attracted each other, and famous dishes such as chicken Marengo inevitably featured on the menu.

Yet, for much of the time, *haute cuisine* failed fully to live up to its reputation. It repeatedly underwent a cycle of renewal followed by stagnation, as rigidity and boredom set in, and as the old methods became invalid in the face of new challenges posed by broad social trends. Chicken Marengo had been born in a golden age – the age of Carême, the great chef primarily responsible for codifying *haute cuisine* and providing an organized, rational basis for his profession. Unfortunately, the effect of genius can be stultifying rather than inspirational. By the mid-nineteenth century, following Carême's death in 1833, standards were perceived to be in decline, and it was during this period that novelists such as Mary Braddon and William Makepeace Thackeray began to condemn chicken Marengo as over-familiar. Then, in the late nineteenth century, *haute cuisine* underwent a period of renewal in the age of another great chef, Georges-Auguste Escoffier. Along with his contemporaries, Escoffier sought to introduce greater simplicity, lightness, and balance, and reorganized the kitchen staff to make the preparation of dishes quicker and more efficient.

Yet as the decades passed, Escoffier's revived and rationalized *haute cuisine* proved altogether too convenient, and its apparent perfection ended up fostering laziness instead of bold innovation. Mediocre successors lacked his innovative drive, and ignored his emphasis on simplicity. Bound by seemingly inflexible rules and traditions, by the late 1960s *haute cuisine* had become fossilized and discredited. Instead of inventing new sensations, chefs merely repeated the old classics. Dishes were often cooked in advance, and simply reheated when required, with their strongly flavoured sauces being used to override the taste of the often-stale ingredients. The old fears resurfaced that had so beset British tourists a century earlier, about the way French sauces might disguise all kinds of alarming substances. To these were now added concerns about the healthiness of the dishes, including their fat and salt levels. Ordinary roast chicken was seen as a wiser choice than a dish fried in oil and laden with an elaborate, *roux*-based sauce.[21]

Nouvelle cuisine was now the rage. The new emphasis lay on the freshness and quality of the ingredients, the creativity of the chef, and the artistic presentation of the dish. Heavy sauces gave way to light seasoning, and this made chicken Marengo particularly vulnerable, since the sauce was so central to its identity. Indeed, it was not the swings in Napoleon's reputation that the dish followed, but the fortunes of French *haute cuisine*: as one of the best-known dishes, it risked becoming an example of all that was wrong with the old methods. Rather than being a prestigious icon of French culture, it was in danger of being condemned as over-seasoned, over-familiar, and over-pretentious.

Broader forces were also at work. Internationalization, the growth in prosperity, the triumph of supermarkets, and the massive increase in tourism and migration all made it easier for Westerners to experience different foods and cultures. Restaurants served a growing range of cuisines, with traditional French dishes having to compete with exotic food from around the world. At the same time, the desire to protect local ways of life contributed to the growing popularity of France's regional cuisines, and this, too, has sometimes come at the expense of the standardized national dishes.

Yet even if chicken Marengo now has a lower profile, it has adapted surprisingly well to these new and more complex times. The élite *haute cuisine* of professional chefs was just one strand in French cooking, and the fact that simpler versions of chicken Marengo already existed in the ordinary *cuisine bourgeoise* practised by home cooks around the world gave the dish a broader and more resilient base. Its sheer adaptability has also allowed this quintessential emblem of French cuisine to find a wider market by embracing foreign customs and styles. This was exemplified by the success of a New York restaurant in the early 1990s in integrating two cultures: its owners were Haïtian, along with the music and murals, but the waiting staff were mainly French, and customers could opt for either French or Haïtian dishes, including chicken Marengo.[22]

Sometimes chicken Marengo was not simply combined with other cuisines, but completely fused with them. At San Antonio in Texas, for example, a restaurant in the 1980s served it with *guacamole*, a traditional, avocado-based side dish from neighbouring Mexico. At the other end of the spectrum, chicken Marengo could be found 8,500 miles away in the former French colony of Vietnam, but here an omelette replaced the more usual fried egg, and a pork meatball appeared alongside the chicken.[23] These various incarnations bore hardly any resemblance to each other, let alone to the older, and supposedly traditional, dish served in Paris, and yet they hardly had less of a claim to the title of chicken Marengo than some of the wilder flights of fancy by French chefs, or the unappetizing, mass-produced concotions so condemned by the champions of *nouvelle cuisine*.

By continuing to evolve, chicken Marengo therefore survived the oscillations in culinary fashion. Its would-be nemesis, *nouvelle cuisine*, lost its novelty in the 1980s, and many chefs began to merge the old and the new styles in order to exploit the best of both. French *haute cuisine* remains prestigious. Admittedly, it faces greater competition, but competitors can be a positive influence, by encouraging innovation and the maintenance of high standards. The health concerns related to Marengo dishes have also been allayed – by insisting on using lean meat and only a limited amount of oil, cookery books have even been able to include them in weight-loss programmes. Veal Marengo would have been particularly suited for such regimes, because of the meat's relatively low fat content, only veal consumption slumped amid public disgust at the way calves were reared in factory farms.

At the same time, many Westeners have lost interest in cooking altogether. This has provided Marengo dishes with yet another chance to find a gap in the market, by appealing to those who lack the time and inclination to cook from scratch, but who want a whole-some and respectable alternative to fast food. By the early 1970s, chicken Marengo could be bought in London as a ready-cooked take-away, while by the end of the decade two young entrepreneurs were selling it at their local train station in Connecticut, to meet commuters returning home in the evening from New York City. By 1985, supermarkets in Washington DC were trying out a similar concept, by introducing catering kiosks to serve meals for reheating in a microwave. Even some restaurants have now begun selling Marengo take-aways, for customers who want to eat sophisticated dishes in their own homes.[24]

The common theme of such initiatives was a reaction against mediocre, mass-produced food – as was the inclusion of chicken Marengo in efforts to improve the food served to the US Army in the late 1980s.[25] Yet the danger existed that elegant dishes would not only fail to elevate the food industry as a whole, but would actually be dragged down by it. In too many cases, when French cuisine became caught up in the trend towards speed and convenience, its standards were fatally compromised, and this was reflected in the popular fiction of the time. In 1975, the US novelist William Gaddis featured veal Marengo in his satirical masterpiece, *JR*, a study of the corrosive social effects of the preoccupation with money. Inside an apartment in New York City, one of his characters prepares veal Marengo simply by dropping the freeze-dried contents of a packet into hot water. For so stylish and carefully prepared a dish to be reduced to a mere dessicated, and instantly reconstitutable, object was a pithy and yet supremely ironic comment on the throwaway nature of American society, in which quality and style were sacrificed to bland and depersonalized efficiency.[26]

As it turned out, Gaddis's vision was not completely surreal, for chicken Marengo has actually been debased enough to become an airline lunch. Passengers trying to decide between it and beef *burritos* while on a flight in the United States in 1990 were reportedly startled by an announcement asking them not to be upset if they failed to receive their first choice, 'as all our *entrées* taste very much the same'.[27]

Marengo dishes have even gone into space, thus taking to new heights their old role as ambassadors of French culture. In 1988, when a French cosmonaut, Jean-Loup Chrétien, joined the Soviet space station *Mir*, he and his team-mates enjoyed tinned veal Marengo and other of his country's classic dishes, which had been specially modified for eating in zero gravity, to make a change from dehydrated rations. What more ingenious way could have been found of winning the stomachs and minds of the Soviet cosmonauts, while simultaneously broadcasting to the world the fact that France was part of the space age?[28]

No one would deny that the pursuit of convenience has come at a cost in quality, yet the underlying subtleties of these changes are all too easily overlooked. Purists might deplore the debasing of the more traditional recipes for chicken Marengo, but their objections are actually self-defeating, as they highlight one of the most glaring reasons why the popular story of the dish's creation cannot be true. If Dunant had prepared chicken Marengo from scratch in the classic, *haute cuisine* style of the great restaurants, Napoleon would have had to wait several hours before his meal was ready. With quicker and simpler versions becoming predominant in recent decades, more suited for the home kitchen, chicken Marengo has actually taken a step forward rather than back, by drawing closer to the logic of the myth. And the fact that it has done so holds an even deeper significance, since it highlights just how fundamentally today's society has been transformed. Whereas the way in which people ate used to be determined by the norms of their class, it has now become overwhelmingly a matter of personal choice. By eating so quickly, holding working lunches, and habitually fitting their meals around a busy schedule, all too many individualistic Westerners have become Napoleons of the table.

Austrian grenadiers firing volleys.

Chapter 13

Washing Up

♥ ↑ ♥

For all its wastefulness, war can be a surprisingly creative force. Throughout history, it has helped produce and popularize new dishes, sometimes by virtue of necessity, not least when rationing was introduced in Britain during the Second World War. Soldiers, traders, and colonialists have helped spread foods and recipes by coming into contact with different peoples and cultures: kedgeree (a mixture of rice, fish, and hard-boiled eggs) is believed to have originated in an ancient dish called *khichri*, which the British encountered and adapted after arriving in India.[1] At the same time, successive generations of victorious commanders have left their mark on culinary fashion, even if the connection with these famous men often turns out to be illusory on closer examination. Valençay cheeses, for example, are said to owe their distinctive shape – a truncated pyramid – to Napoleon slicing off the tops with a sword, since they supposedly reminded him of the failure of his expedition to Egypt. In reality, he was proud of the expedition, which he cynically portrayed as a glorious success, and the fable about the cheeses may simply have been an excuse to omit the fragile, tapering tops of the pyramids, and avoid the wastage caused by accidental damage.

The glamour of chicken Marengo rests on equally flimsy foundations. The dish was not suddenly improvised for Napoleon on a battlefield, and yet the fact it gave rise to such a potent myth constitutes a fascinating story in its own right. Napoleon had always been adept at self-promotion, but Marengo was the first campaign he fought as head of state, and having the full administrative resources of France at his disposal enabled him to create a formidable propaganda machine with which to shape his image. By spinning a legend around Marengo, he made the battle a core component in his claim to greatness. Chicken Marengo has not only drawn strength from that legend, but has also played its own role in reinforcing it, and has become caught up in its multiple layers of misinformation. Nothing connected with the dish is quite what it seems, and this epitomizes the difficulties both in unravelling the truth about Napoleon himself, and in seeing through the veil of deception that obscures the nature of much of what we eat.

Illusions can be beneficial. Indeed, they form an integral part of the whole experience of eating out. Seated in the calm, pristine surroundings of a restaurant, diners are insulated from the messier reality of what happens in the kitchens next door. They can enjoy a sense of glamour and luxury, and a fleeting illusion, for one evening at least, that they are eating like royalty. They may want to savour the magic link with fame, whether by dining in a world-class establishment, by sitting alongside well-known guests, or by eating a prestigious dish named after a great battle or personality. This is why it is so important for a top chef to have not just a talent for cooking, but a flair for publicity, and an entrepreneurial drive, as was exemplified by the legendary Georges-Auguste Escoffier – it was he, for example, who created peach Melba in the 1890s for the soprano known as Dame Nellie Melba, in order to exploit the popular hunger for some connection with celebrity.

Chicken Marengo was just one of many dishes linked to Napoleon. Of his illustrious band of marshals, Massena lent his name to both a *consommé* (clarified soup) and a dish of eggs; Murat was honoured by fillets of sole; and Suchet immortalized by *poularde Albuféra*, which drew its name from the title of his dukedom.[2] Ney was remembered with a dish of red partridges, and as for the plain-spoken wife of Maréchal Lefebvre, she had her nickname, *Madame Sans-Gêne*, bestowed on a concoction of vanilla ice cream with red-currants. Members of Napoleon's family were also honoured – his youngest brother, prince Jérôme, became a dessert – but it was the two most noted gourmets of the Empire, Talleyrand and Cambacérès, both of them prominent political figures, who accumulated a particularly large number of dishes bearing their name, for they were served by first-rate cooks, and provided them with the motivation to excel.[3]

It was Talleyrand who employed Marie-Antoine Carême, the most famous chef of the age. Carême's life was a rags-to-riches story – or at least that was how he told it. He claimed to have been abandoned as a child by his impoverished father, and to have made his own way in the world, eventually becoming an international celebrity through sheer talent and hard work, first in Talleyrand's service and then in those of a succession of European monarchs. Carême was a creative genius. 'I have dreamed up an infinite number of soups, joints of meat, *entrées*, side dishes, and even sauces,' he boasted.[4] Crucially, he also had that instinctive gift for knowing how to make a dish popular by bestowing a famous title on it, naming a chestnut pudding, for example, after the Russian diplomat, Karl, Count Nesselrode, and one of his soups after the great French writer, Victor Hugo.[5] Could it have been Carême who created – or at least named – chicken Marengo? Possibly, but there are many other candidates, and we are unlikely ever to know for sure. What is certain is that Carême popularized chicken Marengo, by serving the dish for his famous employers, and he did more than anyone else to codify French *haute cuisine* and establish it on a scientific basis. In his greatest book, *L'Art de la cuisine française au dix-neuvième siècle* (completed after his death by a friend, Armand Plumerey, who compiled the last two volumes), he arranged hundreds of recipes into a logical order, so they constituted a systematic body of knowledge.

In Carême's system, chicken Marengo was classified as a poultry *entrée*, and fitted into a flowing sequence of recipes. The *entrées* began with chickens cooked whole, and then progressed to the *fricassées*, where chicken Marengo was grouped with chicken Provençale and its other closest relatives. There followed dishes of breast fillets, or legs, and they in turn gave way to more elaborate options, including a *soufflé* made with eggs and puréed chicken meat, and at the end came the elegant *quenelles*, *boudins*, and *timbales*, which transformed the chicken into something completely unrecognizable from its original form.[6] Chicken Marengo, therefore, was integrated into a balanced, hierarchical system, and owed its global success to the fact it was not an isolated individual in a loose collection of dishes, but a star performer enshrined within an organized French cuisine that could readily be exported and promoted by its practitioners.

ᶲ♞ᶲ

The Empire was a golden age of gastronomy, underpinned by an expanding social élite filled with a heady awareness of its new prestige and power. The widespread passion for fine food was stimulated by a handful of great cooks and gastronomic writers, but also by leading patrons such as Talleyrand, Cambacérès, and some of Napoleon's more refined relatives, notably his uncle, Cardinal Joseph Fesch. In contrast, Napoleon himself has been accused of having a stultifying effect by failing to appreciate fine food. His cooks are generally remembered, if at all, simply as devoted servants, rather than as bold innovators. With all the power and resources at his disposal, it is argued, Napoleon could have done more to foster culinary achievements, in the same way that he over-saw the birth of a great era of French battle painting through his patronage of pioneering artists such as Lejeune, the young staff officer who painted the most memorable picture of Marengo.

Yet this is hardly fair. Napoleon actually employed some out-standingly capable men, such as Hubert Lebeau, his renowned pastry chef, and Louis, marquis de Cussy, one of his prefects of the palace. As for Dunant – the supposed creator of chicken Marengo – he, too, had impeccable qualifications, having previously served in the household of the Condés, one of the most illustrious branches of the Bourbon family. Even so, claim the critics, Napoleon did not make the most of Dunant's talents: his inability to keep to regular mealtimes meant the food was past its best by the time he finally ate, and made it pointless for his cooks to try and dream up sophisticated new dishes.

In fact, Napoleon seemed to discourage innovation – or so commentators have concluded from a notorious incident that occurred in 1806. Its origin can be traced back to the day when Napoleon asked why he was never served *crépinettes de cochon* (pork patties). Dunant replied that they were indigestible, by which he meant they were excessively fatty, but in reality he also regarded them as too vulgar to appear on the imperial table. So next day, he produced a gastronomic version called *crépinettes de perdreaux*, using partridge meat instead of pork. Napoleon seemed to like these genteel patties, but could be unpredictable, especially if his mind was preoccupied by a problem. When Dunant served them again for *déjeuner* a month later, Napoleon took one look, burst into a rage, and overturned the table, spilling all its contents on to the magnificent carpet, before stalking off into his office. It was left to the Grand Marshal of the Palace to soothe the distraught Dunant and dissuade him from resigning. On his advice, Dunant prepared another *déjeuner*, which included a roast chicken. This time, Napoleon complimented him. 'Ah! Dunant,' he said, giving him a familiar tap on the cheek, 'you are happier as my *maître d'hôtel* than I am as emperor.' It was his way of excusing the fit of temper, by blaming it on the strain of his position, and of dismissing it as too unimportant to be remembered for long.[7]

The episode, it might be thought, did nothing to induce Dunant to experiment, yet the reason it was remembered at all was surely because it was extraordinary. If anything, it actually demonstrated the loyalty Napoleon inspired in his servants, and the shortlived nature of his outbursts, for Dunant continued to serve him devotedly for the rest of his reign. Besides, as we have already seen, Napoleon's preference for plain dishes was largely a myth, and his request for pork patties may simply have been another of those occasional attempts he made to prove to himself and others that behind the imperial trappings of power he remained an austere, down-to-earth soldier.

Napoleon in fact had a major beneficial impact on the development of gastronomy, even if his influence was largely indirect. By rewarding his marshals, ministers, relatives, and other prominent figures so lavishly, he enabled them to maintain luxurious households and first-rate cooks, while the banquets for the great ceremonial occasions of his reign, such as his coronation and his son's baptism, provided additional opportunities for Carême and other leading professionals to hone their talents. Most importantly of all, he created an environment favourable for the emergence of gastronomy by helping to end the shortages and upheavals of the Revolution.

Hence the victory of Marengo did not simply share the prestige of its name with chicken Marengo, but contributed to its success by helping to stabilize France. Also crucial to the dish's prominence was Napoleon's instinctive grasp of public relations, for without his intervention, the battle might have received a different name altogether. When Berthier wrote his initial report that evening, he dated it from the 'Battlefield of San-Juliano', since it had been near the village of that name that the decisive climax of the day had unrolled. Yet 'San-Juliano' was then crossed out by Napoleon's secretary, Bourrienne, and replaced with 'Marengo'. The change shifted the focus away from San Giuliano, which would have highlighted the long retreat and narrow outcome, and emphasized instead the earlier, heroic defence of the hamlet of Marengo, 5 miles further forward. Marengo was also a simpler and more memorable name, and undoubtedly served as a more effective marketing tool than chicken Saint Julian.[8]

Bestowing a name on a dish is done partly for the sake of convenience – as with any other system of classification – yet at the same time it is meant to mystify and mislead. Grandiose labels create the impression that cooking is a prestigious, scientific profession, the preserve of experts, rather than an art that can be picked up by mere amateurs. A complex title also promises a large, well-seasoned dish, and hints at a venture into the unknown, while the inclusion of an illustrious word evokes a glamorous location, or a larger-than-life personality, and stirs the diner's imagination, thereby engaging all the senses at the same time.

The sheer longevity of chicken Marengo commands attention. It was far from being the only dish to be named after events or personages of this period, but became more prevalent and longer-lasting than any other, with the possible exception of beef Wellington. So many of the rest have disappeared almost without trace. In some cases, the reason is obvious, as in the case of *chaufroix de mauviettes à la Bonaparte*. Few people today eat *mauviettes* (larks), or go to the time and trouble of making *chaufroix* by coating the cooked meat with a sauce that sets on being chilled.[9] The key with chicken Marengo was that its sheer adaptability enabled it to make the leap from the fully staffed and equipped restaurant kitchen to the stove of a family home without being so simplified as to lose its essential character.

Myths are a useful, even a necessary, component of a great dish, in the same way that they can play a vital role in the life of a society. They fill the void of the unknown, provide a rosy interpretation of the past, and gloss over subjects into which it would be awkward to delve too deeply. They can assuage the bitterness of a defeat, or even deny it altogether, and foster a sense of solidarity. Yet myths tend to outlive their usefulness, and in the long run, through their mindless repetition, they breed complacency, and deaden rather than inspire the mind. Vitality depends on the ability to adapt, and absorb new ingredients, ideas, or methods: this was as true of Napoleon's system of waging war – we saw how effectively he absorbed the lessons of Marengo – as it is of cooking. *Haute cuisine* eventually became discredited because of an excessive regard for traditional, standardized methods, which encouraged laziness and a tendency to look backwards to a supposed golden age, instead of forwards to the boundless possibilities of the future. The belief that there is just one, true, historical recipe for chicken Marengo is therefore the greatest myth of them all. The dish has countless variations, some of them spectacularly different in appearance, and the only ingredient common to them all is the intangible element of mystery that has been so vital to its success.

✷ ✷ ✷

Memorable events are inevitably reduced in popular memory to just one or two dramatic snapshots. When David painted Napoleon crossing the Alps, he created one of the iconic images of history, and managed to encapsulate the entire campaign – even the era as a whole – in a single, frozen moment. Chicken Marengo played a similar role in defining Napoleon's victory, and prolonging it in popular memory. Yet symbols do not remain constant, and in the same way that chicken Marengo's recipe gradually evolved, so too did its underlying meaning and importance. In origin, it was probably a variation on a dish associated with Provence, a region, ironically, that was generally hostile to Napoleon. Adopted as a celebration of one of his victories, it subsequently blossomed instead into an emblem of elegant French cuisine – a strange outcome for a concoction said to have been created on an Italian battlefield, with theoretically Italian ingredients. There was all the more irony in the fact that the national cuisine chicken Marengo supposedly epito-mized did not really exist except in the imagination – what France possessed was an artificial combination of dishes that had been drawn from various regions, and refined and codified in Paris. Indeed, France itself was a largely fictional entity until surprisingly recently. Its borders repeatedly moved, with Lorraine, for example, being absorbed as late as 1766, partly lost in 1871, regained from Germany in 1919, and temporarily lost again during the Second World War. Regional identities have always been strong in France, and, even after Napoleon's reign, most of the population spoke not French, but a local *patois*, or dialect. Right up until the start of the twentieth century, successive governments struggled to penetrate the isolation of vast swathes of the countryside, and to impose the concept of national unity on uneducated peasants whose outlook was altogether more restricted, sometimes to the narrow confines of their village.

None of this prevented chicken Marengo from being perceived as an emblem of France, or at least of a particular interpretation of France – the stylish, sophisticated France of the wealthy Parisian. It actually helped forge the nation that had adopted it, by promoting the concept of a unified and integrated France before one had truly emerged. That was not the only paradox, for this seemingly nationalized dish was exported and transformed into a truly global phenomenon, and in the process actually ended up eclipsing the battle it was meant to commemorate.

How many of the diners who eat it today can locate Marengo on a map, let alone name the defeated Austrian commander? Their ignorance is understandable, yet forms an ironic comment on all the effort Napoleon expended in trying to rewrite the battle. As a lesson in unintended consequences, it is a sobering thought, and has moved a recent historian to describe the way the victory has been forgotten as 'perhaps a little bizarre, and surely a little sad'.[10]

And so chicken Marengo takes on yet another meaning, this time as a poignant reminder of the unfulfilled early promise of Napoleon's rule, before the frenzied wave of rejoicing unleashed by Marengo gave way to the defeats and disillusionment of the following decade. The dish has been seen in many different guises, but of all its multifarious roles, this surely is the most intriguing – as a symbol of dashed hope, offering a final, tantalizing glimpse into what might have been.

Appendix

The Recipe

You may wish to cook chicken Marengo for yourself. Many different recipes exist, but the following, basic version is particularly suited to home cooking, and may be refined with more exotic ingredients such as crayfish – you can find tubs of their tails in many supermarkets, although whole specimens are harder to obtain.

The recipe relies on reduction to thicken the sauce. Add any salt and pepper, if needed, towards the end of stage 6, after the sauce has been reduced. If you would rather not use wine, try diluted lemon juice.

As an alternative to rice, serve the dish with *croûtons*, pasta, mashed potato, or polenta (cornmeal).

If you are using chicken that has been frozen make sure that it is completely defrosted before beginning cooking. Also check that the chicken has been cooked right through before serving, and fry the eggs thoroughly on both sides.

Timings

Preparation time: 15 minutes
Cooking time: 75 minutes
Total time: 90 minutes

Ingredients

Serves 2
(U.S. equivalents are given in parentheses)

2 chicken breast fillets, skinless, each cut into 2 or 3 pieces
1 tablespoon olive oil
1 tablespoon plain (all-purpose) white flour
1 medium-sized onion, peeled and chopped finely
100 g (3½ oz) mushrooms, sliced
150 ml (⅔ cup) dry white wine
150 ml (⅔ cup) stock
2 garlic cloves, crushed
3 tablespoons concentrated tomato purée (tomato paste)
1 teaspoon parsley, chopped finely
150 g (5¼ oz) long-grain rice
2 medium-sized eggs

Method

1. Heat a large frying pan (skillet), and add the olive oil.

2. Dab the chicken pieces dry with a paper towel. Coat thinly in the flour, add to the pan, and sauté over a moderate heat for about 5 minutes, until lightly browned on both sides. (The coating of flour helps the chicken to cook crisply and evenly, without burning.) Remove the chicken pieces from the pan, and put aside in a lidded, medium-sized saucepan.

3. Add the onion and mushrooms to the frying pan, and sauté for about 6 minutes, turning occasionally. Once they are tender, tip them into the saucepan.

4. Remove the frying pan from the heat, and add the wine, stirring and using a spatula to scrape the base of the pan and incorporate the rich residue left from the sautéing. (This is known as deglazing. The addition of the wine must be done away from the heat to avoid the risk of the alcohol igniting.)

5. Pour the enriched wine from the frying pan into the saucepan. Add the stock, garlic, and tomato purée to the saucepan. Stir well. Bring to the boil, then reduce heat and simmer, covered, for 30 minutes.

6. Remove the saucepan lid and simmer for about another 30 minutes, or until the sauce has been reduced. It should become thick enough to coat the back of a metal spoon.

7. While the sauce is reducing, cook the rice, and fry the eggs.

8. Arrange a bed of rice on each plate. Spoon the chicken and sauce on top. Sprinkle with parsley. Garnish each plate with a fried egg.

Napoleon at his command post.

References

The following abbreviations have been used in the references to identify archive sources:

AN: *Archives nationales*, Paris.

SHD: *Service historique de la défense*, Vincennes.

Chapter 1: The Myth *(pages 1–17)*

1. Gruyer, p. 879.
2. According to the Austrians, they lost 963 men killed. French estimates of their own casualties varied, and tended to be understatements, but even the official account of 1805–6 admitted to as many as 1,100 dead. Berthier, p. 51. Herrmann, p. 198. Cugnac, *Campagne*, vol. 2, p. 456.
3. SHD 1M 1362: Observations sur la Bormida. SHD 1M 462: Renseignemens statistiques sur le terrain compris dans le plan du champ de bataille de Marengo, an X, report by Chef de btn J. B. Chabrier, of the Ingénieurs-géographes, to Gén Sanson, Directeur du Dépôt général de la guerre, dated Paris, 3 September 1802. The drainage ditches near Marengo have since been filled in. Trolard, vol. 2, pp. 126, 140.
4. Cugnac, *Campagne*, vol. 2, pp. 380–1.
5. Rauch, p. 372.
6. Adriani, p. 618.
7. However, the often-repeated claim that Melas actually sent a victory despatch to Vienna is another of the myths of Marengo. Herrmann, p. 164.
8. Rauch, p. 373.
9. Cugnac, *Campagne*, vol. 2, p. 400.
10. Cugnac, *Campagne*, vol. 2, p. 413.
11. Dunant's name is sometimes spelled 'Dunan', but he himself included the 't' in his signature. AN O2 23, folio 42: Service du Grand

maréchal du palais, gages de fructidor an XIII.

12. Anon, 'Origine du poulet à la Marengo' (1860), pp. 83–5.

13. Perhaps the tale originated from a confused recollection of Napoleon's subsequent visit to northern Italy at the end of 1807. At that time, one of the local prefects, or chief administrative officials, found him at Chivasso, just 13 miles north-east of Turin, eating fried lampreys and *œufs sur le plat* (eggs baked in an oven). Godard d'Aucourt, p. 75. Coghlan, p. 63. Valéry, *L'Italie*, p. 292.

14. AN O2* 22: Maison de l'empereur, service du Grand maréchal, registre de matricules, nos. 147, 164, 178. Carême and Plumerey, vol. 1, pp. xlv–xlvii.

15. Carême and Plumerey, vol. 1, pp. xlv–liii.

16. Peuchet, p. 172. Herbin de Halle, vol. 7, p. 354. SHD 1M 462: Renseignemens statistiques sur le terrain compris dans le plan du champ de bataille de Marengo, an X, report by Chef de btn J. B. Chabrier, of the Ingénieurs-géographes, to Gén Sanson, Directeur du Dépôt général de la guerre, dated Paris, 3 September 1802.

17. Bourrienne, vol. 4, pp. 126–7.

18. Méneval, vol. 1, pp. 145–50.

19. Roustam, p. xi.

20. Rambuteau, p. 75.

21. Constant, vol. 2, pp. 56–7.

22. Bourrienne, vol. 3, p. 211.

23. Soyer, p. 62.

24. *Almanach des gourmands* (1805), p. 200. Anon, *Le cuisinier méridional* (1835), pp. 43, 170.

25. Blanc. *Le guide des dîneurs* (1815), pp. 15, 94–103. The *Provençaux* in Paris may have been more distinctive and cohesive than other groups, but most of the capital's immigrants during and before Napoleon's rule came from the north and east of France, not the south. Tulard. *Nouvelle histoire*, p. 149.

26. Poulain and Rouyer, pp. 13–14. Soyer, p. 62.

27. Blagdon, vol. 1, p. 444.

28. Beauvilliers, vol. 1, pp. ix–x.

Chapter 2: The Campaign *(pages 18–38)*

1. Petit, pp. 14–16.

2. Petit, pp. 16–17. Constant, vol. 1, p. 57.

3. Constant, vol. 1, p. 56. Petit, p. 13. Bourrienne, vol. 4, p. 82. Cugnac, *Campagne*, vol. 1, pp. 446–7.

4. Napoléon, *Mémoires pour servir*, vol. 1, p. 253. Similar claims about deceiving Melas had already appeared in the French official history of

Marengo. Berthier, pp. 24–5.

5. Napoléon, *Mémoires pour servir*, vol. 1, pp. 254–6.

6. *Gazette nationale, ou le moniteur universel*, 27 germinal an VIII (17 April 1800).

7. Victor, pp. 216–18.

8. Deficiences certainly existed, as was inevitable in a hastily organized formation, but Napoleon subsequently covered up these organizational shortcomings by portraying them as part of a deliberate policy of deception. He claimed that the vast numbers of rations needed for the army arrived only as it reached key towns during its march to Switzerland, so as not to give prior warning of its route. Aulard, vol. 1, pp. 251, 254. Victor, pp. 218–19. Napoléon, *Mémoires pour servir*, vol. 1, p. 255. Berthier, pp. 24–5.

9. 'The enemy has not an inkling of the operation you are undertaking,' Napoleon wrote to Berthier on 2 May. 'I have very reliable intelligence that the Armée de réserve is a subject of mockery at Vienna and in Italy. They do not believe it will be ready before August, and regard it as an assembly of conscripts to complete the Armée du Rhin.' Cugnac, *Campagne*, vol. 1, p. 261. Yet Napoleon may have made this claim simply to try and inject some confidence into the frequently despondent Berthier. Even if the Austrians were in fact ridiculing the Armée de réserve, they might have been doing so merely as a propaganda exercise to boost the morale of their troops.

10. *The Morning Chronicle*, 19 April 1800.

11. Hüffer, *Quellen*, p. 226.

12. Napoleon, *Correspondance*, vol. 6, no. 4819.

13. Lathion, pp. 9, 34–5, 92.

14. Brockedon, vol. 1, p. 78.

15. Thomé, pp. 16, 19. Similarly, David's 1793 painting of the murdered French Revolutionary leader, Jean-Paul Marat, has striking similarities with Michelangelo's *Pietà*, showing the dead Christ. David thereby portrayed Marat as a Republican martyr, just as he depicted Napoleon as the superhuman arbiter of the world's destiny.

16. The bar on members of the Directory commanding the military was contained in Article 144 of the Constitution of Year III. In his correspondence in January–March 1800, Napoleon referred to commanding the Armée de réserve in person. But on 2 April, Berthier was formally appointed its commander.

17. Cugnac, *Campagne*, vol. 1, p. 262.

18. Napoleon, *Correspondance*, vol. 6, no. 4971.

19. Thiers, vol. 1, p. 375.

20. Lathion, pp. 124, 126. Lumbroso, vol. 1, p. xvii. Napoleon did wear a general's uniform at the Battle of Marengo, and it was this uniform

that David borrowed as a model for his painting of the crossing of the Alps.

21. Napoléon, *Mémoires pour servir,* vol. 1, p. 260. Rose, pp. 78–9. Thiers did not invent the detail about the guide being enabled to marry, but was misled by unreliable local accounts. The comte de Plancy, the Prefect of the Doire, claimed to have spoken with Napoleon's guide in June 1805. The guide – if indeed he was genuine – supposedly said that he had told Napoleon he would be able to marry if he could buy some tools to work as a master joiner, instead of simply as a craftsman making furniture. Godard d'Aucourt, pp. 53–4.

22. Lathion, pp. 87, 99. Cugnac, *Campagne,* vol. 1, p. 447. Napoleon, *Correspondance,* vol. 7, nos. 5644, 5832. Bourrienne, vol. 4, p. 82.

23. Napoleon, *Correspondance,* vol. 6, no. 4846.

24. Napoléon, *Mémoires pour servir,* vol. 1, p. 261. Lathion, p. 119.

25. Constant stated that Napoleon rode a horse, La Stirie, at the Grand Saint-Bernard, the same one that later carried him at Marengo. Constant, vol. 2, p. 82.

26. Lathion, p. 111.

27. Napoleon, *Correspondance,* vol. 6, no. 4836.

28. The bulk of Napoleon's own guns were still detained in the Alps, where the isolated Austrian stronghold of Fort Bard held out until 1 June.

29. Hüffer, *Quellen,* pp. 254, 259–60.

30. Hüffer, *Quellen,* pp. 305–6.

31. Neipperg, pp. 22–3. Mras (1823), vol. 3, no. 8, pp. 137–8. Hüffer, *Quellen,* p. 72. According to Bourrienne's memoirs, the double-agent was in fact working for Napoleon, who ordered Bourrienne after Marengo to reward him well. Bourrienne added that the agent was also rewarded by Melas, whom he had successfully misled. Bourrienne, vol. 4, p. 107.

32. Hüffer, *Quellen,* pp. 311–12, 325–6.

33. Zach believed that the French force that took Marengo on the evening of 13 June was only a small force, and that the main body would still come through Sale. Hüffer, *Quellen,* p. 75.

34. Victor, p. 166. Melas had given strict orders for the advance to be made with flags flying and bands playing. By insisting that the flags remained with the regiments, instead of being sent to safety in the rear, he wanted to ensure his troops fought as hard as possible. The sound of the bands was intended to boost morale, and help units keep abreast of each other even when hidden by the vegetation. Hüffer, *Quellen,* pp. 313–14.

35. Rauch, pp. 369–70. Neipperg, who was highly critical of the Austrian commander-in-chief and his team, claimed that Melas failed to

address the troops on the day before the battle. This is refuted by
Rauch's testimony. Neipperg, p. 27.

36. Melas's army order of 14 June (written by Radetzky) emphasized the
    need to advance with concentrated forces. It directed that the troops
    were not to disperse in skirmish order, but to remain closed up in
    pursuit of the French, ready to counter any attempt to rally and
    counter-attack. Hüffer, *Quellen*, p. 313.

Chapter 3: Marengo-Mania *(pages 39–50)*

1. Aulard, vol. 1, p. 435.
2. Cambacérès, vol. 1, p. 510.
3. AN F1c I 103: illuminations pour la bataille de Marengo, messidor an
    VIII.
4. Cugnac, *Campagne*, vol. 1, p. 511.
5. *Journal de Paris*, 30 nivôse an VIII (20 January 1800). Cabanis, pp. 11–
    13, 319. Napoleon, *Correspondance*, vol. 6, no. 4707.
6. Constant, vol. 1, p. 75.
7. Napoleon, *Correspondance*, vol. 6, no. 4949.
8. Napoleon, *Correspondance*, vol. 6, no. 5012.
9. Aulard, vol. 1, pp. 508, 512.
10. La Tour du Pin-Gouvernet, vol. 1, pp. 220–1.
11. Beauharnais, vol. 1, pp. 85–6.
12. *Journal de Paris*, 5 and 19 messidor, and 1 thermidor an VIII (24 June,
    8 and 20 July 1800). Lecomte, pp. 54, 56–7. Aulard, vol. 1, pp. 467,
    528. The subtitle, '*la voiture cassée*', referred to an accident at
    Montereau as Napoleon neared Paris during his return from Italy.
13. Pardoen, pp. 99–108. *Journal de Paris*, 10, 19, and 29 messidor an VIII
    (29 June, 8, 18 July 1800); 16 and 29 brumaire an IX (7, 20 November
    1800).
14. *Journal de Paris*, 20 messidor an VIII (9 July 1800).
15. Robertson, vol. 1, pp. 386–7.
16. *Journal de Paris*, 27 messidor an VIII (16 July 1800).
17. In addition, *gris marengo* was apparently a shade of grey, the same as
    that of Napoleon's overcoat. A *maringote* was a small, two-wheeled cart
    that reputedly came into use soon after the battle, but some sources
    indicate that it instead took its name from the town of Maringues in
    the *département* of the Puy-de-Dôme, where it originated. Du Bois,
    Glossaire, entry for 'maringote'. Anon, *Dictionnaire des dictionnaires*
    (1839), vol. 2, p. 390. France, Centre national de la recherche
    scientifique, vol. 11, pp. 387, 404. Robert, *Le grand Robert*, vol. 6,
    p. 253.
18. Not including merchant vessels or privateers. A privateer called

Marengo was captured by HMS *Albion* in 1803.

19. The last vessel, launched in 1869, and brought into service in 1872, retained the name *Marengo* despite the fall of the Second Empire in 1870, perhaps because it commemorated a Republican victory, won before Napoleon became Emperor. Roche, vol. 1, pp. 295–6.
20. www.onlymelbourne.com.au (accessed 22 May 2010).
21. Michel and Berger-Levrault (firms), p. 798.
22. www.co.iowa.ia.us (accessed 22 May 2010).
23. Owen, vol. 2, p. 935.
24. Hamilton and Brandon, pp. 4–5, 76, 110, 129. Osché and Künzi, pp. 255–6, 260.
25. The Jardin de Marengo became the Jardin de Prague after Algeria won independence.
26. Loyer de la Mettrie, p. 8. Playfair, p. 67.
27. www.nature.jardin.free.fr (accessed 4 June 2010).
28. SHD 1M 610: notes employées par le Gén Mathieu Dumas pour la correction de son 2e volume du précis des événements militaires pour les campagnes de 1799 et 1800 en Italie etc (nouvelle édition), Dampierre to Dumas, 17 July 1800.
29. Gruyer, p. 877.
30. Anon, 'La bataille de Marengo, d'après un témoin bourbonnais' (1911), p. 379.

Chapter 4: Creating a Legend *(pages 51–62)*

1. Kellermann later dismissed the words as an invention. 'It is doubtful if the First Consul made this speech, or if anyone was able to hear him', he wrote. SHD 1M 908/1: copy of Kellermann's notes on *Première relation de la bataille de Marengo*, note ref p. 297.
2. Cugnac, *Campagne*, vol. 2, p. 419. Bourrienne, vol. 4, p. 87.
3. Bonnal de Ganges, p. 260.
4. Cugnac, *Campagne*, vol. 2, pp. 415–16. Bonnal de Ganges, pp. 261–3. Desaix had in fact arrived three days before the battle.
5. Berthier also wrote a second, more detailed report, which he addressed to the Minister of War. Yet another report was written by Berthier's chief-of-staff, Dupont. There were no major differences in their essential points.
6. Cugnac, *Campagne*, vol. 2, p. 458.
7. Fazi du Bayet, p. 310. Pasquier, vol. 1, p. 158.
8. AN 390 AP/4: Fonds Bertrand, voyage en Italie, croquis de la manœuvre du 15 floréal an XIII sur le champ de bataille de Marengo.
9. Bausset, vol. 1, pp. 35–6. Avrillion, vol. 1, pp. 185–6. Constant, vol. 2, p. 195. Napoleon's uniform, worn at Marengo, is now preserved at the

Musée de l'armée at the Invalides, Paris.

10. Cugnac, *Campagne*, vol. 2, pp. 460–1. Camon, p. 41.
11. Berthier, pp. 41–2.
12. Berthier, pp. 48–9.
13. Cugnac, *Campagne*, vol. 2, p. 457. The final published version of events had some surprising inconsistencies: for example, the text referred to Carra Saint-Cyr's division, but the maps, and the order of battle, still listed Monnier as the divisional commander.
14. Camon, p. 44. Napoleon dictated his account of the Battle of Marengo to Gourgaud on 20 September 1816. Las Cases, vol. 3, pt 6, p. 165.
15. France, Dépôt général de la guerre, pp. 292–3.
16. Savary, Bourrienne, and Marmont all subsequently embroidered dubious tales based on this theme about the Bormida bridges in their unreliable memoirs. Lauriston and Gardanne were variously alleged to have been responsible for the failure to destroy – or report the existence of – the bridges, yet it is notable that the career of neither man suffered as a result of Marengo. Gardanne, for example, was awarded a sabre of honour in July 1800, 'for having conducted himself with as much bravery as intelligence at the Battle of Marengo'. *Gazette nationale, ou le moniteur universel*, 12 thermidor an X (31 July 1802), *1er supplément . . . tableaux à annexer à l'arrêté du 27 messidor an X*, p. 19. Savary, vol. 1, p. 265. Bourrienne, vol. 4, p. 98. Marmont, vol. 2, p. 128. Dampierre, pp. 803–4. Napoléon, *Mémoires pour servir*, vol. 1, p. 286. France, Dépôt général de la guerre, p. 312.
17. Junot, vol. 2, p. 179.

Chapter 5: Disputing a Legend *(pages 63–88)*

1. Croker, vol. 2, p. 287.
2. Plumptre, vol. 3, p. 354.
3. SHD 1M 908/1: copy of Kellermann's notes on the Austrian account of 1823, note ref p. 344.
4. Anon, 'La bataille de Marengo, d'après un témoin bourbonnais' (1911), p. 380.
5. Savary, vol. 1, pp. 266–7. Savary was the ADC whom Desaix sent to Napoleon. He (or at least his ghost-writer) later wrote that Desaix marched early in the morning from Rivalta for Novi, and halted on hearing gunfire soon after dawn. But Boudet, who commanded the division under Desaix's orders, stated in his report soon after the battle that the division had set out from Rivalta only towards noon. Neither Boudet nor another key witness, Dalton, mentioned Desaix hearing gunfire or reacting to it. Gunfire alone would have been an inadequate reason for Desaix to have abandoned his detached mission

on his own initiative. Herrmann, pp. 134–5.

6. Kellermann, *Histoire*, p. 176.
7. Cugnac, *Campagne*, vol. 2, pp. 391, 393–401.
8. Bonnal de Ganges, p. 114.
9. Cugnac, *Campagne*, vol. 2, p. 399.
10. Cugnac, *Campagne*, vol. 2, p. 412–13. The *capitaine* was Charles Lefebvre-Desnouëttes, one of Napoleon's ADCs.
11. Ségur, vol. 2, p. 72.
12. Marmont, vol. 2, p. 137. Cugnac, *Campagne*, vol. 2, pp. 412–13, 421, 428.
13. Bourrienne, vol. 4, pp. 127–8. Cugnac, *Campagne*, vol. 2, pp. 412–13.
14. Syntax, pp. 110–12.
15. Constant, vol. 1, pp. 67, 69.
16. Napoleon, *Correspondance*, vol. 6, nos.4927, 5006. Sauzet, p. 300. Bonnal de Ganges, p. 357. Quintin, p. 265. Vidal, p. 22.
17. Cugnac, *Campagne*, vol. 2, p. 420.
18. Chazal, p. 2. Debry, p. 3.
19. Napoleon, *Correspondance*, vol. 6, no. 4953; vol. 8, nos. 6545, 6732. Barbey, pp. 90, 94.
20. AN AF/IV/1050, 1st dossier, folio 35: Denon to Nap, 19 June 1805.
21. Desaix crossed the Alps by the Petit Saint-Bernard pass on 7 June. Bonnal de Ganges, p. 247. Sauzet, p. 273.
22. *Gazette nationale, ou le moniteur universel*, 28 prairial an XI (17 June 1803). Aulard, vol. 1, pp. 437–8. Villiers, p. 268. Pessard, pp. 350, 456. Constant, vol. 1, p. 71. Roquefort, pp. 172, 460. Poisson, pp. 42–3. Fouché, pp. 48, 51. Duval, p. 15. The place Dauphine was located on the Ile de la Cité; it had been renamed place Thionville during the Revolution, and now became known as the place Desaix.
23. Thibaudeau, *Mémoires de A.-C. Thibaudeau*, p. 288. Napoleon, *Correspondance*, vol. 8, no. 6355; vol. 30, p. 83. Biver, pp. 154–5. Gourgaud, vol. 2, pp. 186, 423.
24. *Mercure de France* (25 August 1810), p. 495. Biver, pp. 157–60. Pessard, pp. 456, 1587. Lazare, p. 669. Poisson, p. 183.
25. Méneval, vol. 1, pp. 382–3.
26. Rœderer, p. 10. Hortense, vol. 1, p. 59.
27. Marmont, vol. 2, p. 139.
28. Las Cases, vol. 1, pt 1, p. 246. Camon, pp. 44–6.
29. O'Meara, vol. 1, pp. 237–8. Las Cases, vol. 1, pt 2, p. 10. Gourgaud, vol. 1, p. 59.
30. Bertrand, vol. 2, p. 436.
31. Amalvi, pp. 179–91.
32. Cugnac, *Campagne*, vol. 2, pp. 405–6.

33. Marmont, vol. 2, pp. 133–4.
34. Cugnac, *Campagne*, vol. 2, pp. 419, 458.
35. Kellermann, 'Eclaircissemens historiques', pp. 126–7.
36. Savary, vol. 1, pp. 273–5. The fact that Savary was sent with orders to Kellermann was confirmed by a third party: Marmont wrote that Savary had come to him in the middle of his massed battery, and had asked where Kellermann was located, so he could take him his orders. Marmont had pointed him in the direction. Marmont, vol. 2, p. 140.
37. Savary, vol. 4, pt 2, p. 227.
38. Quérard, vol. 8, p. 495.
39. Kellermann, *Réfutation*, p. 5.
40. Cugnac, *Campagne*, vol. 2, pp. 404–5.
41. Cugnac, *Campagne*, vol. 2, pp. 399–400.
42. Marmont, vol. 2, pp. 132–4.
43. Kellermann himself later claimed that he had to use his superior rank to compel Bessières to charge with the Guard cavalry in the evening of Marengo. SHD 1M 908/1: copy of Kellermann's notes on *Première relation de la bataille de Marengo*, note ref. p. 281; and copy of his notes on *Deuxième relation*, note ref. p. 303.
44. Bourrienne, vol. 4, pp. 124–6.
45. Kellermann stated that he did not recall this particular discussion with Napoleon, but admitted that Napoleon more than once expressed himself favourably, saying he would never forget the charge of Marengo. Kellermann, *Deuxième et dernière réplique*, p. 17. Savary, vol. 4, pt 2, p. 247.
46. Kellermann, 'Eclaircissemens historiques', p. 129.
47. Victor, p. 433.
48. Bourrienne, vol. 4, pp. 71–2.
49. Bourrienne, vol. 4, pp. 121–2.
50. Las Cases, vol. 3, pt 6, p. 9.
51. Cugnac, *Campagne*, vol. 2, p. 412.
52. Marmont, vol. 2, pp. 132–4.
53. This account was by one of Napoleon's corps commanders, Général de division Victor, and can be found in his memoirs. He based it on a second-hand recall of the unpublished recollections of Dupont, the chief-of-staff of the Armée de réserve. Victor, pp. 181, 434.
54. Cugnac, *Campagne*, vol. 1, p. 228.

Chapter 6: Commemorating a Legend *(pages 89–107)*

1. SHD 1M 610: notes employées par le Gén Mathieu Dumas pour la correction de son 2e volume du précis des événements militaires pour les campagnes de 1799 et 1800 en Italie etc. (nouvelle édition), copy

of a letter from Guénand to Napoleon, protesting at his deeds at Marengo being overlooked, 25 June 1800.

2. SHD 1M 610: notes employées par le Gén Mathieu Dumas. By the time he wrote this note, Guénand was already suffering from the chest illness that would kill him in May 1803.

3. Neipperg, p. 32.

4. Varnhagen, *Denkwürdigkeiten*, vol. 2, p. 293.

5. Fillon, 'Carle Vernet', p. 451.

6. Napoleon, *Correspondance*, vol. 28, no. 21780. Vernet needed the money, for his expenses in painting the vast picture, including the construction of a large enough studio, had almost equalled the 20,000 francs he had been paid. AN AF/IV/989, folios 13 and 14: Conseil des ministres, 1 December 1813, reports and draft decrees submitted to Napoleon.

7. Napoleon, *Correspondance*, vol. 10, no. 8687.

8. Napoleon, *Correspondance*, vol. 10, no. 8688.

9. Massobrio, *Che si salga*, p. 26.

10. Napoleon, *Correspondance*, vol. 8, no. 6287.

11. Napoleon, *Correspondance*, vol. 8, nos. 6306, 6337.

12. Napoleon, *Correspondance*, vol. 8, no. 6675.

13. SHD 1M 1385: rapport sur Alexandrie, avec un plan, par le Gén d'Anthouard, 15 December 1813.

14. SHD 1M 1362: copy of Tableaux politiques, statistiques et financières des six nouveaux départements formés du ci-devant Piémont.

15. SHD 1M 462: Renseignemens statistiques sur le terrain compris dans le plan du champ de bataille de Marengo, an X, report by Chef de btn J. B. Chabrier, of the Ingénieurs-géographes, to Gén Sanson, Directeur du Dépôt général de la guerre, dated Paris, 3 September 1802.

16. Ibid.

17. Woloch, p. 231.

18. Napoleon, *Correspondance*, vol. 8, no. 6334.

19. Napoleon, *Correspondance*, vol. 9, no. 7523.

20. Napoleon, *Correspondance*, vol. 9, no. 7154.

21. Napoleon, *Correspondance*, vol. 8, no. 6334.

22. SHD Xn 3: extrait des registres des délibérations du gouvernement de la République, 15 June 1803.

23. SHD Xn 5: contrôle nominatif des militaires faisant partie du camp de vétérans de la 27e Division militaire à l'époque du 12 août 1810. Signed at Bosco, 14 August 1810.

24. Another 8 per cent had died.

25. Calculated from SHD Xn 5: état général de tous les individus reçus au camp de vétérans de la 27e Division militaire, depuis sa formation,

jusqu'au 1er janvier 1809, et de toutes les mutations qui ont eu lieu jusqu'à la même époque. Signed 29 March 1809.

26. Napoleon, *Correspondance*, vol. 12, no. 9817.

27. SHD Xn 1: report to Napoleon about the veterans' camps, 24 March 1815.

28. It is suspected that the pyramid was built near the Cascina Poggi, about 1.75 miles east or north-east of Marengo, where Napoleon apparently conducted the manoeuvres on 5 May 1805. Massobrio, *Che si salga*, pp. 27–30. Oliva, p. 298.

29. Heine, pp. 43–6.

30. Griffin, vol. 1, p. 150.

31. Eustace, vol. 2, p. 324. Valéry, *Voyages*, vol. 5, p. 84. Fillon and Lot, p. 489. Massobrio, *Che si salga*, p. 10. Beaufort, pp. 277–8. Biasoletto, pp. 176–7. Murray, John, *Handbook for travellers in southern Germany*, p. 546. Civalieri-Inviziati, pp. 4–6.

32. Delavo, *L'ingratitude*, p. 14.

33. Anon, *Marengo et ses monuments* (1854), p. 42. Gould, pp. 121–8.

34. Lathion, pp. 129–30.

35. Delavo, *A la mémoire*, pp. 7–8.

36. Gould, p. 119. Delavo, *L'ingratitude*, p. 61.

37. MacFarlane, vol. 2, p. 232.

38. *Journal des débats politiques et littéraires* (4 June 1856), p. 4.

39. Anon, 'To be sold by auction' (1856), p. 541.

Chapter 7: 'It smells of the Revolution' *(pages 108–123)*

1. Similarly, the second edition of *Le parfait cuisinier*, published in 1811, contained thirty-five pages of poultry recipes, yet not a single mention of chicken Marengo, or any variant of it. Raimbault, pp. 92–127.

2. Löbel, vol. 7, p. 269. This particular volume was published in 1817.

3. Wybranowski, pp. 19–20.

4. Anon, *Diary of an excursion to France* (1814), p. 78.

5. Smirnov, Miltchina, and Ospovat, p. 143.

6. Blanc, *Le guide des dîneurs* (1815).

7. Alméras, pp. 127–8. Véron, vol. 1, p. 120; vol. 3, pp. 2–3.

8. Spang, pp. 1–2, 64–5, 149–51, 158, 204, 206.

9. Capefigue, vol. 2, pp. 212–13. Capefigue's research was superficial: *sauce Robert*, for example, had existed for at least a century before the Revolution.

10. Lacroix, p. 17. *Almanach des gourmands* (1805), pp. 201–2.

11. *Almanach des gourmands* (1807), p. 328.

12. *Almanach des gourmands* (1807), pp. 338–9. Reichardt, *Un hiver*, p. 226. *Journal de Paris*, 8 nivôse an IX (29 December 1800).

13. *Journal des débats politiques et littéraires* (10 August 1820), pp. 3–4.
14. Thackeray, *Burlesques*, p. 170. See also Lytton, vol. 1, p. 78.
15. Villiers, p. 12. Pessard, pp. 304, 1265. The place de Marengo has since disappeared as a result of the extension of the rue de Rivoli.
16. Carême, *Le maître d'hôtel*, vol. 2, p. 167. Spang, p. 187.
17. Salgues, pp. 160–1.
18. Spang, pp. 149–51, 158, 204, 206.
19. Shelley, vol. 1, p. 137.
20. Reichardt, *Vertraute Briefe*, pt 2, pp. 195–6.
21. Gozlan, p. 78.
22. Gronow, *Captain Gronow's last recollections*, p. 78. Some editions of Gronow mispell Jacqueminot's name as Jacquinot.
23. The escapade must have occurred before 25 July 1814, which was when Hortense left Saint-Leu for a lengthy health cure at Plombières. Maillard, p. 187.
24. Cochelet, vol. 1, pp. 417–18.
25. Véron, vol. 1, p. 232.
26. Cochelet, vol. 1, pp. 418–19. Doher, p. 71. Labédoyère had fallen in love with Hortense in 1806, but she was already in an unhappy marriage with Napoleon's brother Louis. Hortense, vol. 1, pp. 149–50.
27. Cochelet, vol. 1, pp. 420, 423.
28. Cussy, vol. 1, pp. 59–60.
29. Quintin, pp. 18, 506–7.
30. Kielmannsegge, pp. 179–80.
31. SHD 7 Yd 1157: dossier of GdeD Anatole-Charles-Alexis, marquis de Lawoëstine. SHD 7 Yd 1143: dossier of GdeD Jean-François Jacqueminot. SHD 2 Ye 2402: dossier of Charles-Emmanuel Lecouteulx de Canteleu. Quintin, pp. 434–5.
32. SHD 7 Yd 1143: dossier of GdeD Jean-François Jacqueminot.
33. Cochelet, vol. 1, p. 420. No mention of the escapade is to be found in the officers' dossiers at the Service historique de la défense.
34. Doher, pp. 73, 145.

Chapter 8: Pinnacle of Fame *(pages 124–138)*

1. Lovell, pp. 97–8, 113. Thomas, pp. 1596–9.
2. Anon, 'New cemetery projects' (1825), p. 369.
3. Lytton, vol. 1, p. 79.
4. Anon, 'A palatable pilgrimage' (1838), pp. 493–3. Jewett, vol. 1, p. 312. Vandam, vol. 2, p. 152.
5. O'Meara, vol. 1, p. 62. Abell, p. 35.
6. Mathews, p. 164. Reid, vol. 2, p. 406.
7. Richardin, pp. 358–9.

8. Stanhope, p. 233.
9. Reid, vol. 2, pp. 411–12. C. H. Scott, *The Baltic*, p. 93.
10. Devereux, p. 209. Barnard, p. 297.
11. Hardman, p. 114.
12. Thackeray, *Early and late papers*, p. 32.
13. Cooper, vol. 2, p. 13.
14. Mitchell, pp. 327–8.
15. Kotzebue, vol. 2, pp. 78–9.
16. Sanderson, vol. 1, p. 106. Raffles, pp. 80–1.
17. Jewett, vol. 1, pp. 302–5.
18. Fayot, p. 40. Dix, p. 258.
19. Ranhofer, pp. 432–3.
20. Hassell, p. 50.
21. Anon, 'A gastronomic survey' (1839), p. 470.
22. Thackeray, *Early and late papers*, p. 23.
23. Sala. *Quite alone*, pp. 259–60.
24. Blagdon, vol. 1, pp. 454–6. Montigny, vol. 1, p. 235.
25. Allard, pp. 76–7. Payne, pp. 289–90.
26. *Nouvel almanach des gourmands* (1825), pp. 211–12.
27. Kotzebue, vol. 2, pp. 225–6. Salgues, p. 462.
28. Blanc, *Le guide des dîneurs* (1814), pp. 94–103.
29. Allard, p. 76.
30. Bailey, p. 38.
31. Gribble, pp. 92–3.

Chapter 9: Napoleon and his Meals *(pages 139–160)*

1. Balmain, p. 159. O'Meara, vol. 2, p. 290. Bertrand, vol. 2, pp. 441–2. Saint-Denis, p. 164.
2. Fain, p. 4. Bausset, vol. 1, p. 3. Constant, vol. 2, p. 55.
3. Constant, vol. 2, p. 56. Masson, *Napoléon chez lui* (1921), p. 130. Bausset, vol. 1, p. 3. Méneval, vol. 2, p. 40. Caulaincourt, vol. 2, p. 387. Godard d'Aucourt, pp. 225–6.
4. Lejeune, vol. 1, pp. 251–2. Saint-Denis, p. 28. Masson. *Napoléon chez lui* (1921), p. 137. Avrillion, vol. 1, pp. 151–2. Durand, *Mémoires*, p. 117.
5. Masson. *Napoléon chez lui* (1921), pp. 137–9. Méneval, vol. 1, p. 424.
6. Masson. *Napoléon chez lui* (1921), pp. 136–7. Saint-Denis, p. 26. Marchand, vol. 2, p. 261. Constant, vol. 3, pp. 300–1; vol. 5, p. 38. Méneval, vol. 2, pp. 464–5. Durand, *Mémoires*, p. 117.
7. Marchand, vol. 2, pp. 260–1. Durand, *Mémoires*, p. 115. Bertrand was appointed the Grand Marshal of the Palace in 1813, after a cannonball killed Géraud Duroc, who had hitherto held the post.

8. Masson. *Napoléon chez lui* (1921), pp. 139–40. Saint-Denis, p. 29. Hortense, vol. 2, p. 37. Fain, p. 64. Méneval, vol. 2, p. 41.

9. Ségur, vol. 2, p. 231. Napoleon on this occasion was wearing the blue coat of the *grenadiers à pied* of the Guard.

10. Constant, vol. 1, pp. x–xi.

11. Bausset, vol. 1, pp. 3, 6. Saint-Denis, p. 27. Avrillion, vol. 1, pp. 135–6. Constant, vol. 2, pp. 64–5.

12. Potocka, p. 278. Constant, vol. 2, pp. 55, 155; vol. 6, p. 161. Masson. *Napoléon chez lui* (1921), p. 220. Bausset, vol. 1, pp. 6–7, 9. Méneval, vol. 1, p. 132.

13. Arnault, vol. 4, pp. 7–9. Beugnot, p. 223.

14. Fain, pp. 187, 191. Avrillion, vol. 1, p. 115. Bausset, vol. 1, p. 377. Masson. *Napoléon chez lui* (1921), p. 220. Constant, vol. 2, p. 155.

15. Bausset, vol. 1, p. 378. Las Cases, vol. 2, pt 4, p. 114.

16. Hortense, vol. 2, pp. 28–9. Masson, *Napoléon chez lui* (1921), p. 220. Marchand, vol. 1, pp. 72–3.

17. Masson, *Napoléon chez lui* (1921), pp. 130, 223–4. Avrillion, vol. 2, p. 101. Bausset, vol. 1, p. 7. Constant, vol. 6, p. 159.

18. Fain, p. 193. Bausset, vol. 1, p. 7. Constant, vol. 2, pp. 54–6; vol. 6, p. 159. Rœderer, p. 107. Saint-Denis, p. 163. Masson, *Napoléon chez lui* (1921), p. 269.

19. Masson, *Napoléon chez lui* (1921), p. 218. Abell, pp. 123–4. Hortense, vol. 1, pp. 60–1.

20. Potocka, pp. 261, 274–90.

21. Fain, pp. 3–4, 199–203. Constant, vol. 2, pp. 6, 69. Marchand, vol. 1, p. 49.

22. Masson, *Napoléon chez lui* (1921), pp. 238–9. Bourrienne, vol. 4, p. 315. Constant, vol. 2, p. 73.

23. Saint-Denis, pp. 315–16. Constant, vol. 4, pp. 139–41.

24. Thiard, p. 9.

25. Méneval, vol. 1, p. 142.

26. Avrillion, vol. 1, pp. 259–60. Constant, vol. 1, p. 239. Saint-Denis, pp. 170–1.

27. AN O2 16, folio 5: règlement pour le service de Mr le Grand maréchal du palais. Fain, p. 193. Constant, vol. 1, pp. 172–3.

28. Masson, *Napoléon chez lui* (1921), pp. 129, 220. Constant, vol. 2, pp. 58, 308. Durand, *Mémoires*, p. 39.

29. Réal, vol. 1, pp. 359–60. O'Meara, vol. 2 p. 226.

30. Marchand, vol. 1, p. 47. Las Cases, vol. 1, pt 1, p. 267; vol. 2, pt 3, p. 314. Constant, vol. 2, p. 63.

31. Constant, vol. 1, p. 238.

32. Divova, pp. 84–5. Masson, *Napoléon chez lui* (1921), p. 144. Carême and Plumerey, vol. 5, pp. xxi–xxii.

33. Masson, *Napoléon chez lui* (1921), p. 271. Las Cases, vol. 1, pt 2, pp. 292–4.
34. Fain, p. 10.
35. Calculated from data in Appendix 1 of Guerrini.
36. Fain, pp. 224–5. Thiard, pp. 134–6.
37. Constant, vol. 3, p. 322–3. Fain, p. 245. Bausset, vol. 1, p. 88; vol. 2, pp. 44–5.
38. Constant, vol. 1, p. 56; vol. 2, pp. 284–5. Pils, pp. 143, 228.
39. Warden, pp. 114–18. Lavallette, vol. 1, p. 191. Fain, pp. 226–7. Chłapowski, pp. 12–15.
40. Ségur, vol. 2, pp. 456–9. Thiard, pp. 213–14, 217.
41. Caulaincourt, vol. 2, p. 38.
42. Bausset, vol. 2, pp. 81–2. Constant, vol. 2, p. 285. Saint-Denis, p. 111. Pétiet, p. 34.
43. Buhle, pp. 17–18.
44. Constant, vol. 2, pp. 239–40.
45. Lejeune, vol. 1, pp. 52, 396. Brett-James, p. 241.
46. Bertrand, vol. 1, p. 151.
47. Gourgaud, vol. 1, pp. 273–4, 405; vol. 2, p. 145. Bertrand, vol. 1, p. 151. Las Cases, vol. 4, pt.7, pp. 185–7.
48. Roth, pp. 25–6, 44–5, 48–9, 51, 115, 330–1.
49. Pilcher, p. 56.
50. Masson, *Le sacre*, p. 218.
51. Lanzac de Laborie, vol. 5, pp. 176–7. *Journal des débats*, 16 frimaire an X (7 December 1801).
52. Napoleon said that Parmentier had done mankind a great service, and urged the farmers on the island of Elba to grow them. Pons (de l'Hérault), p. 280. Macdonogh, pp. 203–4. Pitte, p. 102.
53. Napoleon, *Correspondance*, vol. 23, no. 18568. Larsen, p. 144. Modern analysis has shown, in fact, that Rumford's soups did not in themselves meet today's daily recommended intake of calories, partly because of his flawed belief in the nutrional qualities of cooked water. They also contained inadequate amounts of calcium, but did generally provide the necessary protein, potassium, and iron. Heller, pp. 499–500.
54. Tulard, *Nouvelle histoire*, pp. 249, 261.

Chapter 10: **The Belly of an Emperor** *(pages 161–182)*

1. Masson, *Napoléon chez lui* (1910), p. 232; (1921), p. 130. Carême, 'Notice historique', p. 51. Constant, vol. 2, p. 57.
2. Shorter, p. 315. Caulaincourt, vol. 2, p. 387. O'Meara, vol. 1, p. 26. Antommarchi, vol. 1, p. 104. Carême, 'Notice historique', p. 50.

Avrillion, vol. 1, p. 246. Pons (de l'Hérault), p. 250. Maitland, p. 120.

3. Montholon, *Récits*, vol. 1, p. 139. Gourgaud, vol. 1, pp. 59, 61. Dr Walter Henry, surgeon with the 66th Regiment of Foot, described how he caught a dolphin while sailing back to England from Saint Helena in 1821, just weeks after Napoleon's death. He handed it over to the cook, who converted it into chops for dinner. 'The fish turned out excellent', reported Henry, 'with much salmon flavour.' Henry, vol. 2, p. 95.

4. Marchand, vol. 2, p. 26. Las Cases, vol. 1, pt 1, p. 205. Rose, p. 187. Montholon, *Récits*, vol. 1, pp. 143, 145. Gourgaud, vol. 1, pp. 63–4. Saint-Denis, p. 142.

5. Masson, *Napoléon chez lui* (1921), p. 130. Caulaincourt, vol. 2, p. 387. Constant, vol. 2, p. 57. Saint-Denis, p. 162. Marchand, vol. 1, p. 50. Bertrand, vol. 2, p. 134; vol. 3, p. 81.

6. Saint-Denis, p. 162. Pons (de l'Hérault), pp. 67–8. Bertrand, vol. 2, p. 134. Carême, 'Notice historique', p. 50. Marchand, vol. 2, p. 99. Gourgaud, vol. 2, p. 361.

7. Saint-Denis, pp. 122, 162. Bertrand, vol. 3, p. 65.

8. Méneval, vol. 1, p. 416.

9. Malcolm, pp. 48–9. Bertrand, vol. 1, pp. 105, 324. O'Meara, vol. 1, pp. 90–1. Las Cases, vol. 3, pt 5, p. 248. Montholon, *Récits*, vol. 1, p. 353.

10. Potocka, p. 279. Fain, p. 192. Marchand, vol. 1, p. 50. Bausset, vol. 1, pp. 88–9. O'Meara, vol. 1, p. 26. Saint-Denis, p. 162.

11. Masson and Biagi, vol. 1, pp. 35–6.

12. Durand, *Mémoires*, p. 38. Constant, vol. 3, pp. 290–1.

13. AN O2 6, folio 21: soumission pour les volailles et gibier, 27 November 1804.

14. AN O2 16, folio 7: copie du marché passé, pour dépenses de cuisine, 20 May 1807.

15. Méneval, vol. 1, pp. 144–5.

16. Saint-Denis, pp. 162–3. Bertrand, vol. 2, p. 134.

17. Carême, 'Notice historique', p. 49.

18. Raisson and Romieu, pp. 123–4. Masson, *Napoléon chez lui* (1921), p. 222. It has been pointed out that Napoleon's meals would not have impressed a true gastronome. The menus drawn up under the supervision of his prefect of the palace, Bausset, might break some of the key rules of fine dining, for example by including two soups that were too similar to provide a proper balance. But too much emphasis has been laid on such objections. Criticism of prominent practitioners by envious theoreticians is nothing new. The essential point about Napoleon's meals is that they were neither parsimonious nor extravagant. Napoleon may have broken some of the rules of fine

dining, but he nonetheless dined on fine dishes that belied his image as a man who invariably ate plain, straightforward food.

19. Las Cases, vol. 1, pt 1, p. 389.
20. Fain, p. 287. Constant, vol. 1, p. 247; vol. 2, pp. 52–3.
21. Méneval, vol. 2, p. 36.
22. Constant, vol. 2, p. 57.
23. Bausset, vol. 2, p. 44. Saint-Denis, p. 162.
24. Bausset, vol. 2, p. 45. Marchand, vol. 1, p. 50.
25. Las Cases, vol. 1, pt 1, p. 392. Masson, *Napoléon chez lui* (1921), p. 132. Saint-Denis, p. 163.
26. Bingham, pp. 546–7. Abell, p. 78.
27. AN O2 23, folio 178: Maison de l'empereur, service du Grand maréchal du palais, état pour servir au paiement des gages des gens employés au service de la Maison de Leurs Majestés pendant le mois de janvier 1813.
28. In 1806, Napoleon had six carvers (two *chefs-tranchants*, and four *aides-tranchants*). AN O2* 7, folio 12: service du Grand maréchal, dépense ordinaire. The employees in January 1813 included a head carver (*chef-tranchant*), and four carvers (*tranchants*). AN O2 23, folio 178: Maison de l'empereur, service du Grand maréchal du palais, état pour servir au paiement des gages des gens employés au service de la Maison de Leurs Majestés pendant le mois de janvier 1813.
29. Las Cases, vol. 1, pt 1, pp. 266–7.
30. Méneval, vol. 3, pp. 4–5.
31. Caulaincourt, vol. 2, pp. 209, 387.
32. Castellane, vol. 1, p. 153.
33. Soltyk, p. 45. Caulaincourt, vol. 2, pp. 77–8, 116, 139.
34. Napoleon, *Correspondance*, vol. 24, no. 19608.
35. Bertrand, vol. 2, p. 137.
36. Bartel, p. 170.
37. Masson and Biagi, vol. 1, p. 216.
38. Las Cases, vol. 2, pt 4, p. 122. Cronin, p. 21. Bertrand, vol. 3, p. 65. Masson and Biagi, vol. 1, p. 35.
39. Avrillion, vol. 1, pp. 135–6.
40. Marchand, vol. 1, p. 51. Constant, vol. 2, pp. 90, 92. Méneval, vol. 2, p. 38. Roustam, p. 168. Durand, *Mémoires*, p. 40.
41. Reichardt, *Vertraute Briefe*, pt 1, pp. 355–6; Divova, p. 85.
42. Fayot, p. 275.
43. Avrillion, vol. 2, p. 101. Las Cases, vol. 1, pt 1, pp. 390–1. Bausset, vol. 1, pp. 88–9.
44. Las Cases, vol. 2, pt 3, p. 5. Véron, vol. 1, p. 125. Castellane, vol. 1, p. 112.
45. Durand, *Mémoires*, p. 284.

46. *Tirant d'eau* was an expression Napoleon is recorded as having used in various circumstances. He also used it, for example, to describe the capacity of his generals in terms of keenness and courage. Las Cases, vol. 1, pt 1, p. 392; vol. 1, pt 2, p. 10. Fain, pp. 288–9.
47. Maitland, p. 223. Shorter, p. 308. Bingham, p. 541. Cockburn, p. 60. Warden, pp. 27–8. Rose, pp. 122–3. Betsy Balcombe, the teenage daughter of Napoleon's host during his first weeks on Saint Helena, stated that Napoleon lived very simply, cared little what he ate, and 'did not admire highly seasoned dishes'. Abell, pp. 34, 167. But she may have taken this information from the memoirs of Napoleon's servants, rather than from her own memory, for her book was published only in 1844, more than two decades after his death.
48. Cockburn, p. 61. Rose, p. 229.
49. Smetham, pp. 135–6.
50. Home, pp. 251–2.
51. Las Cases, vol. 1, pt 1, pp. 100–1. Gourgaud, vol. 1, pp. 51–2. Montholon, *Récits*, vol. 1, p. 96. Arnault, vol. 4, p. 81. Bingham, p. 542.
52. Younghusband, pp. 150–1. Fain, p. 192.
53. Shorter, p. 60. Henry, vol. 2, pp. 15, 22–3.
54. Switzerland, Napoleon-Museum Arenenberg, p. 109. Broadley, vol. 2, p. 64.
55. AN O2 16, folio 613: bordereau des dépenses faites pour cave pendant le voyage de l'empereur en janvier, février et mars 1814. The total of 17,809 francs 75 centimes was spent between 26 January and 13 April 1814.
56. AN O2 16, folio 48: état pour servir au paiement des gages des gens employés au service de la Maison de LL MM pendant le mois d'avril année 1810.
57. Bertrand, vol. 2, p. 134. Napoleon also claimed that *déjeuner* was his biggest meal, and that he ate little at *dîner*, but this was untrue. He made the claim in 1818, at a time when he faced the prospect of having to simplify his meals because of the illness of Pierron, his *chef d'office*, and was undoubtedly trying to convince himself, and his companions, that the prospect of retrenchment was nothing to be feared.
58. Bausset, vol. 1, pp. 7–8. Caulaincourt, vol. 2, p. 387. Avrillion, vol. 2, p. 101. O'Meara, vol. 1, p. 26. Bourrienne, vol. 3, p. 211. Saint-Denis, pp. 29, 163. Constant, vol. 2, pp. 6, 57. Durand, *Mémoires*, p. 38. Masson, *Napoléon chez lui* (1921), p. 227.
59. Saint-Denis, p. 163.
60. O'Meara, vol. 2 p. 257. Bartel, p. 65. Masson and Biagi, vol. 1, p. 90. Las Cases, vol. 1, pt 1, p. 391; vol. 2, pt 3, pp. 259–60.
61. Rœderer, vol. 2 p. 114.

62. Constant, vol. 2, pp. 57–8. Bourrienne, vol. 1, p. 576.

63. Thiard, pp. 154–5.

64. Masson, *Napoléon chez lui* (1921), pp. 133–4. Saint-Denis, p. 163–4. Durand, *Mémoires*, p. 293. Las Cases, vol. 1, pt 2, pp. 313–14.

65. Bausset, vol. 1, p. 7; vol. 2, pp. 81–2. Marchand, vol. 1, p. 50; vol. 2, pp. 161–2, 248. Constant, vol. 1, p. 244; vol. 2, p. 285; vol. 5, pp. 61–2. Rapp, p. 201.

66. Maitland, p. 223. Bingham, pp. 541, 543. Saint-Denis, p. 163.

67. Bausset, vol. 2, p. 251. Constant, vol. 2, pp. 87–8. Las Cases, vol. 2, pt 4, p. 246. Fain, p. 288.

68. Réal, vol. 1, pp. 197–8.

69. Constant, vol. 2, p. 88; vol. 3, pp. 302–3. Méneval, vol. 1, pp. 144–5.

Chapter 11: Saint Helena *(pages 183–191)*

1. Marchand, vol. 2, pp. 119–20.

2. Balmain, p. 110.

3. Henry, vol. 2, p. 54.

4. Montchenu, pp. 118–19.

5. Carême, 'Notice historique', p. 50. Beatson, pp. 184–5, 329–30. Barnes, pp. 179–80.

6. Rose, p. 236.

7. Carême, 'Notice historique', p. 50. Masson, 'Les cuisiniers', p. 249. Duncan, pp. 145–6, 218. Beatson, p. xxxvii.

8. Marchand, vol. 2, pp. 265–6. Saint-Denis, p. 210. Pons (de l'Hérault), pp. 280, 291.

9. Balmain, pp. 233–4, 237–8. Lutyens, p. 32, 54. Montchenu, pp. 187–9.

10. Masson, 'Les cuisiniers', pp. 254–8, 261.

11. Cabanès, *Au chevet*, p. 148. Las Cases, vol. 1, pt 1, p. 389. Saint-Denis, p. 184.

12. Napoleon, *Correspondance*, vol. 24, no. 19365.

13. Méneval, vol. 2, p. 35.

14. Constant, vol. 2, p. 59–60.

15. Pasquier, vol. 2, pp. 85–6.

16. 'I was suffering from indigestion, as a result of a joint cooked in garlic', was the remark attributed by Bertrand to Napoleon on Saint Helena. Bertrand, vol. 2, p. 437.

17. Las Cases, vol. 3, pt 6, p. 134.

18. Mathews, p. 165. Le Doulcet, vol. 3, pp. 160–1. Petre, pp. 248–9. Napoleon could be breathtakingly inconsistent. While blaming setbacks on illness, he was keen to portray himself as invariably fit and healthy. On Saint Helena, he repeatedly denied that he had ever had any problems with his digestion. 'I am luckier than you', he

supposedly said on learning that Las Cases was prone to stomach-ache. 'In my whole life, I have never been troubled by either my head or my stomach.' Las Cases, vol. 3, pt 5, p. 167.

19. Roustam, p. 161.
20. Howard, p. 197. Hillemand, pp. 59–60. Marchand, vol. 2, p. 290. Bertrand, vol. 3, pp. 89, 113, 115, 118, 122–3, 127–30, 130, 131, 193. Lutyens, p. 94.
21. Campana, p. 204. Montholon, *Récits*, vol. 2, p. 548. Marchand, vol. 2, p. 326. Bertrand, vol. 3, p. 195.

Chapter 12: Rebranding a Legend *(pages 192–206)*

1. Dayot, *Napoléon*, p. 396.
2. Johnson, 'Report', p. 15. The original of the 'Napoleon' pear tree was raised from seed by a gardener at the Belgian city of Mons in 1808. It was then bought by the abbé Duquesne and named after Napoleon. It was first sent to the United Kingdom in 1816 by a prolific raiser of new pear varieties, Dr Van Mons of Brussels. Some confusion arose over the origins of the 'Napoleon' pear, since Dr Van Mons himself created a different type, called the 'Empereur de France'. The 'Bigarreau Napoléon' cherry tree originated in France, and was introduced to the United States in the 1820s. Another cherry tree was called 'Waterloo', as its fruit was first perfected soon after the battle, and ripened in June. Downing, pp. 183, 401. Braddick, p. 160. Loudon, book 1, pt 1, p. 76. Anon, 'Cherries' (1827), p. 261. Kenrick, p. 278.
3. The British Commonwealth favours the unimaginative title of vanilla, cream, or custard slice, but for inhabitants of the United States, Eastern Europe, Scandinavia, and China, it is a Napoleon cake or pastry.
4. Jouy, vol. 2, p. 11.
5. Bouchencour was probably based on not one, but several real-life people, including both Monsieur Boucher, who worked for Talleyrand after serving in the Condé household, and Louis, marquis de Cussy, one of the great culinarians of the age, a friend of the gastronomic writer Grimod de la Reynière, and a prefect of the palace in Napoleon's household from May 1812. Could Cussy have been the creator of chicken Marengo? One morning, Napoleon is said to have praised some *poulet à la tartare* that he had for *déjeuner,* saying that although he usually found chicken bland, the dish was excellent. Cussy thereupon offered to serve him a new style of chicken for each and every day of the year. Did Cussy really know as many as 365 different ways of preparing chicken? He assured Napoleon he did, and gained his approval to try the experiment. As the days passed,

Napoleon grew more intrigued by the chicken dishes he was eating, and eventually, so it was said, he acquired such a taste for this fine food that he became a real gastronome. Unfortunately, it is a dubious tale, not least as it apparently originated with Grimod de la Reynière, whose anecdotes tend to be taken far more seriously than is warranted. Even if true, it does not necessarily mean that Cussy personally invented 365 different chicken dishes, but simply that he knew the recipes. The story is also suspiciously reminiscent of the challenge that Talleyrand set Carême, of producing a different menu for each day of the year. Raisson and Romieu, p. 125. Desnoiresterres, pp. 230, 235, 281. Kelly, p. 76.

6. Gringo, pp. 331–3.
7. Cobb, p. 256. Richardson, p. 330. Bright, p. 132.
8. Leacock, *Short circuits,* p. 318.
9. Anon, 'A duke on cooks' (1884), p. 101.
10. Lipman, pp. 59–60.
11. Kennedy, pp. 231–2.
12. Claiborne, Craig, '1957's three most often requested recipes were casseroles', in *The New York Times* (26 December 1957), p. 33. Claiborne, Craig, 'Readers' choice', in *The New York Times* (27 December 1964), p. 155.
13. Striffler, p. 18.
14. Heggan, pp. 175–82. For similar examples, see Higgins, p. 24; and Kyne, p. 280.
15. Similarly, in *Blighted blues* (2005) by Maurice Ené, one of the characters explains that they are disposing of their burnt chicken Marengo, and will have to phone for a pizza. Ené, p. 169. Wilcox, pp. 198–9.
16. Wesley, p. 248.
17. Braddon, vol. 1, p. 190.
18. Similarly, the Irish writer Dorothea Conyers in her novel *A lady of discretion* (1938) has dinner guests praising the meal prepared by their hosts' new cook, yet secretly longing for ordinary roast mutton instead of chicken Marengo. Conyers, p. 201. Leacock, *Funny pieces,* p. 169.
19. Ford, p. 230.
20. Ralph, p. 620.
21. Shane, Edie, and Gloria Schwartz, 'Have your diet and eat out too', in *The New York Times* (9 July 1978), p. WC13.
22. Starkey, Joanne, 'French or Caribbean? Take your choice', in *The New York Times* (7 April 1991), p. LI15.
23. Restaurant review, in *Texas monthly* (September 1983), vol. 11, issue 9, p. 104. Levy, Paul, 'Hanoi harvest', in *The Observer* (22 December 1991), p. 78.

24. Anon, 'Grub's up', in *The Observer* (5 March 1972), p. 28. Robertson, Nan, 'Haute cuisine for the commuter', in *The New York Times* (31 March 1979), p. 14. Sugarman, Carole, 'Today's Taste™', in *The Washington Post* (17 February 1985), p. K1. Rosen, Amy, 'The new restaurant-turned-larder', in *Maclean's*, Toronto (1 September 2008), vol. 121, issue 34, p. 59.
25. Johnson, Robert, 'Does an army travel on nouvelle cuisine?', in *The Wall Street Journal*, New York (22 May 1987), p. 1.
26. Gaddis, pp. 623–4.
27. Dullea, Georgia, 'Metropolitan diary', in *The New York Times* (3 October 1990), p. C2.
28. Chrétien had previously taken French cuisine into space in 1982 for the space station *Salyut 7* – the first time French cuisine had gone into orbit. In 1985, French astronaut Patrick Baudry entertained his US colleagues to gourmet dining on the Space Shuttle *Discovery*.

Chapter 13: Washing Up *(pages 207–215)*

1. Burton, pp. 83–4.
2. Escoffier, *Le guide*, pp. 256, 352, 557. Filippini, p. 165.
3. Nisbet and Massena, pp. 64, 170. Escoffier, *Le guide*, p. 867.
4. Carême, *Le cuisinier parisien*, p. 13.
5. Fayot, p. 259. Kelly, p. 95. Nisbet and Massena, p. 112.
6. Carême and Plumerey, vol. 4, pp. 413–25. Carême did not live long enough to include chicken Marengo, and other warm *entrées*, in this crowning achievement of his life's work. They formed part of the fourth volume, which was compiled by Plumerey, but was based on Carême's cooking.
7. Carême and Plumerey, vol. 1, pp. xlix-l.
8. Another alternative name was given by Kellermann on 15 June, when he wrote a report about his role in the 'Battle of Alessandria' (*bataille d'Alexandrie*). Cugnac, *Campagne*, vol. 2, pp. 403, 414.
9. Dubois and Bernard, pt 1, p. 414.
10. Haythornthwaite, p. 54.

Bibliography

Abell, Lucia Elizabeth. *Recollections of the Emperor Napoleon, during the first three years of his captivity on the island of St Helena*. London, 1844.

Adriani, Giovambatista. *Monumenti storico-diplomatici degli archivi Ferrero-Ponziglione e di autre nobili case subalpine, dalle fine del secolo XII al principio del XIX*. Turin, 1858.

Albert, Maurice. *Les théâtres des boulevards, 1789–1848*. Paris, 1902.

Alessandria. Società di Storia della Provincia. *Centenario della battaglia di Marengo: memorie storiche del periodo napoleonico*, 2 vols. Alessandria, 1900.

Alexandre, Arsène-Pierre-Urbain. *Histoire de la peinture militaire en France*. Paris, 1890.

Allard, Léon. *L'impasse des couronnes*. Paris, 1880.

d'Alméras, Henri. *La vie parisienne sous le consulat et l'empire*. Paris, 1909.

Amalvi, Christian. 'Le mythe du général Desaix', in *Annales historiques de la Révolution française* (April–June 2001), no. 324, pp. 179–91.

Anon. *Paris et ses modes, ou les soirées parisiennes*. Paris, 1803.

——. *Manuel de la cuisine, ou l'art d'irriter la gueule, par une société de gens de bouche*. Metz, 1811.

——. *Le nouveau cuisinier impérial, ou l'art de faire la cuisine, mis à la portée de tout le monde . . . par un officier de bouche*. Paris, 1813.

——. *Diary of an excursion to France in the months of August and September 1814, in a series of letters*. Edinburgh, 1814.

——. *Dictionnaire des protées modernes, ou biographie des personnages vivans qui ont figuré dans la Révolution française, depuis le 14 juillet 1789, jusques et compris 1815, par leurs actions, leur conduite ou leurs écrits*. Paris, 1815.

——. 'Profanation du cénotaphe du général Desaix', in *Bibliothèque historique, ou recueil de matériaux pour servir à l'histoire du temps* (1818), vol. 3, pp. 28–32.

——. 'New cemetery projects and cemeteries', in *The London magazine* (July 1825), new series, vol. 2, no. 7, pp. 363–70.

——. 'Cherries', in *American farmer* (2 November 1827), vol. 9, no. 33, pp. 260–1.

——. *Le cuisinier méridional, d'après la méthode provençale et languedocienne.* Avignon, 1835.

——. 'A chapter on gourmanderie, or, a peep at the restaurants of Paris', in *Bentley's miscellany* (1838), vol. 2, pp. 228–38.

——. 'A palatable pilgrimage to the eating-houses in Paris', in *Bentley's miscellany* (1838), vol. 2, pp. 485–95.

——. 'Parisian cafés', in *Bentley's miscellany* (1838), vol. 2, pp. 543–52.

——. 'A gastronomic survey of the dining-houses in London', in *Bentley's miscellany* (1839), vol. 5, p. 470.

——. *Dictionnaire des dictionnaires, ou vocabulaire universel et complet de la langue française, reproduisant le dictionnaire de l'Académie française . . .*, 2 vols. Brussels, 1839.

——. 'Rise and progress of culinary literature and cookery', in *The Foreign quarterly review* (April 1844), vol. 33, pp. 98–114.

——. 'A chapter on the art of eating', in *The Daguerreotype: a magazine of foreign literature and science, compiled chiefly from the periodical publications of England, France, and Germany* (1847), vol. 1, pp. 518–24.

——. *Notices sur les tableaux de bataille peints par le général baron Lejeune.* Toulouse, 1850.

——. *Marengo et ses monuments.* Paris, 1854.

——. 'To be sold by auction – Marengo', in *The Leader: a political and literary review* (7 June 1856), vol. 7, issue 324, p. 541.

——. 'Origine du poulet à la Marengo', in *Almanach de la bonne cuisine et de la maîtresse de maison* (1860), 3rd year, pp. 83–5.

——. *Cookery for English households, by a French lady.* London, 1864.

——, 'A duke on cooks', in *Punch, or the London Charivari* (1 March 1884), vol. 86, p. 101.

——. 'La bataille de Marengo, d'après un témoin bourbonnais', in *Bulletin de la société d'émulation du Bourbonnais* (November 1911), vol. 19, pp. 377–81.

——. 'Impressions of Boston', in *Life* (18 April 1912), vol. 59, issue 1538, p. 834.

Antommarchi, François. *Mémoires du docteur F. Antommarchi, ou les derniers momens de Napoléon*, 2 vols. Paris, 1825.

Appert, Charles. *The art of preserving all kinds of animal and vegetable substances for several years.* London, 1811.

Archambault, Julien. *Le cuisinier économe, ou éléments nouveaux de cuisine, de pâtisserie et d'office*, 3rd edition. Paris, 1825.

Arnault, Antoine-Vincent. *Souvenirs d'un sexagénaire*, 4 vols. Paris, 1833.

Arnold, James R. *Marengo and Hohenlinden: Napoleon's rise to power.* Reissued Barnsley, 2005.

Audiguier. *Coup-d'oeil sur l'influence de la cuisine et sur les ouvrages de M. Carême.* Paris, 1830.

Aulard, François-Victor-Alphonse. *Paris sous le consulat: recueil de documents pour l'histoire de l'esprit public à Paris,* 4 vols. Paris, 1903–9.

Avrillion, Marie-Jeanne-Pierrette [and Charles-Maxime Catherinet de Villemarest]. *Mémoires de mademoiselle Avrillion, première femme de chambre de l'impératrice, sur la vie privée de Joséphine, sa famille et sa cour,* 2 vols. Paris, 1833.

Bailey, Henry Christopher. *Forty years after: the story of the Franco-German war, 1870.* London, 1914.

Balmain, Alexander Antonovitch, Count. *Napoleon in captivity: the reports of Count Balmain, Russian commissioner on the island of St Helena, 1816–1820.* Trans. and ed. by Julian Park. New York, 1927.

Bann, Stephen. *Paul Delaroche: history painted.* London, 1997.

Barbey, Frédéric. *Les pierres parlent.* Lausanne, 1940.

Barillo, Madeline. *The wedding sourcebook planner,* 2nd ed. Lincolnswood, Illinois, 2000.

Barnard, E. G. 'A peep into palm land', in *The Ludgate.* London (August 1898), vol. 6, p. 297.

Barnes, John. *A tour through the island of St Helena.* London, 1817.

Bartel, Paul. *La jeunesse inédite de Napoléon, d'après de nombreux documents.* Paris, 1954.

de Bausset, Louis-François-Joseph, baron. *Mémoires anecdotiques sur l'intérieur du palais et sur quelques événemens de l'empire,* 5 vols. Paris, 1827–9.

Bazin, Christian. *Kléber l'indomptable.* Paris, 2003.

Beatson, Alexander. *Tracts relative to the island of St Helena, written during a residence of five years.* London, 1816.

Beaufort, Emily Anne, afterwards Smythe, Viscountess Strangford. *The eastern shores of the Adriatic in 1863, with a visit to Montenegro.* London, 1864.

de Beauharnais, Eugène. *Mémoires et correspondance politique et militaire du prince Eugène,* 10 vols. Ed. by Pierre-Emmanuel-Albert, baron du Casse. Paris, 1858–60.

Beauvilliers, Antoine. *L'art du cuisinier,* 2 vols. 2nd ed. Paris, 1816.

Beeton, Isabella Mary. *The book of household management.* London, 1863.

——. *Mrs Beeton's dictionary of every-day cookery.* London, 1865.

[Berkheim, Carl Christian, Baron von]. *Lettres sur Paris, ou correspondance de M***, dans les années 1806 et 1807.* Heidelberg, 1809.

Bernède, Allain. 'Autopsie d'une bataille: Marengo, 14 juin 1800', in *Revue historique des armées* (December 1990), no. 181, pp. 33–47.

Bertaud, Jean-Paul. 'Les compagnons d'armes de Desaix', in *Annales historiques de la Révolution française* (April–June 2001), no. 324, pp. 39–45.

Bertaut, Jules. *La vie à Paris sous le premier empire.* Paris, 1943.

Berthier, Louis-Alexandre. *Relation de la bataille de Marengo, gagnée le 25 prairial an 8, par Napoléon Bonaparte, Premier Consul, commandant en personne l'armée française de réserve, sur les autrichiens, aux ordres du Lieutenant-Général Melas.* Paris, 1805–6.

Bertrand, Henri-Gratien, comte. *Cahiers de Sainte-Hélène,* 3 vols. Ed. by Paul Fleuriot de Langle. Paris, 1949–59.

Beugnot, Jacques-Claude, comte. *Mémoires du comte Beugnot, 1779–1815.* Ed. by Robert Lacour-Gayet. Paris, 1959.

Biasoletto, Dottore Bartolomeo. *Relazione del viaggo fatto nella primavera dell'anno 1838 dalla Maestà del Re Federico Augusto di Sassonia nell'Istria, Dalmazia e Montenègro.* Trieste, 1841.

Bigarré, Auguste-Julien. *Mémoires du général Bigarré: aide de camp du roi Joseph, 1775–1813.* Paris, 1893.

Bingham, Sir George Ridout. 'Napoleon's voyage to St Helena', in *Blackwood's Edinburgh Magazine* (July–December 1896), vol. 160, pp. 540–9.

Biver, Marie-Louise, comtesse. *Le Paris de Napoléon.* Paris, 1963.

[?Blagdon, Francis William]. *Paris as it was and as it is; or a sketch of the French capital, illustrative of the effects of the Revolution . . . in a series of letters written by an English traveller, during the years 1801–2, to a friend in London,* 2 vols. London, 1803.

Blanc, Alexandre-Auguste-Philippe-Charles. *Une famille d'artistes: les trois Vernet, Joseph, Charles, Horace.* Reissued Paris, 1907.

[Blanc, Honoré]. *Le guide des dîneurs, ou statistique des principaux restaurans de Paris.* Paris, 1814.

[——]. *Le guide des dîneurs, ou statistique des principaux restaurans de Paris,* 2nd ed. Paris, 1815.

Blanvillain, J.-F.-C. *Le Pariseum, ou tableau de Paris en l'an XII (1804).* Paris, 1804.

Blot, Pierre. *What to eat, and how to cook it: containing over one thousand receip[e]s, systematically and practically arranged, to enable the housekeeper to prepare the most difficult or simpler dishes in the best manner.* New York, 1863.

Bois, Jean-Pierre. 'Napoléon et les anciens soldats: le rêve et l'ordre', in *Revue historique des armées* (December 1990), no. 181, pp. 73–81.

Bonnal de Ganges, Edmond. *Histoire de Desaix: armées du Rhin, expédition d'Orient, Marengo, d'après les archives du dépôt de la guerre.* Paris, 1881.

de Bonneval, Armand-Alexandre-Hippolyte, marquis. *Mémoires anecdotiques du général marquis de Bonneval, 1786–1873.* Paris, 1900.

Boulart, Jean-François, baron. *Mémoires militaires du général baron Boulart sur les guerres de la république et de l'empire,* Paris, 1892.

Boulay de la Meurthe, Alfred, comte. *Correspondance de Talleyrand avec le premier consul pendant la campagne de Marengo: extrait de la Revue d'histoire diplomatique.* Laval, 1892.

Bourdin, Philippe. 'Le sultan dévoilé: Desaix en Egypte d'après ses notes de campagne', in *Annales historiques de la Révolution française'* (April–June 2001), no. 324, pp. 47–62.

de Bourrienne, Louis-Antoine Fauvelet [and Charles-Maxime Catherinet de Villemarest]. *Mémoires de M. de Bourrienne, ministre de l'état; sur Napoléon, le directoire, le consulat, l'empire et la restauration,* 10 vols. Paris, 1829–30.

Braddick, John. 'List of select new pears introduced by John Braddick', in *The Gardener's magazine and register of rural and domestic improvement* (1827), vol. 2, pp. 159–60.

Braddon, Mary Elizabeth. *The lovels of Arden,* 3 vols. London, 1871.

Branda, Pierre. 'Le Grand maréchal du palais: protéger et servir', in *Napoleonica: la revue historique en ligne publiée par la Fondation Napoléon* (May–August 2008), no. 1, pp. 2–43.

Brégeon, Jean-Joël. *Kléber: le dieu Mars en personne.* Paris, 2002.

Bret, Patrice. 'Le "guerrier philosophe"', in *Annales historiques de la Révolution française* (April–June 2001), no. 324, pp. 69–82.

Brett-James, Antony. *Europe against Napoleon: the Leipzig campaign, 1813, from eyewitness accounts.* London, 1970.

Bright, Florence. *A girl capitalist.* London, 1902.

Broadley, Alexander Meyrick. *Napoleon in caricature, 1795–1821,* 2 vols. Intro. by John Holland Rose. London, 1911.

Brockedon, William. *Illustrations of the passes of the Alps, by which Italy communicates with France, Switzerland, and Germany,* 2nd ed, 2 vols. London, 1836.

Browet, Emile-Paul. 'Malmaison et Navarre de 1809 à 1812: journal de Piout', in *Revue des études napoléoniennes* (January–June 1926), 25th year, vol. 26, pp. 215–32.

Brown, George Ingham. *Scientist, soldier, statesman, spy: Count Rumford, the extraordinary life of a scientific genius.* Reissued Stroud, 2001.

Brownstein, Rachel M. *Tragic muse: Rachel of the Comédie-Française.* London, 1995.

Bruce, Evangeline. *Napoleon and Josephine: an improbable marriage.* Reissued London, 1996.

Buckingham and Chandos, Richard Plantagenet Temple Nugent Brydges Chandos Grenville, Duke of. *The private diary of Richard, Duke of Buckingham and Chandos,* 3 vols. London, 1862.

Buhle, Carl. *Erinnerungen aus den Feldzügen von 1809 bis 1816, entlehnt aus den Papieren eines Veteranen der sächsischen Armee,* 2nd ed. Lobau, 1848.

[ed. Bulos, Antoine]. *Bourrienne et ses erreurs, ou observations sur ses mémoires,* 3 vols. Brussels, 1830–1.

Bülow, Dietrich Heinrich, Freiherr von. *Histoire des campagnes de Hohenlinden et de Marengo par M. de Bülow, contenant les notes que Napoléon fit sur cet ouvrage en 1819, à Ste Hélène.* Trans. by Charles-Louis de Sevelinges. Ed. by Major Emmett. London, 1831.

Burnet (officier de bouche). *Dictionnaire de cuisine et d'économie ménagère.* Paris, 1836.

Burt, Raymond A. *French battleships, 1876–1946.* London, 1990.

Burton, David. *The Raj at table: a culinary history of the British in India.* Reissued London, 1994.

Cabanès, Dr Augustin. *Au chevet de l'empereur.* Paris, 1924.

——. *Dans l'intimité de l'empereur.* Paris, 1924.

Cabanis, André. *La presse sous le consulat et l'empire, 1799–1814.* Paris, 1975.

[Cadet de Gassicourt, Charles-Louis]. *Cours gastronomique, ou les dîners de Manant-Ville: ouvrage anecdotique, philosophique et littéraire,* 2nd ed. Paris, 1809.

de Cambacérès, Jean-Jacques Régis. *Mémoires inédits: éclaircissements publiés par Cambacérès sur les principaux événements de sa vie politique,* 2 vols. Ed. by Laurence Chatel de Brancion. Paris, 1999.

Camon, Hubert. *Génie et métier chez Napoléon.* Paris, 1930.

Campana, Ignace Raphäel. *Marengo: étude raisonnée des opérations militaires qui ont eu pour théâtre l'Italie et l'Allemagne au printemps 1800, d'après la correspondance et les mémoires de Napoléon.* Paris, 1900.

Capefigue, Jean-Baptiste-Honoré-Raymond. *Histoire des grandes opérations financières,* 3 vols. Paris, 1855–8.

Carême, Marie-Antonin. *Le maître d'hôtel français, ou parallèle de la cuisine ancienne et moderne, considérée sous le rapport de l'ordonnance des menus selon les quatre saisons,* 2 vols. Paris, 1822.

——. *Le cuisinier parisien, ou l'art de la cuisine au dix-neuvième siècle: traité élémentaire et pratique des entrées froides, des socles et de l'entremets de sucre,* 2nd ed. Paris, 1828.

——. 'Notice historique et culinaire sur la manière dont vivait Napoléon à Sainte-Hélène', in *Revue de Paris* (1833), vol. 46, pp. 47–52.

Carême, Marie-Antonin, and Armand Plumerey. *L'art de la cuisine française au dix-neuvième siècle,* 5 vols. Ed. by Charles-Frédéric-Alfred Fayot. Paris, 1833–47.

de Castellane, Esprit-Victor-Elisabeth-Boniface, comte. *Journal du maréchal de Castellane, 1804–1862,* 5 vols. Paris, 1895–1897.

de Caulaincourt, Armand-Augustin-Louis. *Mémoires du général de Caulaincourt, duc de Vicence, grand écuyer de l'empereur,* 3 vols. Ed. by Jean Hanoteau. Paris, 1933.

Chandler, David. 'Adjusting the record: Napoleon and Marengo', in *On the Napoleonic wars: collected essays*. London, 1994.

Chappet, Alain, Roger Martin, and Alain Pigeard. *Le guide Napoléon: 4000 lieux pour revivre l'épopée*. Paris, 2005.

Chaptal, Jean-Antoine-Claude, comte de Chanteloup. *Mes souvenirs sur Napoléon*. Paris, 1893.

Chazal, Jean-Pierre. *Tribunat: discours prononcé par Chazal, dans le séance du 2 messidor an 8*. Paris, 1800.

Chłapowski, Adam Dezyderyusz. *Mémoires sur les guerres de Napoléon, 1806–1813*. Trans. by Jan V. Chelminski and Alphonse-Marie Malibran. Paris, 1908.

Ciotti, Bruno. 'La dernière campagne de Desaix', in *Annales historiques de la Révolution française* (April–June 2001), no. 324, pp. 83–97.

Civalieri-Inviziati, Annibale. *La colonna di Marengo*. Turin, 1894.

Clary und Aldringen, Karl Joseph, Fürst von. *Trois mois à Paris lors du mariage de l'empereur Napoléon 1er et de l'archiduchesse Marie-Louise*, 2nd ed. Paris, 1914.

Clifford, Kay. *A temporary affair*. London, 1982.

Cobb, Irwin Shrewsbury. *From place to place*. Reissued 2007.

Cochelet, Louise. *Mémoires sur la reine Hortense et la famille impériale*, 2 vols. Ed. by Frédéric Lacroix. Paris, 1836.

Cockburn, Sir George. *Buonaparte's voyage to St Helena; comprising the diary of Rear Admiral Sir George Cockburn, during his passage from England to St Helena, in 1815*. Boston, 1833.

Coghlan, Francis. *Handbook for travellers in northern Italy: arranged and written upon a new plan, with all the lines of railways and steam packets, never before published . . .* London, 1856.

Cole, Sir Galbraith Lowry. *Memoirs of Sir Lowry Cole*. Ed. by Maud Lowry Cole and Stephen Gwynn. London, 1934.

Constant [Wairy, Louis-Constant, and Charles-Maxime Catherinet de Villemarest, *et al.*]. *Mémoires de Constant, premier valet de chambre de l'empereur, sur la vie privée de Napoléon, sa famille et sa cour*, 6 vols. Paris, 1830.

Constant de Rebecque, Benjamin-Henri. *Tribunat: discours de Benjamin Constant, sur les victoires de l'armée d'Italie, séance du 3 messidor an 8*. Paris, 1800.

Conyers, Dorothea. *A lady of discretion*. London, 1938.

Cooper, James Fenimore. *The Redskins; or, Indian and Injin: being the conclusion of the Littlepage manuscripts*, 2 vols. Reissued New York, 1852.

Cordingly, David. *Billy Ruffian: the Bellerophon and the downfall of Napoleon, the biography of a ship of the line, 1782–1836*. London, 2003.

Cornet, Dr Paul. *Alimentation des malades: l'application diététique dans le traitement des maladies des voies digestives, avec 200 formules de préparations d'aliments.* Paris, 1901.

Coudreux, Alexandre. *Lettres du commandant Coudreux à son frère, 1804–1815.* Ed. by Gustave Schlumberger. Paris, 1908.

Croker, John Wilson. *The Croker papers*, 3 vols. Ed. by Louis J. Jennings. London, 1884.

Cronin, Vincent. *Napoleon.* Reissued London, 1990.

de Crossard, Jean-Baptiste-Louis, baron. *Mémoires militaires et historiques pour servir à l'histoire de la guerre depuis 1792 jusqu'en 1815 inclusivement*, 6 vols. Paris, 1829.

[Croze-Magnan, Simon-Célestin]. *Le gastronome à Paris: épître à l'auteur de la Gastronomie, ou l'homme des champs à table.* Paris, 1803.

de Cugnac, Gaspar-Jean-Marie-René, comte. *Campagne de l'armée de réserve en 1800*, 2 vols. Paris, 1900–1.

——. 'Mort de Desaix à Marengo', in *Revue des études napoléoniennes* (July–August 1934), vol. 39, year 23, no. 147, pp. 5–32.

de Cussy, Ferdinand, chevalier. *Souvenirs du chevalier de Cussy: garde du corps, diplomate et consul général, 1795–1866*, 2 vols. Ed. by Marc, comte de Germiny. Paris, 1909.

Dampierre, Achille. 'Lettres sur la campagne de Marengo', in *La Revue de Paris* (15 June 1900), pp. 787–810.

Dauncey, Hugh, and Keith Reader. 'Consumer culture: food, drink and fashion', in ed. Nicholas Hewitt. *The Cambridge companion to modern French culture.* Cambridge, 2003.

David, Elizabeth. *Harvest of the cold months: the social history of ice and ices.* Ed. by Jill Norman. London, 1994.

——. *French provincial cooking*, Revised ed. London, 1997.

David, Jacques-Louis-Jules. *Le peintre Louis David, 1748–1825: souvenirs et documents inédits.* Paris, 1880.

Davis, Maggie. *Miami midnight.* New York, 1999.

Dayot, Armand. *Napoléon raconté par l'image, d'après les sculptures, les graveurs et les peintres.* Paris, 1895.

——. *Les Vernet: Joseph, Carle, Horace.* Paris, 1898.

——. *Carle Vernet: étude sur l'artiste, suivie d'un catalogue de l'œuvre gravé et lithographié et du catalogue de l'exposition rétrospective de 1925.* Paris, 1925.

Debry, Jean-Antoine-Joseph. *Tribunat: discours prononcé par Jean Debry, sur le message relatif à la victoire de Maringo, séance du 3 messidor an 8.* Paris, 1800.

Delavo, Jean-Antoine. *L'ingratitude de Napoleon III: appel adressé à l'opinion publique.* Brussels, 1861.

——. *A la mémoire de mes chers soldats français morts à la bataille de Marengo: les douleurs et espérances d'un vieux patriote italien.* Nice, 1889.

Delécluze, Etienne-Jean. *Louis David, son école et son temps: souvenirs.* Paris, 1855.

Desaix, Louis-Charles-Antoine. *Journal de voyage du général Desaix: Suisse et Italie, 1797.* Ed. by Arthur Chuquet. Paris, 1907.

Desnoiresterres, Gustave Le Brisoys. *Grimod de la Reynière et son groupe, d'après des documents entièrement inédits.* Paris, 1877.

Devereux, Roy, pseud. [Margaret Rose Roy Pember-Devereux]. *Side lights on South Africa.* London, 1899.

Divova, Elisabeth Petrovna. *Journal et souvenirs de Madame Divoff.* Ed. by Sergyei Nikolaevich Kaznakov. Paris, 1929.

[Dix, John]. *Lions: living and dead; or, personal recollections of the great and gifted.* London, 1852.

Doher, Marcel. *Charles de la Bédoyère, 1786–1815: aide de camp de l'empereur.* Paris, 1963.

Downing, Andrew Jackson. *The fruits and fruit trees of America: the culture, propagation, and management.* Reissued Bedford, Massachusetts, nd.

Doyle, Sir Arthur Conan. *Uncle Bernac: a memory of the empire.* London, 1897.

Du Bois, Louis. *Glossaire du patois normand.* Ed. by Julien Travers. Caen, 1856.

Dubois, Urbain, and Emile Bernard. *La cuisine classique: études pratiques, raisonnées et démonstratives de l'école française appliquée au service à la russe,* 2 vols. Paris, 1856.

Ducrest, Georgette. *Mémoires sur l'impératrice Joséphine, ses contemporains, la cour de Navarre et de la Malmaison,* 3 vols. Paris, 1828.

Dufey, Pierre-Joseph-Spiridion. *Nouveau dictionnaire historique des environs de Paris.* Paris, 1825.

Dumas, Alexandre. *Impressions de voyage,* 2 vols. Brussels, 1835.

——. *The company of Jehu,* 2 vols. Trans. by Katharine Prescott Wormeley. London, 1895.

Duncan, Francis. *A description of the island of St Helena, containing observations on its singular structure and formation, and an account of its climate, natural history, and inhabitants.* London, 1805.

Durand (cuisinier). *Le cuisinier Durand, cuisine du Midi et du Nord,* 8th ed. Nîmes, 1863.

Durand, Sophie. *Mémoires sur Napoléon, l'impératrice Marie-Louise, et la cour des Tuileries, avec des notes critiques faites par le prisonnier de Sainte-Hélène.* Paris, 1828.

Durande, Amédée. *Joseph, Carle et Horace Vernet: correspondance et biographies.* Paris, 1863.

Duval, Amaury. *Les fontaines de Paris, anciennes et nouvelles.* New ed. Paris, 1828.

[Dwight, Theodore]. *A journal of a tour in Italy, in the year 1821, with a description of Gibraltar . . . by an American.* New York, 1824.

Ehrard, Antoinette. 'Autour de la statue de Desaix par Nanteuil, place de Jaude à Clermont-Ferrand', in *Annales historiques de la Révolution française* (April–June 2001), no. 324, pp. 161–78.

Ellwanger, George Herman. *The pleasures of the table: an account of gastronomy from ancient days to present times.* London, 1902.

Elphinstone, George Keith, 1st Viscount Keith. *The Keith papers: selected from the papers of Admiral Viscount Keith,* 3 vols. Ed. by William Gordon Perrin and Charles Christopher Lloyd. London, 1927–55.

Elting, John Robert. *Swords around a throne: Napoleon's Grande Armée.* Reissued London, 1989.

Ené, Maurice Ogochukwu. *Blighted blues.* London, 2005.

Ernouf, Alfred-Auguste, baron. *Le général Kléber.* Paris, 1867.

Escoffier, Georges-Auguste, *et al. Le guide culinaire: aide-mémoire de cuisine pratique,* 4th ed. Paris, 1929.

——. *The complete guide to the art of modern cookery: the first translation into English in its entirety of Le guide culinaire.* Trans. by H. L. Cracknell and R. J. Kaufmann. 1979. Reissued London, 1981.

——. *Auguste Escoffier: souvenirs inédits: 75 ans au service de l'art culinaire.* Marseille, 1985.

Esposito, Vincent Joseph, and John Robert Elting. *A military history and atlas of the Napoleonic wars.* Reissued London, 1999.

Eustace, Rev. John Chetwode. *A tour through Italy, exhibiting a view of its scenery, its antiquities, and its monuments,* 2 vols. London, 1813.

Fain, Agathon-Jean-François, baron. *Mémoires du baron Fain, premier secrétaire du cabinet de l'empereur.* Paris, 1908.

Faul, Michel. *Les aventures militaires, littéraires et autres de Etienne de Jouy de l'Académie française.* Biarritz, 2009.

ed. Fayot, Charles-Frédéric-Alfred. *Les classiques de la table, à l'usage des praticiens et des gens du monde.* Paris, 1843.

de Fazi du Bayet, comte. *Les généraux Aubert du Bayet, Carra Saint-Cyr et Charpentier: correspondances et notices biographiques, 1757–1834.* Paris, 1902.

Ferguson, Priscilla Parkhurst. *Accounting for taste: the triumph of French cuisine.* London, 2004.

ed. Ffrench, Yvonne. *News from the past, 1805–1887: the autobiography of the nineteenth century.* London, 1934.

Fierro, Alfred. *La vie des Parisiens sous Napoléon.* Saint-Cloud, 2003.

Filippini, Alessandro. *The Delmonico cook book: how to buy food, how to cook it, and how to serve it.* Revised ed. London, 1893.

Fillon, Benjamin. 'Carle Vernet: lettre au maréchal Berthier (1806)', in *Nouvelles archives de l'art français* (1872). Paris, pp. 451–2.

Fillon, Benjamin and Henri Lot. 'Les monuments commemoratifs des victoires de Dego, Montenotte, Mondovi et Marengo (1805)', in *Nouvelles archives de l'art français* (1874–5). Paris, pp. 487–99.

Floquet, Charles. *Pontivy-Napoléonville: une cité impériale*. Pontivy, 2003.

de Font-Réaulx, Hyacinthe. *Le général Kléber*. Limoges, 1891.

Fontaine, Pierre-François-Léonard. *Journal, 1799–1853*, 2 vols. Paris, 1987.

Forbes, James. *Letters from France, written in the years 1803 and 1804, including a particular account of Verdun, and the situation of the British captives in that city*, 2 vols. London, 1806.

Ford, Simeon. *A few remarks*. London, 1903.

Fouché, Maurice. *Percier et Fontaine: biographie critique*. Paris, 1905.

Fournier-Sarlovèze, Raymond. 'Le général Lejeune', in *La Revue de l'art ancien et moderne* (January–June 1901), vol. 9, 5th year, pp. 161–82.

Fraisse, François-Joseph. *Un poulet à la Marengo*. Paris, 1907.

France. Centre national de la recherche scientifique. *Trésor de la langue française: dictionnaire de la langue du XIXe et du XXe siècle, 1789–1960*, multivolume. Paris, 1971– .

——. Comité national français de géographie, Commission de géographie historique, Centre national de la recherche scientifique. *Alimentation et régions: actes du colloque 'Cuisines, régimes alimentaires, espaces régionaux' réunis par Jean Peltre et Claude Thouvenot, Nancy 24–27 septembre 1987*. Nancy, 1989.

——. Dépôt général de la guerre. 'Rapprochement entre diverses relations de la bataille de Marengo', in *Mémorial du Dépôt général de la guerre, imprimé par ordre du ministre* (1828), vol. 4, pp. 268–344.

——. Musée national des châteaux de Malmaison et Bois-Préau. *Marengo: une victoire politique*. Paris, 2000.

——. Official Publications. *Etiquette du palais impérial*. Paris, 1808.

——. Société savoisienne d'histoire et d'archéologie. *La deuxième campagne d'Italie et les conséquences de la bataille de Marengo: actes du colloque international de Chambéry, 9–10 novembre 2000*. Ed. by Maurice Messiez, and Christian Sorrel. Chambéry, 2001.

ed. Freedman, Paul H. *Food: the history of taste*. London, 2007.

Frémeaux, Paul. *With Napoleon at St Helena: being the memoirs of Dr John Stokoe, naval surgeon*. Trans. by Edith S. Stokoe. London, 1902.

Funck, Karl Wilhelm Ferdinand von. *In the wake of Napoleon, being the memoirs, 1807–1809, of Ferdinand von Funck, lieutenant-general in the Saxon army and adjutant-general to the King of Saxony*. Ed. by Philip Henry Oakley Williams. London, 1931.

Gaddis, William. *JR*. Reissued London, 1993.

Gainot, Bernard. 'Les mots et les cendres', in *Annales historiques de la Révolution française* (April–June 2001), no. 324, pp. 127–38.

Gajal, Mathurin. *Pétition des anciens vétérans du camp d'Alexandrie*. Paris, 1829.

Galignani and Co., A. and W. (firm). *New Paris guide, to which is added a description of the environs*. Paris, 1841.

Garat, Dominique-Joseph. *Eloge funèbre des généraux Kléber et Desaix, prononcé le 1er vendém. an 9, à la place des Victoires*. Paris, 1800.

[Gardeton, César]. *Nouveau guide des dîneurs, ou répertoire des restaurants à la carte et à prix fixe*. Paris, 1828.

Gaudin, Martin-Michel-Charles, duc de Gaëte. *Notice historique sur les finances de France, de l'an 8 (1800) au 1er avril 1814*. Paris, 1818.

George, Mademoiselle [Weimer, Marguerite-Joséphine]. *Mémoires inédits de Mademoiselle George*. Ed. by Auguste-Paul-Arthur Cheramy. Paris, 1908.

Gervais, Capitaine. *A la conquête de l'Europe: souvenirs d'un soldat de la Révolution et de l'empire*. Ed. by Louise-Henry Coullet. Paris, 1939.

Gioannini, Marco, and Giulio Massobrio. *Marengo: la battaglia che creò il mito di Napoleone*, 2nd ed. Milan, 2000.

Gleig, George Robert. *The life of the Duke of Wellington*. Reissued London, 1939.

Godard d'Aucourt, Adrien, comte de Plancy. *Souvenirs du comte de Plancy, 1798–1816*, 2nd ed. Paris, 1904.

Gore, Catherine Grace Frances. *Cecil: or, the adventures of a coxcomb*. London, 1845.

Gorrequer, Gideon. *St Helena during Napoleon's exile: Gorrequer's diary*. Ed. by James Kemble. London, 1969.

Gould, William M. *Zephyrs from Italy and Sicily*. New York, 1852.

Gourgaud, Gaspard, baron. *Sainte-Hélène: journal inédit de 1815 à 1818*, 2 vols. Ed. by Emmanuel-Henri, vicomte de Grouchy and Antoine Guillois. Paris, 1899.

Gozlan, Léon. 'Le Château d'Ecouen', in *Revue de Paris* (1835), new series, vol. 17, pp. 73–129.

Graham, J. C. 'The French connection in the early history of canning', in *Journal of the Royal Society of Medicine* (May 1981), vol. 74, pp. 374–81.

Gribble, Francis. *Rachel: her stage life and her real life*. London, 1911.

Griffin, Rev. Edmund Dorr. *Remains of the Rev. Edmund D. Griffin*, 2 vols. Ed. by Francis Griffin. New York, 1831.

Gringo, Harry, pseud. [Henry Augustus Wise]. *Tales for the marines*. Reissued Boston, 1857.

Gronow, Rees Howell. *Reminiscences of Captain Gronow, formerly of the Grenadier Guards, and MP for Stafford: being anecdotes of the camp, the court, and the clubs, at the close of the last war with France*. London, 1862.

——. *Recollections and anecdotes: being a second series of reminiscences of the camp, the court, and the clubs*, 2nd ed. London, 1863.

——. *Celebrities of London and Paris; being a third series of reminiscences and anecdotes of the camp, the court, and the clubs, containing a correct account of the coup d'état.* London, 1865.

——. *Captain Gronow's last recollections; being the fourth and final series of his reminiscences and anecdotes,* 2nd ed. London, 1866.

Gruyer, Antoine. 'Miettes de l'histoire: un récit de la bataille de Marengo', in *Le carnet historique et littéraire* (1898), pp. 877–80.

Guerrini, Maurice. *Napoléon et Paris: trente ans d'histoire.* Paris, 1967.

Günther, Reinhold. *Geschichte des Feldzuges von 1800 in Ober-Deutschland, der Schweiz und Ober-Italien.* Frauenfeld, 1893.

Guy, Christian. *Une histoire de la cuisine française.* Paris, 1962.

Haine, W. Scott. *The world of the Paris café: sociability among the French working class, 1789–1914.* London, 1996.

Hamilton and Brandon, Jill Douglas-Hamilton, Duchess of. *Marengo: the myth of Napoleon's horse.* Reissued London, 2001.

Hamley, Sir Edward Bruce. 'The campaign of Marengo', in *Journal of the Royal United Service Institution* (1861), vol. 4, p. 25.

Hardman, Sir William. *A mid-Victorian Pepys: the letters and memoirs of Sir William Hardman, MA, FRGS.* Ed. by Stewart Marsh Ellis. London, 1923.

Hassell, Agostino von, *et al. Military high life: elegant food histories and recipes.* New Orleans, 2006.

Haythornthwaite, Philip. *Die hard! dramatic actions from the Napoleonic wars.* London, 1996.

Heggan, Christiane. *The search.* Richmond, 2007.

Heine, Heinrich. *Italien.* Reissue of part of the 'Reiserbilder'. Berlin, 1919.

Heller, R. A. '"Let them eat soup" – Count Rumford and Napoleon Bonaparte', in *Journal of Chemical Education* (August 1976), vol. 53, no. 8, pp. 499–500.

Henry, Dr Walter. *Events of a military life: being recollections after service in the Peninsular war, invasion of France, the East Indies, St Helena, Canada, and elsewhere,* 2 vols. London, 1843.

Herbin de Halle, P. Etienne, *et al. Statistique générale et particulière de la France et de ses colonies,* 7 vols. Paris, 1803.

Herrmann, Dr Alfred. *Marengo.* Münster, 1903.

Hervé, Peter. *How to enjoy Paris: being a guide to the visiter of the French metropolis,* 2 vols. London, 1816.

Herz, Micheline. 'From "The Little Corporal" to "Mongénéral": a comparison of two myths', in *Yale French Studies* (1960), no. 26, pp. 37–44.

Higgins, George V. *The agent.* Reissued Harpenden, 2000.

Hillairet, Jacques. *Dictionnaire historique des rues de Paris,* 2 vols. 8th ed. Paris, 1985.

Hillemand, Dr Pierre. *Pathologie de Napoléon.* Paris, 1970.

Hollins, David. *Marengo 1800.* Oxford, 2000.

Holtz, Georg, Freiherr von. *Die innerösterreichische Armee, 1813 und 1814* (vol. 4 of Alois Veltzé, ed. *1813–1815: Osterreich in den Befreiungskriegen*). Vienna, 1912.

Home, George. *Memoirs of an aristocrat, and reminiscences of the Emperor Napoleon, by a midshipman of the Bellerophon.* Edinburgh, 1837.

Horn, Jeff. 'Building the new regime: founding the Bonapartist state in the department of the Aube', in *French historical studies* (Spring 2002), vol. 25, no. 2, pp. 225–63.

Hortense, Queen of Holland. *The memoirs of Queen Hortense*, 2 vols. Ed. by Prince Napoléon and Jean Hanoteau. Trans. by Arthur Kingsland Griggs and Frances Mabel Robinson. London, 1928.

Houssaye, Henry. *Waterloo 1815.* Reissued Evreux, 1987.

Howard, Dr Martin. *Napoleon's poisoned chalice: the Emperor and his doctors on St Helena.* Stroud, 2009.

Hüffer, Hermann. *Quellen zur Geschichte der Kriege von 1799 und 1800. Zweiter Band: Quellen zur Geschichte des Krieges von 1800.* Leipzig, 1900–1901.

——. *Der Krieg des Jahres 1799 und die zweite Koalition*, 2 vols. Gotha, 1904–5.

Hughes, Kathryn. *The short life and long times of Mrs Beeton.* Reissued London, 2006.

Huguenaud, Karine. 'Une rivalité d'artistes autour de la bataille de Marengo', in *Revue du souvenir napoléonien* (April–May 2006), 69th year, no. 464.

Hyde de Neuville, Jean-Guillaume, baron. *Mémoires et souvenirs du baron Hyde de Neuville*, 3 vols. Paris, 1888–92.

Imbert de Saint-Amand, Arthur-Léon, baron. *La cour de l'impératrice Joséphine.* Paris, 1889.

Italy. Turin, Galleria civica d'arte moderna e contemporanea. *Giuseppe Pietro Bagetti, pittore di battaglie, vues des campagnes des Français en Italie (1796 e 1800): i disegni delle campagne napoleoniche della GAM di Torino.* Turin, 2000.

Jackson, Basil. *Notes and reminiscences of a staff officer, chiefly relating to the Waterloo campaign and to St Helena matters during the captivity of Napoleon.* Ed. by Robert Cooper Seaton. London, 1903.

James, Kenneth. *Escoffier: the king of chefs.* London, 2002.

Jewett, Isaac Appleton. *Passages in foreign travel*, 2 vols. Boston, 1838.

Johnson, Dorothy. *Jacques-Louis David: art in metamorphosis.* Princeton, NJ, 1993.

Johnson, Joseph. 'Report of the committee on fruits and vegetables', in *The Southern agriculturist, and register of rural affairs, adapted to the southern section of the United States* (January 1839), vol. 12, pp. 15–16.

Johnston, Velda. *The face in the shadows*. Reissued London, 1973.

de Jomini, Antoine-Henri, baron. *Histoire critique et militaire des guerres de la Révolution*, 15 vols. New edition. Paris, 1820–4.

Jourdan, Annie. 'Bonaparte et Desaix, une amitié inscrite dans la pierre des monuments?', in *Annales historiques de la Révolution française* (April–June 2001), no. 324, pp. 139–50.

de Jouy, Etienne [Victor-Joseph Etienne]. *Le centenaire: roman historique et dramatique en six époques*, 2 vols. Paris, 1833.

Junot, Laure Permon, duchesse d'Abrantès. *Mémoires de madame la duchesse d'Abrantès*, 10 vols. Paris, nd.

Kellermann, François-Christophe-Edmond. *Histoire de la campagne de 1800, écrite d'après des documents nouveaux et inédits*. Paris, 1854.

Kellermann, François-Etienne. 'Eclaircissemens historiques sur la Bataille de Marengo', in *Bibliothèque historique, ou recueil de matériaux pour servir à l'histoire du temps* (1818), vol. 4, pp. 126–9.

[——]. *Réfutation de M. le duc de Rovigo, ou la vérité sur la bataille de Marengo*. Paris, 1828.

[——]. *Deuxième et dernière réplique d'un ami de la vérité à M. le duc de Rovigo*. Paris, 1828.

Kelly, Ian. *Cooking for kings: the life of Antonin Carême, the first celebrity chef*. London, 2003.

Kennedy, Hugh A. *Waifs and strays: chiefly from the chess-board*. London, 1862.

Kenrick, William. *The new American orchardist: or an account of the most valuable varieties of fruit, adapted to cultivation in the climate of the United States*. Boston, 1833.

Kielmannsegge, Auguste Charlotte, Gräfin von. *Memoiren der Gräfin Kielmannsegge über Napoleon I*. Dresden, 1927.

Klein, Charles. *The music master: a play in three acts*. New York, 1935.

Kotzebue, August-Friedrich-Ferdinand von. *Mes souvenirs de Paris en 1804*, 2 vols. Trans. from German 2nd edition. Paris, 1805.

Künzi, Frédéric. *Bonaparte: bicentenaire du passage des Alpes, 1800–2000*. Martigny, 2000.

Kyne, Peter Bernard. *Two make a world*. London, 1933.

de La Tour du Pin-Gouvernet, Henriette-Lucie, marquise. *Journal d'une femme de cinquante ans, 1778–1815*, 2 vols. Paris, 1913.

Labadini, Ausano. *Milano ed alcuni momenti del Risorgimento Italiano*. Milan, 1909.

Lacroix, Paul. *Directoire, consulat et empire: mœurs et usages, lettres, sciences et arts, France 1795–1815*. Paris, 1884.

Langlois, Claude. 'Le plébiscite de l'an VIII, ou le coup d'état du 18 pluviôse an VIII', in *Annales historiques de la Révolution française*

(January–March 1972), 44th year, no. 207, pp. 43–65; (April–June 1972), 44th year, no. 208, pp. 229–46; (July–September 1972), 44th year, no. 209, pp. 390–415.

de Lanzac de Laborie, Léon. *Paris sous Napoléon*, 8 vols. Paris, 1904–13.

Larousse, Librairie (firm). *Larousse gastronomique*. Ed. by Robert J. Courtine. Paris, 1984.

Larsen, Egon. *An American in Europe: the life of Benjamin Thompson, Count Rumford*. London, 1953.

de Las Cases, Emmanuel-Auguste-Dieudonné, comte. *Mémorial de Sainte-Hélène: journal de la vie privée et des conversations de l'empereur Napoléon, à Sainte Hélène*, 4 vols (in 8 parts). London, 1823.

Lathion, Lucien. *Bonaparte et ses soldats au Grand-Saint-Bernard, d'après les documents de l'armée*. Neuchâtel, 1978.

de Lavallette, Antoine-Marie Chamans, comte. *Mémoires et souvenirs du comte Lavallette*, 2 vols. Paris, 1831.

Lazare, Félix, and (Louis). *Dictionnaire administratif et historique des rues de Paris et de ses monuments*. Paris, 1844.

Le Doulcet, Louis-Gustave, comte de Pontécoulant. *Souvenirs historiques et parlementaires du comte de Pontécoulant*, 4 vols. Paris, 1861–93.

Leacock, Stephen. *Short circuits*. London, 1928.

——. *Funny pieces: a book of random sketches*. London, 1937.

Lecomte, Louis-Henry. *Napoléon et l'empire racontés par le théâtre, 1797–1899*. Paris, 1900.

Legrand d'Aussy, Pierre-Jean-Baptiste. *Histoire de la vie privée des François, depuis l'origine de la nation jusqu'à nos jours*, 3 vols. New ed, revised by Jean-Baptiste Bonaventure de Roquefort. Paris, 1815.

ed. Leibowitz, Herbert A. *Parnassus: twenty years of poetry in review*. Ann Arbor, Michigan, 1994.

Lejeune, Louis-François, baron. *Mémoires du général Lejeune*, 2 vols. Paris, 1895.

Lemaire, Jean. *Le testament de Napoléon: un étonnant destin, 1821–1857*. Paris, 1975.

Lentz, Thierry. 'La légende de Desaix', in *Annales historiques de la Révolution française* (April–June 2001), no. 324, pp. 151–9.

Lipman, Elinor. *The ladies' man*. London, 1999.

Livy. *The history of Rome, by Titus Livius*. Trans. by George Baker, 6 vols. Reissued New York, 1823.

Löbel, Renatus Gotthelf, *et al. Conversations-Lexikon, oder encyclopädisches Handwörterbuch für gebildete Stände*, 7 vols. Stuttgart, 1814–19.

Long, Freda Margaret. *The soldier's woman*. London, 1987.

Longford, Lady Elizabeth. *Wellington: the years of the sword*. Reissued London, 1972.

Loudon, John Claudius. *An encyclopaedia of gardening: comprising the theory and practice of horticulture, floriculture, arboriculture, and landscape-gardening.* Reissued London, 1835.

Lovell, Caroline Couper. *The golden isles of Georgia.* Boston, 1932.

Loyer de la Mettrie, Louis. *Biographie du Colonel Marengo.* Paris, 1854.

Lumbroso, Alberto. *Mélanges Marengo.* Frascati, 1903.

de Luternan, Karl. 'Paris en 1810', in *Revue de Paris* (August 1950), pp. 54–67.

Lutyens, Engelbert. *Letters of Captain Engelbert Lutyens, orderly officer at Longwood, Saint Helena, Feb 1820 to Nov 1823.* Ed. by Sir Lees Knowles. London, 1915.

Lytton, Sir Edward Bulwer. *Pelham; or, the adventures of a gentleman*, 3 vols. London, 1828.

Macdonogh, Giles. *A palate in revolution: Grimod de la Reynière and the Almanach des Gourmands.* London, 1987.

MacFarlane, Charles. *A glance at revolutionized Italy: a visit to Messina, and a tour through the Kingdom of Naples, the Abruzzi, the Marches of Ancona, Rome, the States of the Church, Tuscany, Genoa, Piedmont . . . in the summer of 1848*, 2 vols. London, 1849.

Maillard, André. *Saint-Leu-la-Forêt à travers les siècles.* Paris, 1936.

Maitland, Sir Frederick Lewis. *Narrative of the surrender of Buonaparte and of his residence on board HMS Bellerophon.* London, 1826.

Malcolm, Clementina, Lady. *A diary of St Helena, 1816, 1817: the journal of Lady Malcolm, containing the conversations of Napoleon with Sir Pulteney Malcolm.* Ed. by Sir Arthur Wilson. London, 1899.

de Malglaive, Louis-Marie. *Marengo (Alger) en 1848.* Versailles, 1909.

Malte-Brun, Conrad. *Universal geography, or a description of all the parts of the world*, 9 vols. Edinburgh, 1834.

Manning, Robert. *Book of fruits: being a descriptive catalogue of the most valuable varieties of the pear, apple, peach, plum and cherry, for New-England culture.* Salem, 1838.

de Marbot, Jean-Baptiste-Antoine-Marcellin, baron. *Mémoires du général baron de Marbot*, 3 vols. Paris, 1891.

Marchand, Louis-Joseph-Narcisse, comte. *Mémoires de Marchand, premier valet de chambre et exécuteur testamentaire de l'empereur*, 2 vols. Ed. by Jean Bourguignon and Henry Lachouque. Paris, 1952–5.

Markham, J. David. *Napoleon and Dr Verling on St Helena.* Barnsley, 2005.

de Marmont, Auguste-Frédéric-Louis Viesse. *Mémoires du maréchal duc de Raguse de 1792 à 1841*, 3rd ed., 9 vols. Paris, 1857.

Marshall-Cornwall, Sir James. *Napoleon as military commander.* Reissued New York, 1998.

Martha-Beker, Félix, comte de Mons. *Le général Desaix: étude historique.* Paris, 1852.

Massobrio, Giulio. *Che si salga di pietra in pietra, come su quella d'Egitto: sulle tracce della Pyramide de Marengo*. Marengo, 2009.

Massobrio, Giulio, *et al. Marengo: dalla battaglia al museo*. Marengo, 2009.

Masson, Frédéric. *Napoléon chez lui: la journée de l'empereur aux Tuileries*. Reissued Paris, 1910 and 1921.

——. *Le sacre et le couronnement de Napoléon*. Paris, 1908.

——. 'Les cuisiniers de Napoléon à Sainte-Hélène', in *Autour de Sainte-Hélène*, 2nd series. Paris, 1909.

——. *Napoléon à Sainte-Hélène, 1815–1821*. Paris, 1912.

Masson, Frédéric and Guido Biagi. *Napoléon inconnu: papiers inédits, 1786–1793, accompagnés de notes sur la jeunesse de Napoléon, 1769–1793*, 2 vols. Paris, 1895.

Mathews, William. *Hours with men and books*. Chicago, 1877.

Maurice, Arthur Bartlett. *Fifth avenue*. New York, 1918.

Maxwell, Constantia Elizabeth. *The English traveller in France, 1698–1815*. London, 1932.

McErlean, John Michael Peter. *Napoleon and Pozzo di Borgo in Corsica and after, 1764–1821: not quite a vendetta*. Lewiston, New York, 1996.

McIntosh, Charles. *The practical gardener, and modern horticulturist*, 2 vols. London, 1828–9.

de Méneval, Claude-François, baron. *Mémoires pour servir à l'histoire de Napoléon 1er depuis 1802 jusqu'à 1815*, 3 vols. Paris, 1894.

Ménière, Dr Prosper. *Journal du docteur Prosper Ménière*. Ed. by Dr Emile Ménière. Paris, 1903.

Mennell, Stephen. *All manners of food: eating and taste in England and France from the Middle Ages to the present*. Oxford, 1985.

Menzies, Sutherland. 'A chat about good cheer', in *Fraser's magazine* (December 1881), no. 624; new series, no. 144, pp. 762–76.

Mercer, Cavalié. *Journal of the Waterloo campaign*. Reissued London, 1985.

de Metz, Jean. *Aux pays de Napoléon: l'Italie, 1796–97, 1800*. Grenoble, 1911.

Michel, Albin and Berger-Levrault (firms). *Dictionnaire national des communes de France*. Revised ed. Paris, 2001.

Miot, André-François, comte de Mélito. *Mémoires du comte Miot de Mélito, ancien ministre, ambassadeur conseiller d'état et membre de l'institut*, 3 vols. Ed. by Wilhelm August von Fleischmann. Paris, 1858.

Mitchell, James. *A tour through Belgium, Holland, along the Rhine, and through the north of France, in the summer of 1816*. London, 1816.

Moitte, Adelaïde-Marie-Anne. *Un ménage d'artistes sous le premier empire: journal inédit de Madame Moitte . . . 1805–1807*. Ed. by Paul Cottin. Paris, 1932.

Monnier, Raymonde. 'Vertu antique et nouveaux héros', in *Annales historiques de la Révolution française* (April–June 2001), no. 324, pp. 113–25.

de Montchenu, Claude-Marie-Henri, marquis. *La captivité de Sainte-Hélène, d'après les rapports inédits du marquis de Montchenu.* Ed. by Georges Firmin-Didot. Paris, 1894.

de Montesquiou, Anatole. 'Marie-Louise et le roi de Rome', in *Revue de Paris* (May 1948), pp. 51–80.

de Montesquiou-Fezensac, Raymond-Emery-Philippe-Joseph, duc. *Souvenirs militaires de 1804 à 1814,* 4th ed. Paris, 1870.

de Montholon, Charles-Jean-François-Tristan, marquis. *Récits de la captivité de l'empereur Napoléon à Sainte-Hélène,* 2 vols. Paris, 1847.

——. *Lettres du comte et de la comtesse de Montholon, 1819–1821.* Ed. by Philippe Gonnard. Paris, 1906.

Montigny, Louis-Gabriel. *Le provincial à Paris: esquisses des mœurs parisiennes,* 3 vols. Paris, 1825.

Moorehead, Caroline. *Dancing to the precipice: Lucie de la Tour du Pin and the French Revolution.* Reissued London, 2010.

Morse, John Torrey. *Life and letters of Oliver Wendell Holmes,* 2 vols. London, 1896.

Mras, Karl. 'Geschichte des Feldzuges 1800 in Italien, nach östreichischen Originalquellen bearbeitet', in *Oestreichische militärische Zeitschrift* (1822), vol. 3, no. 7, pp. 16–55; vol. 3, no. 8, pp. 173–200; vol. 3, no. 9, pp. 283–313; vol. 4, no. 10, pp. 80–107; vol. 4, no. 11, pp. 165–203; vol. 4, no. 12, pp. 239–92; (1823), vol. 3, no. 7, pp. 3–27; vol. 3, no. 8, pp. 119–55; vol. 3, no. 9, pp. 235–72.

Mühlbach, Luise, pseud. [Clara Mundt]. *Napoleon in Germany: Napoleon and the Queen of Prussia, a historical novel.* Trans. by F. Jordan. Reissued New York, 1906.

Murray, John (firm). *The hand-book for travellers in Switzerland and the Alps of Savoy and Piedmont.* Reissued London, 1840.

——. *Handbook for travellers in southern Germany: being a guide to Würtemberg, Bavaria, Austria, Tyrol, Salzburg, Styria . . . ,* 9th ed. London, 1864.

——. *A handbook for visitors to Paris: containing a description of the most remarkable objects, with general advice and information for English travellers in that metropolis, and on the way to it,* 3rd ed. London, 1867.

de Nadaillac, Rosalie de Rancher, marquise, duchesse d'Escars. *Mémoires de la marquise de Nadaillac, duchesse d'Escars.* Paris, 1912.

Napoleon I, Emperor of the French. *Mémoires pour servir à l'histoire de France, sous Napoléon, écrits à Sainte-Hélène, par les généraux qui ont partagé sa captivité, et publiés sur les manuscrits entièrement corrigés de la main de Napoléon,* 8 vols. Ed. by Gaspard, baron Gourgaud, and Charles-Jean-François-Tristan, marquis de Montholon. Paris, 1823–5.

——. *Correspondance de Napoléon I, publiée par ordre de l'empereur Napoléon III,* 32 vols. Paris, 1858–70.

——. *Lettres inédites de Napoléon Ier, an VIII – 1815*, 2 vols. Ed. by Léon Lecestre. Paris, 1897.

——. *Lettres de Napoléon à Joséphine*. Ed. by Dr Léon Cerf. Paris, 1929.

Néaimi, Sadek. 'Desaix devant Thèbes', in *Annales historiques de la Révolution française* (April–June 2001), no. 324, pp. 63–7.

Neipperg, Adam Adalbert, Graf von. 'Aperçu militaire sur la bataille de Marengo', in *La Revue de Paris* (July–August 1906), 13th year, vol. 4, pp. 5–36.

Nemnich, Philippe-André. *Une enquête économique dans la France impériale: le voyage du Hambourgeois Philippe-André Nemnich, 1809*. Ed. by Dr Odette Viennet. Paris, 1947.

Nisbet, Anne-Marie, and Victor-André Massena. *L'empire à table*. Paris, 1988.

de Norvins, Jacques, baron Marquet de Montbreton. *Souvenirs d'un historien de Napoléon: mémorial de J. de Norvins*, 3 vols. Ed. by Léon de Lanzac de Laborie. Paris, 1896–7.

Oberlé, Gérard. *Les fastes de bacchus et de Comus: ou histoire du boire et du manger en Europe, de l'antiquité à nos jours, à travers les livres*. Paris, 1989.

Oliva, Pietro. *Marengo antico e moderno*. Alessandria, 1842.

O'Meara, Barry Edward. *Napoleon in exile; or, a voice from St. Helena*, 2 vols. London, 1822.

Onfray, Michel. *Le ventre des philosophes: critique de la raison diététique*. Paris, 1989.

Osché, Philippe and Frédéric Künzi. *Les chevaux de Napoléon*. Aosta, 2002.

Owen, Thomas McAdory. *History of Alabama and dictionary of Alabama biography*, 4 vols. Chicago, 1921.

Page, Edward Beynon, and Peter Wilfred Kingsford. *The master chefs: a history of haute cuisine*. London, 1971.

Palmer, Alan. *Alexander I: tsar of war and peace*. London, 1974.

Palmer, Arnold. *Movable feasts: changes in English eating-habits*. Reissued Oxford, 1984.

Papillard, François. *Cambacérès*. Paris, 1961.

Pardoen, Marie-Hélène. 'Marengo en chantant', in *Annales historiques de la Révolution française* (April–June 2001), no. 324, pp. 99–108.

Parienté, Henriette, and Geneviève de Ternant. *Histoire de le cuisine française*. Paris, 1994.

de Pasquier, Etienne-Dennis, duc. *Mémoires du chancelier Pasquier*, 6 vols. Ed. by Edme-Armand-Gaston, duc d'Audiffret-Pasquier. Paris, 1893–5.

Pattyn, J.-J. 'Regard d'un peintre: la bataille de Marengo', in *Gloire et empire: revue de l'histoire napoléonienne* (July–August 2006), no. 7, pp. 87–9.

Payne, Arthur Gay. *Choice dishes at small cost*. London, 1909.

Pessard, Gustave. *Nouveau dictionnaire historique de Paris*. Paris, 1904.

Pétiet, Auguste, baron. *Souvenirs militaires de l'histoire contemporaine*. Paris, 1844.

Petit, Joseph. *Marengo, or the campaign of Italy by the Army of Reserve*, 2nd ed. London, 1801.

Petre, Francis Loraine. *Napoleon's last campaign in Germany, 1813*. Reissued London, 1974

Peuchet, Jacques. *Statistique élémentaire de la France*. Paris, 1805.

Pilbeam, Pamela. *The middle classes in Europe, 1789–1914: France, Germany, Italy and Russia*. Basingstoke, 1990.

Pilcher, Jeffrey M. *Food in world history*. London, 2006.

Pils, François. *Journal de marche du grenadier Pils, 1804–1814*. Ed. by Raoul de Cisternes. Paris, 1895.

Pinkard, Susan. *A revolution in taste: the rise of French cuisine, 1650–1800*. Cambridge, 2009.

Pinkerton, John. *Recollections of Paris, in the years 1802–3–4–5*, 2 vols. London, 1806.

Pitte, Jean-Robert. *French gastronomy: the history and geography of a passion*. Trans. by Jody Gladding. New York, 2002.

Planta, Edward. *A new picture of Paris; or, the stranger's guide to the French metropolis*. Reissued London, 1816.

Playfair, Sir Robert Lambert. *Supplement to the bibliography of Algeria from the earliest times to 1895*. London, 1898.

Plumptre, Anne. *A narrative of a three years' residence in France, principally in the southern departments, from the year 1802 to 1805*, 3 vols. London, 1810.

Poisson, Georges. *Napoléon 1er et Paris*. Paris, 2002.

Polybius. *The general history of Polybius*. Trans. by James Hampton. 5th ed, 2 vols. Oxford, 1823.

Pons (de l'Hérault), André. *Souvenirs et anecdotes de l'île d'Elbe*. Ed. by Léon-Gabriel-Jean-Baptiste Pélissier. Paris, 1897.

Potocka, Anna, comtesse. *Mémoires de la comtesse Potocka, 1794–1820*. Ed. by Casimir Stryienski. Paris, 1897.

Poulain, Jean-Pierre. 'Sens et fonction des appellations culinaires au XIXe siècle', in *Sociétés: revue des sciences humaines et sociales* (November 1985), no. 6, pp. 20–3.

Poulain, Jean-Pierre, and Jean-Luc Rouyer. *Histoire et recettes de la Provence et du comté de Nice*. Toulouse, 1987.

Poumiès de la Siboutie, Dr François-Louis. *Souvenirs d'un médecin de Paris, 1789–1863*. Paris, 1910.

Pozzo di Borgo, Carlo Andrea, Count. *Correspondance diplomatique du comte Pozzo di Borgo, ambassadeur de Russie en France, et du comte de Nesselrode, depuis la restauration des Bourbons jusqu'au congrès d'Aix-la-Chapelle, 1814–1818*, 2 vols. Ed. by Carlo, Count Pozzo di Borgo. Paris, 1890–7.

Priestley, John Boyton. *Out of town* [volume one of *The image men*]. London, 1968.

Prince, William. *A short treatise on horticulture*. New York, 1828.

Prince, William Robert, and (William). *The pomological manual: or, a treatise on fruits*. New York, 1831.

Quaglia, Lucien. *La Maison du Grand-Saint-Bernard des origines aux temps actuels*. Martigny, 1972.

Quatremère de Quincy, Antoine-Chrysostôme. *Notice historique sur la vie et les ouvrages de M. Carle Vernet*. Paris, 1837.

Quérard, Joseph-Marie. *La France littéraire, ou dictionnaire bibliographique*, 10 vols. Paris, 1827–39.

Quintin, Danielle, and (Bernard). *Dictionnaire des colonels*. Paris, 1996.

Quoy-Bodin, Jean-Luc. 'La Franc maçonnerie dans les armée[s] de la Révolution et de l'empire: le cas des généraux', in *Revue de l'institut Napoléon* (1981), no. 137, pp. 68–89.

———. *L'armée et la franc-maçonnerie: au declin de la monarchie sous la Révolution et l'empire*. Paris, 1987.

Raffles, Thomas. *Letters during a tour through some parts of France, Savoy, Switzerland, Germany, and the Netherlands, in the summer of 1817*. New York, 1818.

Rahden, Wilhelm von. *Wanderungen eines alten Soldaten*, 3 parts. Berlin, 1846–51.

Raimbault, A. T. *Le parfait cuisinier, ou le bréviaire des gourmands*, 2nd ed. Paris, 1811.

Raimbourg, Patrick. *De la cuisine à la gastronomie: histoire de la table française*. Paris, 2005.

Raisson, Horace-Napoléon, and Auguste Romieu. *Code gourmand: manuel complet de gastronomie, contenant les lois, règles, applications et exemples de l'art de bien vivre*, 4th ed. Brussels, 1828.

Ralph, Julian. 'The industrial region of northern Alabama, Tennessee and Georgia', in *Harper's new monthly magazine*. (December 1894–May 1895), p. 620.

de Rambuteau, Charles-Philibert Barthelot, comte. *Mémoires du comte de Rambuteau*. Paris, 1905.

Ranhofer, Charles. *The epicurean: a complete treatise of analytical and practical studies on the culinary art*. Evanston, Illinois, 1920.

Rapp, Jean. *Mémoires du général Rapp, aide-de-camp de Napoléon, écrits par lui-même*. Paris, 1823.

Ratti, Guido. 'A la périphérie du mythe: célébrations et histoires de Marengo au XIXe siècle', in ed. Grange, Daniel J., and Dominique Poulot. *L'esprit des lieux: le patrimoine et la cité*. Grenoble, 1997, pp. 401–17.

Rauch, Josef. *Erinnerungen eines Offiziers aus Altösterreich*. Ed. by Dr Arthur Weber. Munich, 1918.

Réal, Pierre-François, comte. *Les indiscrétions d'un préfet de police de Napoléon*, 2 vols. Reissued Paris, 1986.

Reichardt, Johann Friedrich. *Vertraute Briefe aus Paris geschrieben in den Jahren 1802 und 1803*, 3 parts. Hamburg, 1804.

——. *Un hiver à Paris sous le consulat*. Trans. by Arthur Laquiante. Paris, 1896.

Reid, Thomas Wemyss. *The life, letters, and friendships of Richard Monckton Milnes, first Lord Houghton*, 2 vols. London, 1890.

Richardin, Marie-Ernest-Edmond. *La cuisine française: l'art du bien manger.* Paris, 1907.

Richardson, Frank. *There and back.* London, 1904.

Riquelme, Daniel. *Cuentos de la guerra y otras páginas.* Santiago, 1931.

Rivaud, J. *La ville des victoires sur le champ de bataille de Marengo, dédiée au premier consul de la république française.* Paris, 1803.

Robert, P. C. *La grande cuisine simplifiée, art de la cuisine nouvelle mise à la portée de toutes les fortunes.* Paris, 1845.

Robert, Paul. *Le grand Robert de la langue française: dictionnaire alphabétique et analogique de la langue française*, 9 vols. 2nd ed, revised by Alain Rey. Paris, 1985.

Roberti, G. 'Miettes de l'histoire: une nourrice inconnue de Napoléon Ier', in *Le Carnet historique et littéraire* (1898), pp. 797–8.

Robertson, Etienne Gaspard. *Mémoires récréatifs, scientifiques et anecdotiques*, 2 vols. Paris, 1840.

Roche, Jean-Michel. *Dictionnaire des bâtiments de la flotte de guerre française de Colbert à nos jours*, 2 vols. Toulon, 2005.

Rodger, Alexander Bankier. *The war of the Second Coalition, 1798–1801: a strategic commentary.* Oxford, 1964.

Rœderer, Pierre-Louis, comte. *Journal du comte Pierre-Louis Rœderer.* Ed. by Maurice Vitrac. Paris, 1909.

de Roquefort, Baptiste. *Dictionnaire historique et descriptif des monumens religieux, civils et militaires de la ville de Paris.* Paris, 1826.

Roques, Joseph. *Histoire des champignons comestibles et vénéneux*, 2nd ed. Paris, 1841.

ed. Rose, John Holland. *Napoleon's last voyages: being the diaries of Admiral Sir Thomas Ussher, RN, KCB, on board the 'Undaunted', and John R. Glover, secretary to Rear Admiral Cockburn, on board the 'Northumberland'*, 2nd ed. London, 1906.

Rossetti, Gabriele. *Gabriele Rossetti: a verified autobiography.* Trans. and supplemented by William Michael Rossetti. London, 1901.

Roth, Jonathan P. *The logistics of the Roman army at war: 264 bc – ad 235.* Leiden, 1999.

Rothenberg, Gunther Erich. *Napoleon's great adversary: Archduke Charles and the Austrian army, 1792–1814.* Reissued Staplehurst, 1995.

Rothwiller, Antoine-Ernest, baron. *Histoire du deuxième régiment de cuirassiers, ancien Royal de cavalerie, 1635–1876*. Paris, 1877.

Rousseaux-Berrens, Yvonne. 'La gastronomie à Paris sous le consulat et l'empire', in *Revue de l'institut Napoléon* (1961), pp. 51–6, 95–103, 131–48; (1962), pp. 1–13, 67–80, 109–14.

Roustam (mamelouk). *Souvenirs de Roustam: mamelouk de Napoléon 1er*. Ed. by Paul Cottin. Paris, 1911.

Saint-Denis, Louis-Etienne. *Souvenirs du mameluck Ali, Louis-Etienne Saint-Denis, sur l'empereur Napoléon*. Paris, 1926.

Sala, George Augustus. *Quite alone*. London, 1864.

——. *A journey due south: travels in search of sunshine*, 2nd ed. London, 1885.

Salgues, Jacques-Barthélemy. *De Paris, des mœurs, de la littérature et de la philosophie*. Paris, 1813.

Samanni, Dominique. 'La bouillabaisse', in *Marseille: la revue culturelle de la ville de Marseille* (December 2005), no. 211, pp. 60–72.

Sand, George. *Oeuvres autobiographiques*. Ed. by Georges Lubin, Paris, 1970.

Sanderson, John. *The American in Paris*, 2 vols. London, 1838.

Sartelon, Antoine-Léger. *Chambre des députés: rapport fait au nom de la commission centrale, par M. Sartelon, sur la pétition des vétérans des camps de Juliers et d'Alexandrie*. Paris, 1814.

Sauzet, Armand. *Desaix: le 'sultan juste'*. Paris, 1954.

Savant, Jean. *Napoleon in his time*. Trans. by Katherine John. London, 1958.

Savary, Anne-Jean-Marie-René [Antoine Bulos]. *Mémoires du duc de Rovigo, pour servir à l'histoire de l'empereur Napoléon*, 4 vols. Paris, 1828.

Scheltens, Henri. *Souvenirs d'un grenadier de la Garde*. Ed. by Michel Legat. Paris, 2004.

Schnapper, Antoine. *David: témoin de son temps*. Fribourg, 1980.

Scott, Charles Henry. *The Baltic, the Black Sea, and the Crimea: comprising travels in Russia, a voyage down the Volga to Astrachan, and a tour through Crim Tartary*. London, 1854.

Scott, John. *A visit to Paris in 1814: being a review of the moral, political, intellectual, and social condition of the French capital*, 4th ed. London, 1816.

de Ségur, Philippe-Paul, comte. *Histoire et mémoires*, 7 vols. Paris, 1873.

Shelley, Frances, Lady. *The diary of Frances Lady Shelley*, 2 vols. Ed. by Richard Edgcumbe. London, 1912–1913.

Shephard, Sue. *Pickled, potted and canned: the story of food preserving*. London, 2000.

ed. Shorter, Clement. *Napoleon and his fellow travellers, being a reprint of certain narratives of the voyages of the dethroned Emperor on the Bellerophon and the Northumberland to exile in St Helena: the romantic stories told by George Home, Captain Ross, Lord Lyttleton, and William Warden*. London, 1908.

Siegfried, Susan Locke. 'Naked history: the rhetoric of military painting in postrevolutionary France', in *The art bulletin: a quarterly published by the College Art Association* (June 1993), vol. 75, no. 2, pp. 235–58.

Six, Georges. *Dictionnaire biographique des généraux et amiraux français de la Révolution et de l'empire, 1792–1814*, 2 vols. Paris, 1934.

Smetham, Henry. *C. R. S. and his friends, being personal recollections of Charles Roach Smith, F.S.A. and his friends.* London, 1929.

ed. Smirnov, A., Véra Miltchina, and Alexandre Ospovat. *Les russes découvrent la France au XVIIIe et au XIXe siècle.* Trans. by Camille Lambert, *et al.* Paris, 1990.

Sokolowski, Michel. *Les pistolets de combat du premier consul Napoléon Bonaparte à Marengo.* Paris, 1980.

Soltyk, Roman. *Napoléon en 1812.* Paris, 1836.

Soult, Jean-de-Dieu. *Mémoires du maréchal-général Soult, duc de Dalmatie*, 3 vols. Paris, 1854.

Soyer, Alexis. *A shilling cookery for the people: embracing an entirely new system of plain cookery and domestic economy.* London, 1855.

Spang, Rebecca L. *The invention of the restaurant: Paris and modern gastronomic culture.* London, 2000.

Sparrow, Elizabeth. *Secret service: British agents in France, 1792–1815.* Woodbridge, 1999.

Stanhope, Philip Henry, 5th Earl Stanhope. *Notes of conversations with the Duke of Wellington, 1831–1851.* Reissued London, 1938.

Steinberger, Michael. *Au revoir to all that: the rise and fall of French cuisine.* London, 2009.

Stivens, Dallas George. *Jimmy Brockett: portrait of a notable Australian.* Reissued London, 1961.

Stouff, Louis. *La table provençale: boire et manger en Provence à la fin du Moyen Age.* Avignon, 1996.

Striffler, Steve. *Chicken: the dangerous transformation of America's favorite food.* London, 2005.

Stürmer, Bartholomaus, Baron von. *Napoléon à Sainte-Hélène: rapports officiels du baron Stürmer, commissaire du gouvernement autrichien.* Ed. by H. Schlitter. Trans. by Jacques St-Cère, pseud. [Armand Rosenthal]. Paris, 1888.

Switzerland. Napoleon-Museum Arenenberg. *Napoleon I in the mirror of caricature: a collection catalogue of the Napoleon Museum Arenenberg, with 435 cartoons dealing with Napoleon I.* Zürich, 1998.

Syntax, Dr, pseud. *The life of Napoleon: a Hudibrastic poem in fifteen cantos, by Doctor Syntax, embellished with thirty engravings by G. Cruikshank.* London, 1815.

Teissèdre, F., Librairie historique (firm). *La bataille de Marengo et ses préliminaires racontés par quatre témoins.* Paris, 1999.

Thackeray, William Makepeace. *The confessions of Fitz-Boodle; and some passages in the life of Major Gahagan.* New York, 1853.

——. *Early and late papers, hitherto uncollected.* Ed. by James Thomas Fields. Boston, 1867.

——. *Burlesques.* London, 1869.

de Thiard, Auxonne-Marie-Théodose, comte de Bissy. *Souvenirs diplomatiques et militaires du général Thiard.* Paris, 1900.

Thibaudeau, Antoine-Claire, comte. *Mémoires sur le consulat, 1799 à 1804, par un ancien conseiller d'état.* Paris, 1827.

——. *Mémoires de A.-C. Thibaudeau, 1799–1815.* Paris, 1913.

Thiers, Adolphe. *Histoire du consulat et de l'empire,* 21 vols. Paris, 1845–84.

Thomas, Kenneth H. 'Le marquis de Montalet', in *Généalogie et histoire de la Caraïbe* (April 1996), no. 81, pp. 1596–9.

[Thomé, Antoine]. *Vie de David, premier peintre de Napoléon.* Brussels, 1826.

Thompson, James Matthew. *Napoleon Bonaparte.* Reissued Oxford, 1990.

Tomkinson, William. *The diary of a cavalry officer in the Peninsular war and Waterloo campaign, 1809–1815.* Ed. by James Tomkinson, 2nd ed. London, 1895.

Toogood, Harriett. *The treasury of French cookery: a collection of the best French recipes, arranged and adapted for English households.* London, 1866.

Toussaint-Samat, Maguelone. 'Contes et légendes des *Trois frères provencaux,*' in *Marseille: la revue culturelle de la ville de Marseille* (December 2005), no. 211, pp. 28–9.

Trolard, Eugène. *Pèlerinage aux champs de bataille français d'Italie,* 2 vols. Paris, 1893.

Trollope, Frances Milton. *Paris and the Parisians in 1835,* 2 vols. London, 1836.

Tronchet, Louis. *Picture of Paris: being a complete guide to all the public buildings and curiosities in that metropolis,* 6th ed. London, 1817.

Trubek, Amy B. *Haute cuisine: how the French invented the culinary profession.* Philadelphia, Pennsylvania, 2000.

Truchsess von Waldburg, Ludwig Friedrich. *A narrative of Napoleon Buonaparte's journey from Fontainebleau to Frejus, in April, 1814.* London, 1815.

Tulard, Jean. *Nouvelle histoire de Paris: le consulat et l'empire, 1800–1815.* Paris, 1970.

——. 'Desaix fut-il un général politique?', in *Annales historiques de la Révolution française* (April–June 2001), no. 324, pp. 109–12.

Tulard, Jean, and Louis Garros. *Itinéraire de Napoléon au jour le jour, 1769–1821.* Paris, 1992.

Ude, Louis-Eustache. *The French cook: a system of fashionable and economical cookery, adapted to the use of English families,* 10th ed. London, 1829.

Uffindell, Andrew. *Napoleon's immortals: the Imperial Guard and its battles, 1804–1815*. Stroud, 2007.

Unwin, Sir Brian. *Terrible exile: the last days of Napoleon on St Helena*. London, 2010.

Vachée, Jean-Baptiste-Modeste-Eugène. *Napoléon en campagne*. Paris, 1913.

Valéry, Antoine-Claude. *Voyages historiques et littéraires en Italie, pendant les années 1826, 1827 et 1828; ou l'indicateur italien*, 5 vols. Paris, 1831–3.

——. *L'Italie confortable: manuel du touriste*. Paris, nd.

Vandam, Albert Dresden. *An Englishman in Paris: notes and recollections*, 2 vols. London, 1892.

Varnhagen von Ense, Carl August Ludwig Philipp. *Denkwürdigkeiten und vermischte Schriften*, 6 vols. Mannheim, 1837–42.

——. *Sketches of German life, and scenes from the war of liberation in Germany*. Trans. by Sir Alexander Duff Gordon. London, 1847.

Verdot, C. *Historiographie de la table, ou abrégé historique, philosophique, anecdotique et littéraire des substance alimentaires et des objets usuels, employés par tous les peuples de la terre anciens et modernes*. Paris, 1833.

Vernet, Antoine-Charles-Horace (Carle). *Le campagne napoleoniche in Italia: battaglie ed episodi disegnati da Carle Vernet*. Rome, nd.

Véron, Dr Louis-Désiré. *Mémoires d'un bourgeois de Paris*, 5 vols. Reissued Paris, 1856–7.

Vialles, Pierre. *L'archichancelier Cambacérès, 1753–1824, d'après des documents inédits*. Paris, 1908.

Viard, Alexandre. *Le cuisinier impérial, ou l'art de faire la cuisine et la pâtisserie pour toutes les fortunes*. Paris, 1806.

——. *Le cuisinier impérial, ou l'art de faire la cuisine et la pâtisserie pour toutes les fortunes*, 7th ed. Paris, 1812.

——. *Le cuisinier impérial, ou l'art de faire la cuisine et la pâtisserie pour toutes les fortunes*, 8th ed. Paris, 1814.

——. *Le cuisinier royal, ou l'art de faire la cuisine et la pâtisserie, pour toutes les fortunes*, 9th ed. Paris, 1817.

Viard, Alexandre, and Monsieur Fouret. *Le cuisinier royal, ou l'art de faire la cuisine, la pâtisserie et tout ce qui concerne l'office*, 10th ed. Paris, 1820.

——. *Le cuisinier royal, ou l'art de faire la cuisine, la pâtisserie et tout ce qui concerne l'office, pour toutes les fortunes*. 11th ed. Paris, 1822.

Viard, Alexandre, and Messieurs Fouret and Délan. *Le cuisinier royal*, 20th ed, Paris, 1846.

Vichot, Jacques. *Répertoire des navires de guerre français*. Paris, 1967.

Victor [Claude-Victor Perrin]. *Extraits des mémoires inédits de feu Claude-Victor Perrin, duc de Bellune*. Paris, 1843.

Vidal, Philippe-Jean. 'Les "Desaix"', in *Annales historiques de la Révolution française* (April–June 2001), no. 324, pp. 21–37.

Villiers, Pierre. *Manuel du voyageur à Paris, ou Paris ancien et moderne.* Reissued Paris, 1814.

Warden, William. *Letters written on board His Majesty's Ship the Northumberland, and at Saint Helena,* 5th ed. London, 1816.

Watson, George L. de St M. *A Polish exile with Napoleon.* London, 1912.

Weber, Eugen. *Peasants into Frenchmen: the modernization of rural France, 1870–1914.* London, 1979.

Weil, Maurice H. *Le prince Eugène et Murat, 1813–1814,* 5 vols. Paris, 1901.

Wesley, Mary. *The vacillations of Poppy Carew.* Reissued London, 1987.

Wilcox, James. *Miss Undine's living room.* 1987. Reissued London, 1996.

Wilmot, Catherine. *An Irish peer on the Continent, 1801–1803: being a narrative of the tour of Stephen, 2nd Earl Mount Cashell, through France, Italy, etc.* Ed. by Thomas U. Sadleir. London, 1920.

Wilson-Smith, Timothy. *Napoleon and his artists.* London, 1996.

Woloch, Isser. *The French veteran from the Revolution to the Restoration.* Chapel Hill, 1979.

Wybranowski, Antoni. *Wiersze różne.* Lublin, 1817.

Yorke, Henry Redhead. *Letters from France, in 1802,* 2 vols. London, 1804.

Younghusband, Catherine. 'Letters from St Helena', in *Blackwood's magazine* (August 1947), vol. 262, no. 1582, pp. 144–54.

Articles

In addition to the articles listed within the bibliography and references, there are many others too numerous to list, including those in the *Almanach des gourmands*, the *Nouvel almanach des gourmands*, the *Journal des débats*, the *Mercure de France, Le Figaro, The New York Times,* and *The Washington Post.*

Index